On African Music

On African Music

Techniques, Influences, Scholarship

KOFI AGAWU

OXFORD
UNIVERSITY PRESS

Oxford University Press is a department of the University of Oxford. It furthers the University's objective of excellence in research, scholarship, and education by publishing worldwide. Oxford is a registered trade mark of Oxford University Press in the UK and certain other countries.

Published in the United States of America by Oxford University Press
198 Madison Avenue, New York, NY 10016, United States of America.

Library of Congress Cataloging-in-Publication Data
Names: Agawu, V. Kofi (Victor Kofi), author.
Title: On African music : techniques, influences, scholarship / Kofi Agawu.
Description: New York, NY : Oxford University Press, 2023. |
Includes bibliographical references and index.
Identifiers: LCCN 2023004756 (print) | LCCN 2023004757 (ebook) |
ISBN 9780197664070 (paperback) | ISBN 9780197664063 (hardcover) |
ISBN 9780197664094 (epub) | ISBN 9780197664100
Subjects: LCSH: Music—Africa—History and criticism. |
Music—Social aspects—Africa. | Music—African influences.
Classification: LCC ML3760.A443 2023 (print) | LCC ML3760 (ebook) |
DDC 780.96—dc23/eng/20230131
LC record available at https://lccn.loc.gov/2023004756
LC ebook record available at https://lccn.loc.gov/2023004757

DOI: 10.1093/oso/9780197664063.001.0001

Paperback printed by Marquis Book Printing, Canada
Hardback printed by Bridgeport National Bindery, Inc., United States of America

The publisher gratefully acknowledges support from the General Fund of the American Musicological Society, supported in part by the National Endowment for the Humanities and the Andrew W. Mellon Foundation.

To my students, past and present,
and in memory of Akin Euba (1935–2020)

Contents

Acknowledgments

Many thanks to friends and colleagues for helpful and stimulating conversations about the issues addressed in this book—Christopher Matthay, Ron Radano, Teju Olaniyan, Daniel Avorgbedor, George Dor, Patrick Mensah, Olakunle George, Bode Omojola, Melanie Plesch, Daniel Biro, and Kwasi Ampene. As always, discussions with Christie Agawu were fundamental in shaping my thinking on several topics; to her I owe the framing of Chapter 5.

These essays began life as lectures to various audiences in Africa, Europe, and North America. I am grateful to colleagues and students who invited me to speak at seminars, conferences, colloquia, and workshops. I am pleased to acknowledge the following audiences:

Chapter 1. University of Cape Coast, Ghana, 2010; Society for Ethnomusicology, Philadelphia, 2011; George Eastman Lectures, Oxford University, 2013; City University, London, 2013.

Chapter 2. Harvard University, 2006; University of Paris (1), 2008; Society for Musicology in Ireland and the Royal Musical Association, Dublin, 2009; University of Georgia, Athens, 2017; 50th Annual Conference on African Linguistics (ACAL 50), University of British Columbia, Vancouver, 2019.

Chapter 3. King's College, London, 2008; Society for Ethnomusicology, Middletown, CT, 2008; Music Conservatory and University of Amsterdam, 2008; Indiana University, 2008; Royal Museum for Central Africa, Tervuren, Belgium, 2009; University of Oxford, UK, 2010; University of Ghana, Legon, 2010; University of Cape Coast, Ghana, 2010; Temple University, Philadelphia, 2010; University of Wisconsin, Madison, 2011; Boston University Music Society, 2011; Annual Conference of the Association of Nigerian Musicologists (ANIM), Nsukka, Nigeria, 2012; McGill University, 2009; Royal Holloway, University of London, 2012; RMA Research Student Conference, Southampton, UK, 2013; University of Miami, Coral

Gables, 2014; University of California, Los Angeles, 2016; University of Alabama, 2016.

Chapter 5. 38th Annual Meeting of the Society for Music Theory, St. Louis, 2015; Cornell University, 2016; Universidade Nova de Lisboa (FCSH/NOVA), Lisbon, 2016; Gesellschaft für Musiktheorie International Music Theory Lecture, Berlin, 2022.

Chapter 6. First International Conference on Analytical Approaches to World Music, Amherst, MA, 2010.

Chapter 7. University of Oxford, UK, 2010.

Earlier versions of the essays have appeared as follows:

Chapter 1. *Resiliency and Distinction: Beliefs, Endurance and Creativity in the Musical Arts of Continental and Diasporic Africa. A Festschrift in Honor of Jacqueline Cogdell DjeDje*, edited by Kimasi L. Browne and Jean N. Kidula (Richmond, CA: MRI Press, 2013).

Chapter 3. *Audible Empire: Music, Global Politics, Critique*, edited by Ronald Radano and Tejumola Olaniyan (Durham, NC: Duke University Press, 2016). Portuguese translation by José H. Padovani in *Revista Vórtex* 9 (2021). https://doi.org/10.33871/23179937.2021.9.1.20.

Chapter 4. *Circuit, musiques contemporaines* 21 (2011).

Chapter 6. *The Dawn of Music Semiology: Essays in Honor of Jean-Jacques Nattiez*, edited by Jonathan Dunsby and Jonathan Goldman (Rochester, NY: University of Rochester Press, 2017).

Special thanks to Nathaniel Mitchell for preparing the music examples and to Norm Hirschy and Rachel Ruisard of Oxford University Press for their interest, advice, and support during the preparation of this text.

Introduction

These are exciting days for lovers of African music. At no other time in the continent's history has there been such a massive proliferation of musical forms and performances. Ritual, entertainment, work, worship, and play regularly provide the conditions of possibility for a plethora of creative acts. Forms of professional, semi-professional, and amateur music-making are ubiquitous in village and city, at home and abroad. Enabled and aided by a vast range of expanded media resources, African music is also disseminated daily in diverse recorded forms. To say that African music as a performing and performed art is thriving today is to state the obvious—indeed, it is to risk saying something banal.[1]

Academic scholarship on African music, which always—and perhaps necessarily—lags behind practice, has reacted positively to some of these developments. If we date the modern revival of printed research to the year 1980—and this merely for the sake of one symbolic act—we might begin to outline that history by pointing to the twenty-volume *New Grove Dictionary of Music and Musicians* (1980), which, despite its "inherent European bias," gave unprecedented coverage to African countries.[2] The *New Grove*'s 2001 revised successor, now extending to twenty-nine volumes, went even further, augmenting the earlier coverage with articles on individual ethnic groups, musicians, instruments, and influential genres. And since *Grove* became

[1] This opening paragraph was written only a few months before the onset of the Covid-19 pandemic in 2020 and the forced sequestration that followed. To rethink this book in light of the pandemic's ravages would be difficult, if not impossible. I would have to contend with the erosion of all sorts of categories, some political, others social and still others conceptual. On the horizon today (May 2022), however, is the optimism engendered by the availability of vaccines and the gradual resumption of our old routines. These developments encourage me to retain a sense of optimism about returning to the old normal, and to think of the pandemic as an intermezzo, a historical parenthesis, perhaps even a bad dream. To put it that way is not to suggest that the pre- and post-pandemic periods will come to be seen as continuous—how could they be? It is simply to acknowledge the extremity of the moment itself without rushing into a premature assessment of its ramifications.

[2] In 1985, James Koetting gave notice of this coverage in the flagship journal of the Society for Ethnomusicology, describing it as "wide-ranging [and] up-to-date" and "supersed[ing] anything available for the general study of African music," in "Sub-Saharan Africa," *Ethnomusicology* 29 (1985), 314–317.

On African Music. Kofi Agawu, Oxford University Press. © Oxford University Press 2023.
DOI: 10.1093/oso/9780197664063.001.0001

available online in 2001, these resources have multiplied still. A new and developing bibliographical resource, *Oxford Bibliographies Online*, includes entries on topics such as "East and West Africa," "North Africa," "Music, Dance, and the Study of Africa," "Traditional Music," "Central African Republic," "Fela," "Nketia," "Post-Colonialism," and "Ethnomusicology," among others.[3]

There's more. A little over two decades ago, the first ever English-language encyclopedia on African music was published by Garland. Under the editorship of Ruth M. Stone, it featured contributions by senior scholars as well as several emerging ones. In the last three decades alone, numerous monographs (by Omojola, Fernando, Ampene, Muller, Charry, Arom, Olaniyan, Dor, Nzewi, Kubik, Kidula, Chikowero, Eyre, Jaji, Ndaliko, Klein, Feld, Busse Berger, and Perman, among many others), book-length ethnographies (by Askew, Tang, Gunderson, Djèdje, Reed, Friedson, Nannyonga-Tamusuza, Vallejo, Kyker, Steingo, Kafumbe, and Impey, among many others), and scores of articles in professional journals have appeared, testifying to the vibrancy of research. Book series emphasizing African music have been inaugurated (at Temple University Press and at Cambridge University Press, for example), while some journals have devoted whole or partial issues to African music (*Research in African Literatures* in 2001, *Trans* in 2005, *Music Theory Online* in 2010, *The World of Music* in 2014 and 2015, and *Perspectives of New Music* [forthcoming]). New imaginings of African music's imbrication in other domains undertaken by historians, philosophers, literary theorists, and anthropologists have appeared (see, for example, the diverse disciplinary affiliations of contributors to *Audible Empire: Music, Global Politics, Critique* (2016), edited by Ronald Radano and Tejumola Olaniyan). The explosion on the internet of African content remains astounding. Then, too, conferences, symposia, and festivals continue to be held in Africa, China, Australia, Europe, and the United States to celebrate the music of our continent. We hear of newly formed professional associations like the ICTM Study Group on African Musics, PASMAE (Pan African Society for Musical Arts Education), ANIM (Association of Nigerian Musicologists), and MUSIGA (Musicians Union of Ghana). And as regards the training of scholars, master's, and doctoral degrees continue to be earned at institutions worldwide for research into African and African-diasporic music.

[3] *Oxford Bibliographies Online* (http://www.oxfordbibliographies.com). For a comprehensive bibliography, see John Gray, *Music of Sub-Saharan Africa: an International Bibliography and Resource Guide* (Nyack, NY: African Diaspora Press, 2018).

Significant, too, is the increasing participation of African scholars—individuals born in the tradition—in the process of knowledge production. This badly needed and long overdue demographic change has engendered a reordering of scholarly priorities; it is also puncturing existing paradigms and pointing the way to a more ethical and diverse scholarship. No longer the exclusive preserve of card-carrying ethnomusicologists, knowledge about African music is being produced under a variety of disciplinary aegises: cultural studies, musicology, religion, cognitive studies, linguistics, anthropology, area studies, sound studies, diaspora studies, ecomusicology, music education, music theory, and postcolonial theory, among others. Such knowledge is also sometimes woven thematically into broader interdisciplinary projects. While universal agreement about scholarly procedure and research priorities is still a long way off—we're still reckoning with conceptual differences, some of them fundamental, regarding language and definitions of key terms, geo-cultural representation, the competing perspectives of insiders and outsiders, the very nature of music's ontology, and practical issues in symbolic representation—incorporation of the voices of those who belong simultaneously to the classes of researcher and researched has enhanced African musicology's profile.

It is against this broad background that I have assembled seven essays on aspects of theory and practice in African music as a contribution to ongoing discussion and debate in African musicology. The bulk of them originate in the George Eastman Lectures in Music that I was privileged to deliver at Oxford University in 2013. The remaining essays are drawn from a keynote address to the Society for Music Theory in 2015 and from talks given to audiences in Africa, Europe, and the United States over the last decade and a half. But for a couple of passages of necessary close reading in Chapters 1 and 4, I have in mind a general, humanistic readership rather than jargon-wielding specialists. I also have in mind communities of continent-based readers whose curiosities are not necessarily shaped by the current preoccupations of the Western academy.

This is not the first time I've ventured into the territories explored in this book. In an earlier book, *Representing African Music: Postcolonial Notes, Queries, Positions* (2003), I sought to affirm certain scholarly practices, interrogate others, and encourage debate about certain beliefs and practices that had assumed axiomatic status in African musicology. So I broached issues like the shape of the archive, fieldwork, material discrepancies among differently-positioned scholars, the use of metropolitan rather than African languages, the obsession with rhythm, difference production, analysis, and the ethics of representation. Although the present book retains something of the interrogative spirit of that earlier book, critique as such is *not* the main goal here; rather, I seek to engage more fully with issues dealt with only in passing in previous publications. Having set out an agenda for students wishing to delve more deeply into these collective repertories in *The African Imagination in Music* (2016; French translation, *L'Imagination africaine en musique*, 2020), I focus here on a handful of issues, many of them familiar but still warranting sustained discussion: the minimalist impulse, iconicity as a prevalent modality, tonality's dominating and colonizing impact, African pianism as an avenue for creativity within the insufficiently-acknowledged realm of art music, how the discipline of music theory can benefit from deeper engagement with African music, ethno-theory as a problematic discourse, and the ubiquity of rhythm studies. Each chapter is notionally complete in itself, so the essays may be read in whatever order the reader chooses. It is my hope, however, that resonances (and unavoidable repetition) among them will confer on the collection as a whole a cumulative value that exceeds the value of individual essays.

What, then, are the concerns of individual chapters?

Establishing the *what* and *how* of music-making is basic to sound analysis. Although compositional strategies take different forms, I argue in Chapter 1 that a minimalist impulse lies at the heart of African creativity. Large tracts of musical thought are routinely spun from a minimum of resources—two or three pitches, a pair of contrasting timbres, or nuggets of distinctly shaped rhythms subjected to extensive repetition. Calling this mode "minimalist" and therefore appropriating a term from European music historiography is meant to facilitate analysis, encourage cross-cultural exploration, and ultimately engender admiration for the achievements of African musicians working in predominantly oral traditions who have developed extraordinary abilities to make much out of little.

Chapter 2, "Iconicity: Gift or burden?," proceeds from the premise that human attempts to grasp reality are invariably mediated. Semiotician C. S. Peirce, for example, sought to understand such attempts by formulating a universal algebra of equations. One particular trichotomy of modes of signification, icon-index-symbol, although only a tiny part of Peirce's algebra, has proved fruitful and suggestive for conceptual exploration in a variety of fields, and it will serve here as a point of reference for approaches to meaning-making. While the symbolic mode is well known to Africanists—Africa, indeed, is a land awash in symbols—the indexical and iconic modes have not received as much attention. My interest in this chapter is in the iconic mode, the most immediate and rampant. What are the principal manifestations of iconicity in African (musical) culture? By assembling a number of vivid instances of auditive and visual iconicity, I begin to develop an answer to this question. I don't stop at description and illustration, however, but go on to inquire briefly into what might be considered iconicity's "developmental" potential. Seeking socioeconomic value for a purely technical device is admittedly a contentious move, but I will suggest that the iconic mode be understood as limited, and that its ubiquity be considered an ambiguous "gift."

All music-making presupposes the existence of musical systems. Designed to orient rather than constrict music-making, such systems may be explicit and codified, or implicit and resident in the minds and memories of performers and their audiences. Of the many systems employed by contemporary African musicians, one in particular, tonality, a system of manifestly foreign (European) origins, has gained increasing visibility since it was introduced in the nineteenth century by Christian missionaries, but it has not received as much comment as its ubiquity might warrant. What forms of tonality were exported to Africa, and what sorts of traces have they left on the African soundscape? What was that soundscape like before tonality arrived? If tonality is akin to a language, how has it been "spoken" in Africa, and how has it shaped the musical consciousness of producers and consumers of African music? Chapter 3, "Tonality as a Colonizing Force," addresses these questions and concludes that this symbolically freighted musical resource—an ideological package, no less—has functioned as a colonizing force, enabling forms of creativity while at the same time inhibiting the pursuit of many potential avenues to creativity beholden to indigenous expression.

On-paper composition is the subject of Chapter 4, "African pianism and the challenge of art music." While the best-known African repertories fall roughly into two broad categories, traditional music (which emanates from traditional, pre-colonial segments of society) and popular music (which is a largely urban, commercial, and modern activity), there exists a third repertory, art music, that came into being in the nineteenth century in the wake of European Christian missionization and subsequent colonial presence. Although not as prominent as the other two, the practice of art music is far from insignificant; its identity and creative possibilities are topics of growing interest to composers and critics. African pianism, a movement within African art music, is the brainchild of the Nigerian composer, scholar, and performer, Akin Euba (1935–2020). It was given further visibility by Ghanaian-American scholar and pianist, William Chapman Nyaho (b.1958), who not only edited the first ever anthology of piano music by composers of the Black Atlantic for Oxford University Press in 2007, but subsequently recorded selected items from the anthology. What specific challenges does the composition of art music bring to African composers, and how might the steps taken by currently active composers encourage the development of this dimension of African creativity? The Oxford anthology prompts reflection on these and related questions.

Academic research into music theory in the Western academy has traditionally focused on Western "classical" music. Recent globalizing and post-globalizing trends have engendered a broadening of repertories to include non-canonical music (including popular music), non-Western music (from Southeast Asia, India, China, and Africa), and miscellaneous sound sources, be they ringtones, protest songs, or urban soundscapes. In Chapter 5, I welcome these new developments and suggest that the quotidian practice of music theory in the Anglo-American academy stands to be enriched by greater contact with Black African music as well. At the core of the chapter are eight platforms, presented synoptically and drawn from my *African Imagination in Music*, upon which the engagement with African music might proceed. Setting these platforms into relief requires that we rehearse music theory's previous encounters with the non-West. Here it emerges that the non-West has never been absent from the Western imaginary, but has played variable roles at different points in history. These roles foster a range of attitudes, from puzzlement and downright dismissal of the music of others through exoticization to acknowledgment of strong organizing principles followed by genuine appreciation. To "rethink music theory with African aid," therefore, is to retrieve from the margins of theory's own history the sorts of engagement that have become ethical imperatives in our time. I end the chapter on a pedagogical note by advocating two practices: transcription (of African musics into various standard notations to facilitate analysis) and contrapuntal reading (after Edward Said), with its potential to unveil unsuspected parallels between compositions and performances of diverse, perhaps even far-flung origins, and in the process, expose deep-lying convergences in the ways in which human beings imagine and make music.

Knowledge producers divide into universalists and particularists, absolutists and relativists. Among particularists is a group espousing something called *ethnotheory*, a species of theory that ostensibly gives pride of place to indigenous categories of thought, including the words and formulations of indigenous musicians. Since ethnotheory in principle announces a difference from theory, we must first ask, "What is ethnotheory?" We might follow that with a second question, "What do African musicologists stand to gain from adopting ethno-theoretical frameworks?" Without wishing to undervalue indigenous knowledge, nor to underestimate its potential for self-empowerment, I nevertheless take a stand in Chapter 6 against ethno-theory. Following in the footsteps of anti-ethnophilosophers, I question ethnotheory's coherence and argue that, on political and intellectual grounds, it is both a limited and a limiting concept.

Chapter 7, "African Rhythm Studies," builds on the widely circulated view that rhythm is the single most distinctive quality of African music—a view reflected not only in the popular imagination but also in the musicological literature. Why is there such intense interest in African rhythm? Although possibly interesting from the point of view of race-based reception and attribution, developing a comprehensive answer to that question will require more space than is available here. What is doable, however, is addressing "who" and "what" questions: who has written technically about African rhythm in the last one hundred years or so, and what have they claimed in the way of explanatory theory? I provide brisk summaries of the writings of some two dozen authors and then go on to observe some of the routines of theory-making. Rhythm remains salient in scholarship because it appears to be more fully elaborated in African music than in other world repertories. The assumptions made by scholars, the institutional contexts in which theories are produced, and the fact that the body of scholarship is strangely non-cumulative insofar as subsequent writers do not always build on their predecessors' findings—these are some of the features of the discourse.

Achieving an emancipated discourse is, I believe, a widely shared ambition for African music scholarship among progressives. It requires a careful sifting of alternatives based on an intelligent recognition of Africa's historically specific needs and desires. In these essays, I seek to engage just a handful of issues that I believe are pertinent to the pursuit of that ambition, and I do so from within the institutional discourses of music studies. There are ultimately no guarantees to this kind of exercise, except perhaps the silent rewards entailed in any analytical proceeding, the satisfaction that comes from proximity to sonic materials, and the edification that accrues from reflecting on the nature of their relatedness.

1

The Minimalist Impulse

Among the wonders of African creativity is the ability of certain individuals to spin large tracts of musical thought out of a minimum of resources: two or three pitches, a pair of contrasting timbres, or nuggets of distinctly shaped rhythms. The animating impulse, which may be described as *minimalist*, is widespread throughout Africa, and it is the aim of this chapter to acknowledge its symbolic importance and to lay bare a few of its enabling mechanisms. Although the term *minimalism* has not yet made it into the mainstream of African musicology (it emerges, for example, in writings by Martin Scherzinger and others aligning Steve Reich's music with African music), there is an implicit belief that the aesthetic of African polyphonic and polyrhythmic practices is minimalistic at the core.[1] Anyone familiar with traditional music from Uganda, the DRC, the Central African Republic, Nigeria, Cameroon, Ghana, or the Côte d'Ivoire (among numerous others) will readily call to mind styles and idioms marked by extensive or even obsessive repetition. Insofar as the minimalist manner is constituted by repetition, a device long associated with much African music, the chapter's main claim is not new; nor should it be controversial. What may be new, and what I hope will bring insight, is the process of thinking through these familiar repertories once again as intentional acts motivated by an unspoken minimalist aesthetic. Designating this a "minimalist" mode and therefore appropriating a term from European music historiography should facilitate analysis, encourage cross-cultural exploration, and ultimately engender admiration for the achievements of African musicians working in predominantly oral traditions who have developed extraordinary abilities to make much out of little.

I first define minimalism by contrasting "Western" conceptions emerging specifically in the 1950s and 1960s with African conceptions, whose origins,

[1] Scherzinger, "Afro-Electric Counterpoint," in *Rethinking Reich*, edited by Sumanth Gopinath and Pwyll ap Sîon (New York: Oxford University Press, 2019). Throughout his treatise, *African Polyphony and Polyrhythm* (1991), Simha Arom treats the collective repertoires of Central African traditional music as implicitly minimalist.

On African Music. Kofi Agawu, Oxford University Press. © Oxford University Press 2023.
DOI: 10.1093/oso/9780197664063.003.0001

although yet to be definitively established, are undoubtedly ancient (based on continuities of musical style) and precede the twentieth-century Western practices. A second section samples the sound of African minimalism by commenting briefly on twenty recorded examples of solo and ensemble music selected from a variety of vocal and instrumental African repertories. In Section 3, I dig a bit deeper into musical procedure with an analysis of *Farafinko*, a solo composition by Ivorian balafon virtuoso Aly Keita (b.1969). In a concluding section, I return to a broader perspective with brief remarks about the potential of African minimalism.

Defining Minimalism

Using the word *minimalist* immediately awakens comparisons with the influential movement known as minimalism in Western art music, "one of the most notable developments in late twentieth-century musical culture."[2] According to the conventional narrative, Western minimalism emerged in the 1960s and 1970s in painting, sculpture, literature, and music; its first generation included the composers La Monte Young, Terry Riley, Steve Reich, and Philip Glass. Although their individual styles are internally diversified, these pioneer minimalists shared a commitment to repudiating the values of complexity and alienation associated with musical modernism (as found in the music of Schoenberg and Webern) and replacing them with an accessible, easily heard style based on the essences of musical material. Minimalists foregrounded repetition, treating it not only as a necessary structural device but as a rhetorical option. Along with cellular construction and motivic saturation, minimalist music effected a transformation of the temporal ambience of a performance, highlighting the present or the here and now, discarding a past burdened by nostalgic attachments to musical material, and caring little for a future packaged as so many (empty) promises. These are only the most visible signs of a deep affinity between Western and African minimalism. But there are differences as well. In an effort to characterize African minimalism more precisely, it would be helpful to compare and contrast it with a generalized Western minimalism, bearing in mind that these overarching

[2] Keith Potter, "Minimalism," in *The New Grove Dictionary of Music and Musicians*, ed. Stanley Sadie (New York: Oxford University Press, 2001), vol. 16, p. 716.

categories are necessarily simplified, and that they refer in actuality to a constellation of multifarious practices.[3]

Minimalism, according to Keith Potter, is "a term borrowed from the visual arts to describe a style of composition characterized by an intentionally simplified rhythmic, melodic and harmonic vocabulary."[4] Let us single out three aspects of that definition for a parallel discussion of African minimalism: designation, origins, and intention.

No single term for *minimalism* has so far emerged in black African discourses about music. Nevertheless, there is a plethora of terms that point to a range of qualities associated with minimality. The Ewe lexicon, for example, includes terms for minimum (*nu swɛswɛ*), smallness (*swɛnɔnɔ*), essence (*nua ŋutɔ*), cogent (*zidzi*), and limit (*sefe*). The opposing term, "maximalism," is also missing from metalinguistic designation of musical practice, but there are terms for maximum (*nusi enye lolotɔ*), infinite (*mavɔ*), wide or flowing (*vlayaa*), grand (*gã, lolo*), and superlative (sɔgbɔwu wo katã), to choose only a handful.[5] In making these sorts of comparisons, we should remember that absence is not an indication of a lack but a sign of an alternative distribution of qualities and priorities. It appears that African vocabularies associated with music-making typically refer to names of instruments and genres, encode performance actions, and index word-based functions and meanings (we will return to this issue in connection with ethno-theory in Chapter 6). Thus an abstract term like "minimalism," which was designed to capture a range of individual practices related by their emphasis on minimal resources that are then put through regimes of repetition, phasing, reassertion, and cellular manipulation, is not likely to be in regular circulation unless elicited by an eager ethnographer, imposed from outside the culture, or self-consciously cultivated by an ambitious group leader. The point about designation, then, is simply that although the verbal economies surrounding African performance are not loaded with the term "minimalism" or its synonyms, qualities essential to the term are regularly on display and easily conveyed.

[3] For a cogent and helpful guide to the literature on minimalism, see Robert Fink and Cecilia Sun, "Minimalism," *Oxford Bibliographies Online*, accessed July 8, 2021, https://www-oxfordbibliographies-com.ezproxy.princeton.edu/view/document/obo-9780199757824/obo-9780199757824-0188.xml. See also Quinn, "Minimal Challenges: Process Music and the Uses of Formalist Analysis," *Contemporary Music Review* 25 (2006), 283–294.

[4] Potter, "Minimalism."

[5] Dietrich Frederich Westermann, *Ewefiala or Ewe-English Dictionary* (Berlin: Reimer, 1928).

Second, regarding origins, just as Western minimalism encompassed other arts, so the patterns of African musical minimalism display affinities with visual arts. Inter-domain affinities underpin the African arts. In a number of writings, art historian Robert Farris Thompson has postulated conceptual parallels between visual and temporal art. The unfolding of overall design in Mande-related "country cloths," for example, is likened by Thompson to "a vibrant propensity for offbeat phrasing," just as the patterning of certain narrow-strip textiles is said to be evocative of interlocking patterns in musical execution.[6] Because interlocking typically involves two separate sound patterns entering into each other's spaces and doing so with impunity, the technique is especially felicitous for modeling a form of musical minimalism distributed across a multi-voiced texture. The point is not that African musical minimalism originated from nonmusical arts, but that analogous processes of minimalist structuring may be discerned in both music and visual art.[7]

A more significant dimension of the question of origins is the historical one. What I am calling "Western minimalism" arose at a very specific historical moment (1950s and 1960s) and in reaction to a very specific and recent past of compositional activity, including the following: the modernist revolution of the early decades of the twentieth century; expressionism; the growth, spread and further formalization of serialism; the emergence of other streams of music, including jazz, rock, and popular music; and last but not least, the greater visibility (and audibility) of non-Western music in the Western world, including several projects involving the assembly of numerous ethnographic recordings which then paved the way for the emergence of so-called World Music in the 1990s. Early minimalists like Riley and Reich contributed to a new compositional economy in which ruling techniques of persistent repetition and inflected alignment of textural layers were valued as alternatives to earlier structuring devices. Western minimalism cannot therefore be adequately understood without taking into account antecedent developments spearheaded by musicians active in a variety of traditions, among them Schoenberg, Webern, Boulez, Duke Ellington, Charlie Parker, Miles Davis, and Elvis Presley.

[6] Robert Farris Thompson, *Flash of the Spirit: African & Afro-American Art & Philosophy* (New York: Vintage Books, 1984), 207.

[7] See also Meki Nzewi, *African Music: Theoretical Content and Creative Continuum*, where "bounce-off relationships in space" are likened to cross rhythms or "two with three in music" (pp. 36–38) and Kubik, "African Space/Time Concepts and the 'Tusona' Ideographs in Luchazi Culture: With a Discussion of Possible Cross-Parallels in Music," *African Music* 6 (1987), 53–89.

Minimalism in African music, by contrast, has a much older and largely unwritten history. It would seem, in fact, that minimalism was there in the beginning, that it coincided with some of the earliest manifestations of ensemble music-making. Of course, we can only speculate on such ultimate origins, but what is significant for present purposes is that African minimalism did not emerge as a reaction to the perceived excesses of a prior modernism; composers were in no way expressing dissatisfaction with past practices. Rather, the minimalist impulse appeared almost as a gift. To make music was always already to adopt a minimalistic mode, it would seem.

Western artists in the 1950s and 1960s thus came to discover something that had existed in Africa for centuries, something that defined an original African compositional mode, with its roots in music, language, and dance. That this discovery was made in the political, economic, and social climate of the post-war period in the United States and later Europe is no accident. Thanks to developments in commercial and ethnographic recording initiated in France, the UK, Germany, and the United States, Western musicians could now access diverse sound fields of canonical and noncanonical world repertoires.[8] Steve Reich, for example, a foundational figure in the American minimalist tradition, studied the transcriptions of Southern Ewe music made in the 1950s by the Reverend A. M. Jones, and was intrigued by the ingenious uses of rhythmic repetition in ensemble music. He would later visit Ghana and study drumming (1970), make his own transcriptions of the canonized dance-musics *Gahu* and *Agbadza* following A. M. Jones's example as set out in the latter's magnum opus, *Studies in African Music* (1959), and supplement his interest in African music with study of other World Music, notably music from Indonesia and India. Reich's "sources"—by which I mean inducements to composition—thus include significant encounters with non-Western music.[9] In short, whereas African minimalists pursued minimalist strategies as natural and organic enactments of long-standing conventions, Western minimalists chose a new path in the 1960s in reaction to earlier developments. Some composers sought liberation from the structures and strictures of total serialism, indeterminacy, and complexity; others aimed

[8] Michael Denning, *Noise Uprising: The Audiopolitics of a World Musical Revolution* (London: Verso, 2015).

[9] Steve Reich recounts some of these encounters in *Writings on Music, 1965–2000* (New York: Oxford University Press, 2002). See also Scherzinger, "Gyorgy Ligeti and the Aka Pygmies Project," *Contemporary Music Review* 25 (2006), 227–262; Scherzinger, "Afro-Electric Counterpoint," pp. 259–302; and Michael Tenzer, "That's All It Does: Steve Reich and Balinese Gamelan," in Gopinath and Sîon, *Rethinking Reich*, pp. 303–322.

to achieve accessible and audible results, and still others aimed to encourage wider participation in music-making by people with modest performing abilities. By embracing repetition, Western minimalists were surely embracing the oldest trick in the trade. It remained only to acknowledge that here, as in other realms of creativity, Africa once led the way.

A third factor in distinguishing Western from African minimalism is the matter of intention. If, as Potter says, Western minimalism is "characterized by an *intentionally simplified* rhythmic, melodic and harmonic vocabulary," then African minimalism is both like *and* unlike the West's. It is like the West's in the mundane sense in which all acts of composition and performance are in principle intended by their originators. This does not mean that every last detail of a composition or performance is pre-scripted; it only means that the work's conditions of possibility are laid out in advance by an individual or, in cases of communal composition as encountered among some African communities, a group.[10] Some musical details are consigned to the contingencies of performance, but the fact of prior scripting reinforces the pertinence of the intentionality factor.

African minimalism is unlike its Western counterpart, however, insofar as its compositional imperative at birth already includes a minimalist mandate. In many African traditions, composing in a minimalist manner (for flute and horn ensembles, xylophones, mbiras and other lamellophones, and drum ensembles) is not merely an activity constrained by musical conventions; it responds to aesthetical and ethical considerations as well. The dimensions of subjectivity that allow a Schoenberg, Webern, Cage, Stockhausen, or Lachenmann to opt out of conventions, redefine sound ideals, or redefine their relations to the past, are distributed differently among African composers. The closest African parallels may be glimpsed in the output of composers of art music, such as Akin Euba, Joshua Uzoigwe, Kwabena Nketia, and Justinian Tamusuza (we will return to art music in Chapter 4). But these parallels are put under severe strain when extended to composers of traditional music, for Euba and his colleagues write as individuals for their audiences of choice and with no necessary societal or communal constraint. Poetically, it might be said that the traditional African composer does not elect to compose minimalist music; to compose is always already to adopt a minimalist mode. In this view, compositional resources are gratefully

[10] George Dor, "Communal Creativity and Song Ownership in Anlo-Ewe Musical Practice: The Case of *Havolu*," *Ethnomusicology* 48 (2004): 26–51.

received and treated with reverence. An Aka composer of vocal polyphony or a Southern Ewe composer of drum ensemble music does not approach a pre-compositional resource like the anhemitonic pentatonic scale by entertaining the thought that it is an option to be accepted or rejected; rather, the African composer operating in this tradition accepts this conventional resource as an enabler and directs compositional energies to other domains (e.g., to the composition of topical song texts, or to enriching the drum language by introducing new patterns). Historically, then, minimalism in the sense described above represented a *choice* for Western composers whereas, for many composers in the traditional African sphere, it was—and continues to be—a gift, albeit a constraining gift. (I will make a similar argument about iconicity in the next chapter).

A related issue is that of notation—which again emerges in the context of African art music rather than traditional music. Although improvisatory license is sometimes given to performers of Western minimalist music (e.g., freedom to choose the order in which to play or sing patterns, freedom to determine how many repetitions to take on a given occasion, and freedom to select a register, timbre, or dynamic level—all available, for example, in Terry Riley's *In C* [1964]), many compositions by Reich, Glass, Adams, and others are fully notated; they belong to the tradition of notated Western art music, the "literate tradition," as Taruskin calls it.[11] By contrast, African minimalism, and especially the larger proportion of repertoires belonging to the traditional sphere, generally knows no external written form. Aside from their sporadic appearances in ethnomusicological texts as tokens of descriptive notation, the collective repertoires of traditional music are inscribed in the memories of their composers, performers, and listeners; they are part of a living oral-aural tradition.

The emergence of African art music in the last century-and-a-half has altered the narrative, however. Minimalism is no longer confined to the traditional sphere—the sphere we've been talking about, and the one that has typically supplied essentialized images of *African music* to those minimalist and post-minimalist composers (like Reich) who have freely admitted the influence of its sound and ideals. Like their Western counterparts, some African composers of art music have produced works that utilize procedures associated with "Western" minimalism, but these procedures are more directly sourced from their indigenous heritage. Consider a few examples from the

[11] Richard Taruskin, *The Oxford History of Western Music* (New York: Oxford, 2005).

1992 CD from Kronos Quartet: *Pieces of Africa*.[12] Zimbabwean composer-performer Dumisani Maraire's composition "Mai Nozipo" (Mother Nozipo) (1990) is based on a short, repeated harmonic cycle given profile by a diatonic melody, regulated by a popular clave time-line pattern, and accompanied by a drum. The strings of the Kronos Quartet participate in the rendition of this ostinato, incorporating melodic ornamentation along the way. Strictly speaking, one should recognize the crossing of generic boundaries here, for while the mixture of string quartet and African instruments signals a non-traditional ensemble, indeed the kind of self-conscious orchestration that is more typical of art music, the repeated harmonic-melodic cycle, insofar as it is flavored by functional harmony, is an index of popular rather than traditional music.

Ugandan composer Justinian Tamusuza's "Ekitundu Ekisooka" (1988), heard on the same CD, is even more saturated with repetition. Scored for string quartet, it eschews Maraire's functional harmony and features a consistent pentatonic sound throughout. The combination of sprightly, lively rhythms and brief melodic ideas invokes a traditional idiom, almost as if the piece were a transcription. The sound of the violin in Tamusuza's work may remind some listeners of fiddle playing in other world traditions (Celtic in particular), but the gentle polyphonic writing and percussive pizzicato effects provide the aesthetic distancing that underlies this work's status as art music rather than folk music. And although the African flavors in this work are unmistakable, the resemblance to Reichian minimalism is noteworthy.

Tamusuza's work appears in another collection, this time the second of a two-volume anthology of African piano music published in 2005.[13] "Abakadde Abaagalana Be Balima Akambugu" (Mutual Lovers are Always Successful), scored for soprano, tenor and piano, is 167 bars long, retains a $\frac{6}{4}$ meter throughout, and, like "Ekitundu Ekisooka," utilizes a consistent pentatonic resource in the piano accompaniment; indeed the right hand is limited to perfect fourths, fifths, and octaves while the left hand invests in scale degrees 1, 4 and 5. The vocal parts occasionally incorporate pitches outside the basic pentatonic resource, but such departures, involving the bending of notes and sliding between others in order to capture the nuances of spoken

[12] Kronos Quartet, *Pieces of Africa*, CD (New York: Elektra Nonesuch, 1992).

[13] Justinian Tamusuza, "Abakadde Abaagalana Be Balima Akambugu," in *Towards an African Pianism: Keyboard Music by Composers of the African Diaspora*, edited by Cynthia Tse Kimberlin and Akin Euba (Richmond, CA: MRI Press, 2005).

language, never really disturb the pentatonic horizon. Here too, repetition within a restricted pitch vocabulary confers a minimalist aura.

Other examples of minimalism in African art music may be mentioned briefly. Nigerian composer Joshua Uzoigwe's "Ukom," from his set of piano pieces called *Talking Drums*, affects an obsessive manner reminiscent of 1960s minimalism. The five movements of Volans's "White Man Sleeps" (1985) (also heard on Kronos Quartet's *Pieces of Africa*), chart a slightly different path to minimalism from that of other composers represented on the CD, but they retain an essential gesture of what might be called translation. An enduring impression of some of Volans's early work is of music transcribed directly from African traditional sources, but the evident compositional labor complicates any reading of these works as mere transcriptions. The first movement is virtually a catalogue of devices of repetition. Motives, rhythms, and static chords maintain a constant presence; the tempo and textural alternations in the second movement enhance the minimalist aura in a Stravinskian, block-like manner—not by enveloping listeners through entrainment but by casting them as observers. Finally, Scherzinger's *Masanga* for two pianos (1998), also included in the Euba-Kimberlin anthology, takes advantage of earlier minimalist scores in essaying a harmonically and melodically restricted course. According to the composer, "*Masanga* is a new song using three old chords that are patterned into naïve melody," and he acknowledges the influence of Mwenda Jean Bosco's *Masanga* and thus a nod to the popular music sphere much like Maraire.[14]

In general, African minimalist works in the art music vein display a variety of techniques. Some unwittingly expose the core minimalism of traditional African music by drawing on transcriptions—real or imagined—of traditional African music, while others follow a minimalist imperative based on familiarity with traditional African music. Some are raw exercises in mimicry, being modeled on minimalist works from other traditions. Beyond the markedness of their basic materials, these written compositions by African composers (and numerous others like them) can be placed alongside works by composers like Andriessen, Pärt, Adams, Glass, Nyman, and others.

So far in this chapter, we have drawn on Potter's definition of minimalism to outline some of the grosser parallels and non-parallels between African and Western minimalism. I stopped along the way to acknowledge the work of composers of African art music. Let us now turn to specific products of

[14] Scherzinger, "*Masanga* for Two Pianos (1998)," 291.

the African tradition in order to begin to characterize its sound world more precisely. In inviting readers to listen to African music, I am operating under the belief that certain truths and insight conveyed aurally resist ready verbal specification. There is, in other words, a gap between experience and reported experience; no verbal description can finally convey the full sense of music as heard or felt. This is a frequently acknowledged limitation that honest critics have had to reckon with. I mention it here not merely as a familiar challenge to writing about music, but because listening to African music, the very aural engagement with it, is an activity that continues to require advocacy even today.

The Sound of African Minimalism: A Sampling

If, as I have argued, the aesthetic of African traditional music is fundamentally minimalist, then, given the extraordinarily huge corpus that constitutes African traditional music, coming up with a representative sampling would be a task in itself. Wherever we look and listen, we encounter modalities of minimalist expression: repetition, cyclicity, pulse-orientation, periodicity, groove, ostinato, present-orientation, and a host of others. Whether one takes one's bearings from older compilations of African music, or from participation in live performances, one invariably encounters musical styles animated by persistent, unrelenting repetition. The great xylophone and balafon traditions of East, Southern, and West Africa are cases in point; then there are the one-stringed (gonje) repertories found throughout West Africa, which often feature extensive reiteration of motives. Even more symbolical are ensembles of horns, flutes, and panpipes found throughout Central, East, and Southern Africa, in which the imperatives of group music-making coalesce around periodic regularities and complementary materials.

For the more modest purposes of this chapter, I have assembled a small list of twenty recorded performances to exemplify the basic procedures associated with African minimalism (these are listed in Figure 1.1). Readers are invited to contemplate the regimes of repetition that lie at the core of these performances. I offer brief comments on salient features of each excerpt in hopes of enhancing the reader's appreciation of the variety of structural procedures, but it goes without saying that each excerpt can sustain a deeper, more extensive analysis. I have often insisted that direct aural engagement with the sounding forms of African music, without the

	National/ethnic origin, year	Instrumentation
1	Togo, Kabiyé, 2004. CD, *Orchestres et lithophones Kabiyé* (Paris: Ocora, 2004), track 10.	*Pichanchalassi* lithophone
2	Democratic Republic of the Congo, Nkundo, 1971–72. CD, *Anthologies de la musique congolaise*, Vol. 11: Musique des Nkundo (Tervuren: Fonti Musicali, 2007), track 9.	Female voice with hand clap
3	Ghana, Kusasi, 1976. CD, *Ghana: Music of the Northern Tribes* (New York: Lyrichord, 1976), track 4.	*Gonje* (bowed lute) and voice
4	Democratic Republic of the Congo, Ubangi, 1975. CD, *Anthologies de la musique congolaise*, Vol. 10: Musique de l'Ubangi (Tervuren: Fonti musicali, 1975), track 18.	Male voice, *Kundi* harp
5	Uganda, Ganda, 1972. CD, *Musical Instruments 1: Strings*. Music of Africa Series 27 (Grahamstown, South Africa: International Library of African Music, 200-?), track 2.	*Enanga* 8-stringed bow-harp
6	Burundi, Rundi, 1967. CD, *Burundi: Musiques Traditionnelles* (Paris: Ocora, 1988), track 9.	Two girls' voices
7	Niger, Wodaabe Peuls, c1997. CD, *Introduction aux musiques africaines* by Monique Brandily. Accompanying CD (Cité de la musique: Actes sud, c1997), track 3.	Mixed chorus
8	Democratic Republic of the Congo, N. Boma, 1994. CD, *Petites musiques du Zaïre* (Paris: Buda Musique, 1994), track 12.	Entire village
9	Central African Republic, Ba-Benzele, 1965. CD, *Anthology of World Music: Africa: The Ba-Benzele Pygmies* (Cambridge, MA: Rounder 1998; orig. 1965), track 7.	Two women
10	Central African Republic, Ba-Benzele, 1965. CD, *Anthology of World Music: Africa: The Ba-Benzele Pygmies* (Cambridge, MA: Rounder 1998; orig. 1965), track 1.	*Hindewhu* whistle and voice
11	Zambia, Plateau Tonga, 1957. CD, *Kalimba and Kalimbu Songs, Northern Rhodesia (Zambia), 1952 & 1957* (Utrecht, The Netherlands: Stichting Sharp Wood Productions & Grahamstown, South Africa: International Library of African Music, 1998), track 8.	14-key *kankobela* ("thumb piano")

Figure 1.1 Twenty examples of African minimalism

	National/ethnic origin, year	Instrumentation
12	South Africa, Tswana (Western Transvaal) 200-? CD, *Musical Instruments 4: Flutes & Horns*. Music of Africa Series 27 (Grahamstown, South Africa: International Library of African Music, 200-?), track 2.	4x4 flutes
13	Uganda, Nyoro, 200-? CD, *Musical Instruments 4: Flutes & Horns*. Music of Africa Series 27 (Grahamstown, South Africa: International Library of African Music, 200-?), track 14.	*Makondere* gourd horns
14	Angola, Mbwela/Tucokwe, 1965. CD, *Theory of African Music 1* by Gerhard Kubik. Accompanying CD (Wilhelmshaven, Germany: F. Noetzel, c1994), track 38.	2 tent pegs
15	Angola, Mbwela/Vambwela, 1965. CD, *Theory of African Music 1* by Gerhard Kubik. Accompanying CD (Wilhelmshaven, Germany: F. Noetzel, c1994), track 40.	Drum and percussion stick
16	Angola, Nkhangala/Vankhangala, 1965. CD, *Theory of African Music 1* by Gerhard Kubik. Accompanying CD (Wilhelmshaven, Germany: F. Noetzel, c1994), track 34.	Vibrating leaf
17	Cameroon, Mandara Mountains, 1996. CD, Cameroon: Flutes des Monts Mandara (Paris: Ocora, 1996), track 1.	*Ouldémé* flutes
18	Sara-Kaba, 1967. CD, *Introduction aux musiques africaines* by Monique Brandily. Accompanying CD (Cité de la musique: Actes sud, c1997), track 1.	Xylophone
19	Central African Republic, Banda-Linda, 1983. CD, *Central African Republic: Music of the Dendi, Nzakara, Banda Linda, Gbaya, Banda-dakpa, Ngbaka, Aka Pygmies* (France: Auvidis, 1989), track 8.	Horn ensemble
20	Ghana, 1995. CD, *Opus 1: Pan African Orchestra* (New York: Real World, 1995), track 3.	Pan-African orchestra (with *mmensuon*)

Figure 1.1 Continued

mediation of extensive background information, is a worthwhile and revealing exercise, and I believe the same applies here. Such listening is only a first step, however—the beginning of an adventure. Ideally, the reader would first listen to each of the twenty excerpts, forming his or her own impression of animating procedures, then read the brief comments below, and then listen to the excerpts a second time, this time incorporating whatever information might be helpful from the commentary. Ultimately, my aim is to reinforce the appropriateness of designating these compositions *minimalist*.[15]

Togolese lithophone virtuoso Kpalandao Yurijao invokes a popular rhythm known as *kaleta* in this performance (1). Pulse-oriented, the composition is texturally continuous even though the individual sounds die soon after each stone is struck. Notable here are emergent motifs and an overall illusion that we are hearing several players instead of just one. (2) is a lullaby performed by a woman from the Nkundo group within the DRC. The performance does not have the in-your-face quality of the previous one; rather, the singer uses a B♭-A♭ dyad as the basis of a more extended discourse. One phrase ends on B♭, the next on A♭, a third on B♭ again, and so on. The dyad thus serves as a kind of structural framework, an anchor with a refrain-like quality. Between appearances of the two pitches, the singer uses the remaining pitches of a pentatonic scale to spin short melodic statements. Note the gentle clapping of hands that adds a measure of metrical control despite the free-rhythmic ambience of the whole. Overall, the pacing in this gentle narrative anchored securely by two pitches contrasts with the strident, extraverted quality of the lithophone performance.

From the Kusasi in northern Ghana comes the next performance by one Mr. Akurugu on a one-stringed fiddle locally known as gonje (3). Like the Nkundo singer heard in the previous excerpt, Akurugu draws on a pentatonic resource for what he plays and sings. The minimal manner is evident in the persistent use of fragments of the scale to deliver the song's message. Motives are repeated immediately, returned to later, expanded and contrasted. The singer is wordy in places, but there are moments of song and dance as well. All this takes place within shifts of stylistic register: high style at the beginning of this performance, a low or lower style in the middle, and a high style again at the end.

Another example from the DRC (4), this time of the Ubangi group, features a male voice singing to the accompaniment of a six-stringed harp known as *kundi*. A single prolonged chord serves as backdrop to this narrative, which is delivered in a rapid, quasi-declamatory style. The deliberately restricted melodic range and the syllabic articulation reinforce the speech-like character

[15] Several of these excerpts are mentioned or discussed in *The African Imagination in Music*, but not always under the sign of minimalism.

of the singing, while the rhythmically active but harmonically fixed accompaniment confers a minimalist aura. Listeners who care to count may wish to verify that the performance consists of fifty-seven cycles.

Ugandan bow-harpist Tumusewo Mukasa is featured in the next performance (5) playing the eight-stringed *enanga*. The pitch resource here is pentatonic, and the singer-player starts by rapidly vocalizing a series of syllables as if imitating the sound of playing. (This kind of iconism is a well-established feature of African expression, as we will see in the next chapter.) Then he sings what will turn out to be a carefully calibrated narrative in song, returning to the parlando manner later on. The constancy of the pentatonic resource and the "digital" mode of articulation reinforce the minimalist ambience. Next (6) is an Akazehe greeting performed by two Burundian women. In this fascinating genre of greeting and exchanging news, the duo share a temporal space and pitch reference but use different word-derived motifs to convey their individual messages. The rapid, syllabic enunciation may be heard as an analogue to the *enanga* and lithophone articulations heard previously (5 and 1).

The next two performances feature minimality in the form of drone-like continuity—waves of sound coming toward the listener and then receding. A chorus of Wodaabe Peuls (7) sings and sustains a single sonority. This extended "pedal point" is texturally reinforced from time to time as voices enter and leave the on-going stream. Unlike the examples heard up to now, this one eschews micro-level rhythmic articulation for a continuous—or apparently continuous—sound. Such gesturing toward infinity by means of a continuous rather than broken sound represents one extreme of minimalist procedure. And, for those listeners whose intertextual antennae are active, we might note that the Peuls were doing this sort of thing centuries before La Monte Young composed his *Trio for Strings* in 1958, with its long, sustained notes.

In a similar vein is the lamentation (8) from the North Boma ethnic group of the DRC. An entire village is apparently mourning the death of their chief's son. Weeping is mediated by the pitch C; that is to say, all participants sing and hold that pitch as part of their communal weeping. While one hears fragments of melody descending to middle-C from the minor third above (sometimes intimating a $\hat{3}$-$\hat{2}$-$\hat{1}$ progression), there is co-present a layer of continuous sound. Together with a distant drum beat and sporadic speaking, the resultant sound pits continuous drone against less continuous articulations. Again, the minimal process is evident in the domain of pitch organization, but whereas previous examples featured micro-level articulation, these two performances, (7) and (8), affect a continuous texture.

Another lullaby, this one performed by two Aka women, is heard in (9). Fragments of melody entrusted to each voice are repeated over and over again. Interesting is the asymmetrical arrangement of phrases, which in turn contributes to the open, dynamic quality of the duet. The prominent use of a hocket technique sharpens the jagged contours and adds a percussive quality to the performance. Yet another instance of Aka hocket expression, this time involving voice and "flute" played by a single performer, is heard in (10). Referred to as "Hindewhu," this minimalist essay, made famous by its imitation at the beginning of Herbie Hancock's "Watermelon Man," features 3 + 1 pitches distributed as follows: permutations of F-G-A are interspersed with intonings of the pitch D. The pattern of repetition is unpredictable at first, and meter acquires an elusive and unmarked sense.

The characteristic plucking of individual notes on the mbira often engenders a strong minimalist sense. With its legible and palpable labor of production, a performance such as that in (11) evokes a digital mode. This particular performance was recorded in Zambia, and it features a self-accompanying singer who begins with pace-setting strumming, and then follows it with narrative song. Like the Berceuse heard earlier (2), the song's two alternating phrases feature low-lying ending notes that lie roughly a major second apart. Tonal differentiation at phrase endings reinforces their mutual dependency; if one phrase acquires an interrogative or open quality, the other takes on an affirmative or closed sense. Micro-level repetition animates the performance of the tale. Lacking sung parts, the Tswana flute tune heard in (12) proceeds in a more determined minimalist manner. Its three fragments of melody trace patterns that may be approximated in scale-degree terms as follows: $\hat{6}$-$\hat{5}$-$\hat{3}$-$\hat{2}$, $\hat{6}$-$\hat{5}$-$\hat{5}$-$\hat{3}$-$\hat{2}$ and $\hat{5}$-$\hat{3}$-$\hat{2}$. The succession is subject to constant repetition, and the asymmetrical grouping of onsets (4+5+3) underlines the narrative aura.

The *makondere* horns from Uganda heard in (13) feature stacked ostinatos made up of distinct rhythmic patterns that enliven the texture and convey a dance-like aura. Long-distance hearing will reveal how the constituent motives interact to produce other melodies—emergent melodies, we might say, heard but not played as such by any one instrument. In (14), a different kind of minimalism is heard, one that may be reminiscent of the sound of lithophones in (1). The busy articulation on metal blades invites immediate entrainment, while the reciter reinforces the resultant motive. The means are modest and the human presence is palpable as the reciter seems to run out of breath against the instrument's metronomic rigidity. The minimalist mode sets into relief the material limitations of the performing forces. We might in fact hear in this performance echoes of the interpenetrated voices in the Akazehe singing encountered in (6). Next is a duo performance from Angola comprising a drum and percussion stick (15). The drummer plays an ostinato pattern with a minimally differentiated internal structure, while the percussion stick adds a second pattern, making this a polyrhythmic texture. Indeed, the percussion stick's pattern resembles a West African bell pattern or time line—another marker of minimalism. The timbral distinction between the two instruments ensures an unyielding duality, while the individual rhythmic patterns are shown to be metrically compatible. The performance heard in (16), also from Angola, features an unusual instrument: a vibrating leaf. The instrument is obviously modest from a material point of view. The player's aim is to conjure up as much sound as possible by blowing the leaf. The result is a series of gestural efforts comprising twelve little segments similar in length but variable in the firmness of their pitch identity. Pitch is bent in some of the segments, while the tenth segment is barely audible. This way of stripping things down to a bare but interesting minimum is often encountered in children's play songs throughout the continent. This is experimental minimalism in a juvenile register.

The vibrating leaf lacks pitch, scale, meter, or regular rhythm; in that respect, it is quite different from the performances we have heard so far. Indeed, one may wonder whether it is music at all. One way to answer is to note the affinities between the sound worlds of certain traditional African musics and those of avant-garde European music. I can think, for example, of passages in some of John Cage's prepared piano pieces that are indistinguishable from some African xylophone music; there are moments in Giacinto Scelsi's *Canti del Capricorno* that compare with the lamentation of a Dan woman who has lost her husband; and certain passages in Meredith Monk's "Our Lady of Fate" are reminiscent of Aka singing. Heard simply as sounding surfaces, these passages may be favorably compared, but it is of course the framing that determines their valuation as "music." The fact that each of these particular Euro-American examples evinces a minimal aura is not insignificant for the affinities (*not* influences) I'm trying to draw in this chapter.

Before proceeding further with this description, a provisional generalization may help to further underline the differences between certain environments of traditional African music and those of European avant-garde music. Traditional music is not a music of chance or indeterminacy. Nor is it built on the ostensible rigors associated with on-paper composition. It does not derive from the consuming subjectivities of individuals. To be sure, elements of chance, indeterminacy, abstract rigor, and rampant subjectivity occur sporadically, so the claim being made here is not an absolute one; rather, it refers to an ethos, a set of underlying values, converging tendencies. The essence of African music resides in a network of shared frameworks, each of which inscribes an always-already connected ideology. The communal—as a real or imagined value—is the desired and invariant element among African music's ethical fundaments.

So, although their sound worlds may be similar or even occasionally identical, European avant-garde music and traditional African music proceed from radically different premises. European avant-garde often sports an essential interrogative quality; it explores, reaches for the edge, unsettles, discomfits, challenges, reorients, discovers, extends, etc. African traditional music on the other hand sports an affirmative stance, an affirmation of humanity: communalism, togetherness, and a strategic incompletion awaiting a human (performer's or participant's) completion. And while there are bound to be overlaps between these two worlds at the levels of intention and trace, their premises seem to be significantly different.[16]

The performance recorded in (17) is reminiscent of the Tswana flutes heard in (12), but it may also be affined with the Banda-Linda horn ensemble that we will hear in (19). Recorded in the Mandara mountains in northern Cameroon, this performance features a small group of flutes, each of which contributes a motif to the overall texture. Vocal motives, some of them doubling those played by flutes, others sounding unduplicated in a high register, dominate the texture. Once again, the temporal progression is not predictable, although there is a regulating pulse. As we have seen before, irregular progressions like this often invite a narrative reading. Next (18) is a xylophone performance from Cameroon featuring several ostinato patterns in interlocking fashion. Different emergent melodies claim the listener's attention at different times, while the whole is regulated periodically. Time seems to stand still, performers seem to mark the present continuous tense.

[16] Gross comparisons of this sort sometimes leave some readers uneasy, including those who may suspect that an essentializing or overgeneralizing impulse is at work. But the refusal to compare even as we inhabit an increasingly globalized world is even more objectionable. The point, in any case, is not to postulate absolute, non-overlapping differences but to suggest analogous tendencies in the structural organization of musical material that may or may not be significant.

Again, the busy articulation is reminiscent of the classical minimalism of Reich.

A similar process is evident in a horn ensemble from the Central African Republic (19), each of whose eighteen instruments plays a single note repeated in different rhythmic configurations. Although the ensemble has many components, its resultant sound is reducible to a simple, basic melody—a kind of Ur-melody that may be heard from a distance. This repeated melody serves as foundation for the more overtly minimalist patterns of the horns. The last excerpt (20) is a performance by the Pan African Orchestra of an original but explicitly sourced piece, *mmensuoun*. A time-line pattern played by bells and sporting a [2-2-2-1-2-3] durational pattern starts things off and continues throughout the performance. Then other instruments join with their own patterns: elephant horns, hand claps, small drums, and finally large (fɔntɔnfrɔm) drums. The constancy of the time line confers a minimalist element, serving also as the foundation upon which other instruments ride with their own repeated figures. Responsorial effects are introduced along the way, helping to intensify the affect in this melo-rhythmic feast.

We may draw some preliminary conclusions from listening to these twenty excerpts from various traditional African repertories. First and most obviously, repetition is the key signifier of a minimalist impulse. The kind of repetition we're talking about is not merely that which is ontologically necessary for the articulation of a musical structure, but that which is used idiomatically, expressively, and with rhetorical commitment. Repetition typically occurs on different levels of structure, some of them immediate, others remote. In ensemble performance, combined repeated patterns produce polyrhythm. Repeated patterns tend to be exact rather than varied; acts of variation often follow grammatical constraints. The preference for fixity may well come from the constraints imposed by dance or the choreographic supplement—a set of practical constraints designed to ensure that moving bodies resonate sympathetically.

Second and more technically, African minimalism ranges from a pulse-oriented mode of articulation (in which the pulse is, as it were, in your face) to one in which the pulse is hidden in order to promote the articulation of larger periods. By foregrounding the pulse in these musical idioms, the musical discourse is oriented to the present, to the here and now; hidden pulses by contrast are agents of a future-oriented discourse. Pulse-orientation is sometimes associated with play, and so is found in recreational music and children's game songs, and this contrasts with period-oriented structures that are invariably associated with declamatory narratives or the exposition of non-trivial verbal content, as in performances of epics, genealogies, and histories. Third, the minimalist instinct is equally evident in vocal and instrumental music, allowing us to fantasize identical deep structures for the two forms of material production, structures that are then translated into different material surfaces. A singing duo deploying interlocking patterns (such as the Akazehe greeting, [6]) is easily imagined as the equivalent of a pair of instrumentalists insofar as both ensembles proceed from identical premises; the drum narratives of a lead drummer, interspersed with refrains and waiting patterns, may be compared with the vocal narratives of, for example, the performance of an Nkundo lullaby (2), which combines syllable articulation with a larger trajectory defined by strategically placed goal tones. Even the more continuous textures produced by voices (heard, for example, in drones by Wodaabe Peuls and the North Boma mourners [7 and 8 respectively]) have their equivalents in the continuous sounds of, for example, flute and panpipe ensembles, which simulate droning through overlapping small, proximate steps that come across as unbroken on a less immediate level rather than as discrete points in succession. These sorts of deep-lying parallels appear as casual observations in informal conversations about music, and they speak to deep beliefs about what music means to communities who make it regularly, indeed for whom music-making is not some optional extra in life but a necessary and life-giving activity.

Fourth, minimalism is constrained by certain ethical and aesthetical imperatives that regulate musical composition in African communities. The most important of these stems from a prevailing communal ethos which is most readily expressed in communal dancing. Some Western listeners to African minimalist music are bored because they want to see or hear something happen, something "new," perhaps fulfilling an earlier expectation. They thus betray their own conditioning in the familiar—and I dare say managed—narrative trajectory in which a beginning is followed by intensification leading to climax and closure. What such listeners mistake for sparseness or emptiness in African minimalism, or as a denial of (immediate) fulfillment, is in fact strategic: it is an invitation to the listener-dancer to complete the music by occupying the gaps or spaces inscribed in the musical texture, and to do so with all the temporal resources of an apparently continuous present tense.[17] The participatory element in African

[17] John Miller Chernoff, *African Rhythm and African Sensibility* (Chicago: University of Chicago Press, 1979), 50.

music is not an optional addendum that listeners and dancers embrace as they wish: Participation is structural; it is inscribed in the very fabric of the music; it is a social imperative. To put this more generally, we might say that the African performance ethos is not based on a dialogue in which a skeptical listener says to the composer, "Show me what you can do," as if composers were obliged to put on displays for non-participating observers; the ethos, rather, is a message from the performer-composer to his or her audience: "Let's do it together even as I demonstrate my (advanced) skills." It is possible that the absence of such a communal ethos from certain traditions of music-making elsewhere in the world marks them as categorically different from the music we're exploring in this chapter. And insofar as the communal ethos is not a dispensable option for African performance, it may signal a profound difference between Western and African minimalism. For despite the communalistic pose in Western minimalism's pioneers (Terry Riley, La Monte Young, and even Steve Reich), many later developments (see, for example, Nik Bärtsch's Modulo series) have abstracted core procedures stemming from repetition, complete with the freedom they promise, and reworked them with new, exclusive, and anti-communalistic accents.

Digging Deeper: Aly Keïta's *Farafinko* as Essay in African Minimalism

I spoke earlier of African musicians spinning large tracts of musical thought out of a minimum of resources, and we have listened to a number of recordings from across the continent that exhibit this minimalist manner. It's now time to dig a little deeper. I've chosen for that purpose the opening track of Aly Keïta's absorbing performance on the CD *Farafinko* recorded in 2010.[18] *Farafinko* is a piece for solo balafon, lasts a little over three minutes in this performance, and illustrates many of the ways in which a skilled African musician makes much out of little. Casual listeners may be drawn to Keïta's virtuosic and imaginative playing; some may wonder how he is able to make the balafon sound like an ensemble, as if there was more than one person playing. Some musicians may ask how much of this is improvised

[18] Aly Keïta, *Farafinko*, CD (Vodelée, Belgium: Studio Contre-Jour, 2010). A different version of this piece may be seen on YouTube at https://youtu.be/NoZkNoblOsw.

and how much of it is precomposed. And still others will be curious to know how this particular performance compares to others. While these are all interesting issues, they are not the ones driving the following analysis. I aim instead to identify a few of the procedures that exemplify Keïta's creativity. These procedures are of a structural nature, so they will require representation of the piece in a form that enables readers to identify structures and evaluate the analyst's claims. Example 1.1 offers an annotated transcription

Example 1.1 Annotated transcription of Aly Keita's *Farafinko*, from the album *Farafinko* (2010)

Example 1.1 Continued

of the performance. I want to dwell in a minimalist environment for awhile and suggest ways in which *Farafinko* may be interpreted as a cogent essay in minimalist expression.

Let's begin with the big picture. *Farafinko* is made up of a number of musical ideas (motives, melodies, theme groups) that are introduced, repeated, sometimes elaborated upon, and then recalled in closing. When we're caught up in the moment of Keïta's playing, we are not necessarily reflecting on the evolving architecture, what musicians call the *form* of the work; we

Example 1.1 Continued

may identify with the labor of performance, the alternation of ideas, or even wonder what he's going to do next. Only after the performance, however, do we have a synoptic view of this particular journey. We discover that *Farafinko* is shaped as a palindrome, an ABCBA form, where A, B, and C represent theme areas (they are labeled in Example 1.1). The important point here is not the preciseness of the palindrome but the process of alternating of theme areas. Keïta does not spend a comparable amount of time in each area—nor would one expect him to do so, it being understood that every performance

Example 1.1 Continued

has its exigencies. But the succession of themes within a constant groove is readily audible. The performer's rhetorical manner is to present an idea, ensure through exact repetition that the listener is acquainted with it, and then, especially in the C section, show what can be done with it. Given the consistent energy levels displayed throughout the performance, new themes or ideas are often recognized only in retrospect; yet, because Keïta typically rests his right hand before enunciating a new theme, there are also moments in which listeners anticipate change. Recognition is essential to a proper appreciation of Keïta's art.

Example 1.1 Continued

A word about the transcription. Designed to facilitate reference, Example 1.1 displays *Farafinko* as essentially a two-voice structure: the left hand or bass voice provides the groove by playing an ostinato figure from beginning (m. 3) to end, while the right hand delivers the main content in the form of motives and melodies. (One detail: starting in m. 71, the third beat of each bar introduces a new feature, an eighth-note A. This new form of the ostinato lasts until m. 95, then reverts to the old form.) The left hand serves

Example 1.1 Continued

as an accompaniment or foundation while the right hand carries the burden of speech-making. Aly Keïta's ability to provide his own accompaniment, and to do so with remarkable metronomical precision, is an extraordinary feature of this performance. Not that the melody-accompaniment relationship is mechanically realized. At one point, the performer introduces a time-line pattern above the left hand ostinato (m. 37); in effect, he superimposes a phrasing referent on an accompaniment, as if sounding two accompaniments simultaneously.

Example 1.1 Continued

Some of the decisions made in representing *Farafinko* notationally tap into emerging conventions of representing African music. Most consequential, perhaps, is the use of a $\frac{12}{8}$ time signature. Not only do the rhythmic patterns suggest such a meter, but the introduction of the aforementioned time-line pattern provides external corroboration for the well-formedness of the $\frac{12}{8}$ unit. Less conventionally, I have used phrase markings to indicate the work's constituent phrases—what some theorists call groups.[19] Among other functions, groups demarcate the motivic content of the work. Groups are not always aligned morphologically with meter, however; indeed, some of the excitement in Keïta's performance/composition stems from his combination of a left hand groove that begins on an offbeat (E on the third eighth note of m. 3) and remains so until the end, and a series of melodic phrases that bear variable relations to normative grouping. And as we will see, moments of great intensity are created precisely where phrase and metrical grouping are in non-alignment. Finally, I have used a one-sharp signature to register a hierarchy in tone tendency. *Farafinko* uses an anhemitonic pentatonic set, E-D-B-A-G-(E), and these notes are deployed in such a way that motion to and from them often conveys a sense of goal and therefore of a hierarchy. The pitch E emerges as the tone center on account of its frequent use and its position as goal tone in many of the melodic phrases. Its "tonic" quality is announced early—in the bass ostinato that drives the piece beginning in m. 3.

Let us now take a closer look at the musical materials to appreciate both the resources and the ingredients of this performance. The ostinato or foundation consists of three notes, D-E-G heard in 5 onsets as E-G-D-D-E, all of them eighth notes except the final E, which is a quarter note. This characteristic pentatonic sound [025] has a primal quality, and is often exploited by composers as such. Two qualities contribute to its shape and sense: first, and as previously mentioned, it begins off beat 1 in the $\frac{12}{8}$ meter and ends on beat 3. Many melodic phrases in *Farafinko* will similarly begin off the beat, that is, in places that carry less accentual weight. The effect is to confer a certain dynamism on the phrase motion and, more important, to create tension between the sort of accent that marks the initiation of a musical idea (in this case, the initial E) and that which emerges from metrical positioning (the

[19] See the discussion in Janet Schmalfeldt, "Phrase," in *The Oxford Handbook of Critical Concepts in Music Theory*, edited by Alexander Rehding and Steven Rings (New York: Oxford University Press, 2019). Accessed January 13, 2022. https://doi.org/10.1093/oxfordhb/9780190454746.001.0001.

ostinato's concluding E). The pattern of unaccented beginnings of patterns followed by accented endings is typical of West African rhythmic expression, and may be observed in any number of transcriptions made by scholars. Finally, I have grouped two iterations of the bass ostinato into a single bar because the main motives in theme areas A and B (see bars 1, 17, 27, etc.), which also convey the music's phrasing, are typically one bar long. The ostinato functions at a subphrase level.

Since *Farafinko* features two voices, listeners who have access to this particular metalanguage will likely experience some moments as moving, others as resting. Some sonorities may come across as consonant or stable, others as dissonant or mobile. Consonance and dissonance are qualities manifest in different dimensions, but there are no conventional theories of consonance or dissonance for these West African repertories outside of what can be inferred from the pieces themselves. So here are some speculative thoughts about consonance-dissonance disposition in the pitch dimension. All melodic phrases finish on the notes E, G, or B, often coinciding with bass E. Since these notes combine to form an E minor triad, we may accord it priority, recognizing its role in conveying a sense of ending and resolution. In the articulation of consonance, endings are the most important structural moments; beginnings hold some importance, too, but lack the defining role of endings. All other moments have a transitional value. Since *Farafinko* is consistently pentatonic, the only possibilities for vertical articulation within this two-voice framework are the intervals unisons/octaves, seconds (always major), thirds (major or minor), fourths (always perfect), fifths (always perfect), sixths (always major) and sevenths (always minor). If we now listen to *Farafinko* as a succession of intervals, we get a sense of the disposition of consonance and dissonance. Consider m. 4, for example, where theme area A begins. The intervals between left and right hands are 5-4-1-1-7-4-5-1-6-5-(1) (the last 1 occurs at the start of the next bar); in m. 35, they are 5-1-2-1-6-4-3-4-3-4-2; and in bar 51, they are 7-3-6-5-4-5-4-7-3-2-2. Not much can be concluded from comparing these moments except that unisons occur more at the start of the opening theme; and given the speed at which *Farafinko* is played, hearing every eighth-note resultant as consonant or dissonant is probably impractical. Still, a map of interval succession is revealing. It shows, for example, that the most intense area of "dissonance" occurs in mm. 52–54, where each bar displays an intervallic pattern of 7-7-5-1-1-7-7-7-5-1-1-(7, at start of next bar). This pattern arises because the melody is stuck on the pitch D for three bars, and so forms a 7 with the bass ostinato's E; this seventh frames each sounding of the ostinato in this moment of the performance.

Let us now follow Aly Keïta's narrative from beginning to end. (Please refer to Example 1.1 for the following analysis.)

Bars 1–3.1 These bars are introductory, they establish a pulse, acquaint the listener with the tone system, open up a significant portion of the work's registral space, adumbrate a number of motives, and introduce a sweeping descending gesture that will return from time to time as a closing gesture. From the second eighth-note onset on, the two hands play the "same" pitches an octave apart, and they are heard in the same rhythm. Such "unison" in rhythm and pitch suggests a pristine ground and announces a spirit of cooperation.

Measures 3.2–15.1. Theme A is characterized by constant motion and an internally directed energy. A two-fold statement of the left-hand ostinato in m. 3 prepares for the entrance of the main melody of theme group A in bm.ar 4. This "vamp" will return periodically throughout the piece, serving simultaneously as a boundary marker and a waiting signal. Theme Group A initially unfolds across six bars (4–9) and consists of exactly six repeated phrases. (Phrase marks in the transcription indicate the span of each phrase). After a one-bar rest (bar 10), the melody is sounded again, only four times this time (11–14), making a total of ten iterations. Clearly, we're in for a certain amount of repeated doing in this performance. Repetition in this context occurs at two levels: the left hand ostinato figure occupies a half-bar level, while the main melody occupies a full bar. A feature that contributes to the dynamic quality of Theme A is the off-beat beginning (m. 4), which in turn propels the theme past the bar line as shown by my phrase markings. Toward the end of the performance (mm. 100ff.), Keïta will use a version of the melody that lacks the initial eighth-note rest, as if beginning with the theme's second bar (m. 5), not the first (m. 4). A tiny change, this, but one that helps to distinguish the expository function of these opening bars from the "recapitulatory" function that we encounter late in the performance.

Measures 15–35. The ongoing ostinato, heard by itself in bars 15 and 16, serves the same vamp function as it did previously in bars 3 and 10, and prepares the first statement of Theme B. The larger Theme B area (mm. 15–35) unfolds in phases, not two as in Theme A, but four: mm. 15–20, 21–25, 26–30, and 31–35, all featuring four-bar phrases separated by one-bar vamps. A significant feature of Theme B is the arrangement of its constituent gestures to mimic a question-answer exchange. This is clear from the first phase. The melodic gesture in m. 17, ending on the note B, comes across as a question, whereas that in m. 18, ending on E, provides the answer. The adjacent bars thus display a reciprocal sense that was not present in Theme A. Similarly, mm. 19 and 20 are related respectively as question and answer; note, however, that while the question in m. 19 is the same as the one posed two bars before, the answer in m. 20 is a decorated version of the previous answer in m. 18. This embellished answer (m. 20) incorporates a pair of rising perfect fourths, a characteristic motivic gesture that will feature in the next theme group. Even at this early stage, we're already forming an impression of Keïta's variation technique.

Continuing with our survey of Theme B: The vamp in bar 21 initiates the second phase of this theme area and prepares an exact repeat of the 4-bar question-answer exchange that we heard in the first phase, mm. 17–19. A third phase follows the vamp in m. 26, and features a repeat of Theme B an octave above its previous placement. This higher register is the one in which *Farafinko* started, but it has been notably silent since the opening measure. In addition to its cross-referential value, this moment in m. 27 introduces a new dialogue by presenting recently heard material in a more marked register. The fourth and final phase of Theme B, also introduced by a vamp (m. 31), presents an exact repeat of the previous phase (mm. 27–30). We see then that the entire Theme B area has been remarkably regular and symmetrical. As far as larger temporal profiles go, Theme A may be heard in retrospect as marking time, while Theme B takes a few steps forward through sub-phrase dialogue. Such characterizations provide only a broad orientation, however, and should always be set against opposing tendencies toward stasis manifest at more local levels of structure.

Measures 36–90. While theme areas A and B are each dominated by a single idea, the section I've labeled C is more diversified; it also foregrounds the work mode as distinct from the presentational mode of the two previous sections. Keïta seems to be improvising here, elaborating on various motives, recalling others, and introducing several intensifying gestures. The entire section is akin to a development section, an area in which the composer self-consciously puts material through various paces, displaying his compositional and rhetorical skills, and casting the listener into an observational rather than participatory mode. Where Theme areas A and B invite entrainment, generate a communal feeling, and allow us to sing along, Theme area C asks listeners to stop and behold a master musician at work.

As before, a vamp (bar 36) sets up the first event in this new theme area, but whereas previous themes had been melodies played on the pitched slabs of Keïta's *balafon*, this new idea is realized on the instrument's wooden frame. Aurally distinct, the new timbre turns out to be a well-known West African time-line from the 5-onset [2-2-3-2-3] family of patterns. The new timbre may surprise listeners, but its familiarity from other contexts may charm them as well. A time-line pattern is typically not a theme, so locating the start of Theme C in m. 37 may seem odd at first; however, given the indexical quality enshrined in the preceding "vamp" (m. 36), the time line acquires a more thematic feel. In effect, we are hearing two ostinato patterns starting in m. 37: the ongoing bass ostinato which occupies a half bar, and the time-line pattern, which occupies a full bar. The time-line pattern will occupy eight bars, but the introduction of a new motive at the end of its fourth bar (three E's in m. 40) and the beginning of a new pattern derived from this motive in the eighth (m. 44) replenish the content even as they reinstate the main melodic narrative.

Time-line patterns are widespread in West and Central Africa, serving among other functions as signatures of dances or genres. But they also exist as free-floating rhythmic patterns available for purely musical appropriation. Keïta has chosen an iconic West African pattern, a version of the so-called *clave* pattern typically disposed as a [3-3-4-2-4] inter-onset pattern in duple time. Notable is the resemblance between it and the common variant [2-2-3-2-3], itself structurally prior to the so-called standard pattern [2-2-1-2-2-2-1]. Keita's version [4-5-5-4-6] (counting in sixteenth notes) follows the broad (short-long) contours of the original pattern but tweaks its internal proportions by incorporating more in the way of syncopation.[20]

Like theme areas A and B, Theme area C may also be heard unfolding in phases. There are many more phases than before, however. And whereas A and B respectively feature a temporal profile tending toward circularity or stasis, the patterns in C are more obviously energetical and developmental, reaching several expressive high points.

We may identify five contiguous little phases within Theme area C: 36–50; 51–66; 67–72; 73–81; 82–90. We have already commented on the use of a time-line pattern in the first little phase, bars 36–51, complete with brief "interruptions" in its fourth and eighth iterations. These "interruptions" feature pitched motives that are then extended in the last six bars of the

[20] For a fuller discussion of these sorts of transformation, see Jeff Pressing, "Cognitive Isomorphisms between Pitch and Rhythm in World Musics: West Africa, the Balkans and Western Tonality," *Studies in Music* 17 (1983): 38–61.

phase, culminating in a sweeping closing gesture (mm. 48–50) reminiscent of the very opening of the piece. Also reminiscent of an earlier procedure is the unfolding of ideas in mm. 44.4–46.3, which recall the dialogue in Theme B, mm. 17–20.

An intervening vamp in m. 50 prepares the next little phase of Theme C, mm. 50–66. A salient new device is introduced here to intensify the expression: getting stuck on an individual pitch for a few bars. Three pitches frame the contours of this process: D (52–54), E (55–57), and G (58–59). D is heard thirty-six times in eighth-note succession, E alternates with D in the manner of a trill while incorporating the time-line pattern, and G completes the first part of the ascent in conjunction with two other pitches, A and B, both of which are functionally subsidiary to G. Further intensification (starting in m. 60) takes the form of a high-register ascent in syncopated notes of the ruling pentatonic set, reaches the highest note A in m. 61 and then descends gradually therefrom. Interesting is the incorporation of ascending motivic fourths (bar 63) in the final descent from high A, part of a sweeping closing gesture spread across four bars (mm. 63–66). We may trace the fourths back not only to the start of this phase within theme area C (bar 51), but further back to m. 2 of the composition and to the ever-present bass ostinato that was introduced in m. 3.

Measures 66–67 again signal the completion of one process and the preparation for another. In the next little phase (mm. 66–72), Keïta embarks on another process of melodic intensification. This time he applies the freezing technique to a single motive, E-G-A-A-G, heard at the start of bar 69, and "stuck" for over four bars. The motive itself is heard five times in succession, but what is most striking is its metrical placements. The five appearances begin respectively on the following eighth-note positions within the $\frac{12}{8}$ meter: 1, 9, 5, 1, 9. Positions 1, 5, and 9 are the first, second and third notes within groups of three eighth notes. These shifts in metrical position add to the rhythmical interest of the moment, countering any sense of stasis brought on by the frozen motive.

The next little phase (mm. 72–81) reverts to the frozen-pitch technique applied to two principal pitches, D and B. The pitch D was were frozen not so long ago (see mm. 52ff.), but the process is modified here. Starting in bar 73, D alternates with B for four bars; the pattern also incorporates a time-line pattern in the same way that the E-D alternation in mm. 55–57 did. As for the subsequent E (beginning on the upbeat to m. 77), it is also "frozen" and struck forty-two times in succession. Here, too, the rhythmic disposition carries a whiff of the time-line pattern.

The vamp in 81 announces the next little phase, mm. 81–86. This material is immediately reminiscent of Theme B, especially its responsorial element (mm. 17–18), although it is confined to a higher register for nearly four bars before closing in a lower one. Then follows a final use of the frozen-motive technique starting in m. 87. The motive has five onsets, G-A-B-G-A; like its counterpart in mm. 69–72, its first note appears in the same eighth-note positions of three contiguous bars: 1, 9, 5, 1, 9. The effect is similar: intensification through a simultaneous use of pitch invariance and metrical divergence. The entire theme area C has featured several waves of intensification, but the listener has no way of knowing how many there will be. Only in retrospect do we realize that the freezing of the G-A-B-G-A motive is Aly Keita's last "developmental" act. What follows is a process of recall of material from early on in the movement—a recapitulatory exercise.

Measures 90–98. The vamp in bar 90 prepares a series of recalls. As we have noted, the energy throughout this performance has remained constant and high. Just as the events in Theme area C incorporated cross references to other material, so the recall of Theme B in m. 91 appears without fanfare. The process of recall begins in a high register, however, and only transfers to a lower octave after four bars (m. 95). Significant is the fact that the recapitulation is announced not with the movement's first theme but rather with the second, Theme B. Is the reversal in the order of theme areas formally significant? Perhaps not, given the patterns of recall in Theme area C. Listeners may well be conditioned for temporal flexibility, leading them to predict a general recall rather than a specific thematic order.

Measures 99–107. One may well sense that things are winding down at this point. With the recent return of the symmetries of Theme B, the redundancy that engineers a sense of home-going begins to seem real. When Theme A returns in bar 100, we are prompted further to hear this as the beginning of the end. Unlike Theme B, which returned originally in a higher register (m. 91) before descending to the lower octave (m. 95), Theme A returns in its original register. But there is one telling difference. Theme A begins on a downbeat (bar 100), not on an offbeat as in its earliest appearance (m. 4). One could say that grouping and meter are here aligned. The recording begins to fade from here on, and the last ten bars of the performance are experienced as a structural diminuendo. Turning down the dial signals closure in the most mundane sense, not the kind engineered by the music's syntactical processes. Technology and the market intervene here to define the composition's ontology.

There is obviously more to say about *Farafinko*, more to admire in Aly Keïta's way of proceeding, and more to celebrate in this beautifully calibrated performance-composition. Different listeners will emerge with differing views about what is special here, what is ordinary as distinct from memorable, and where the resonances between *Farafinko* and music more familiar to them might lie. My goal has been to orient us to some of the compositional procedures of African minimalism. I have called *Farafinko* a minimalist essay in part because of the modest resources registered in its pitch and rhythm economies—five pitch classes and a small repertoire of distinct rhythms within a relentless eighth-note pulsation. It is with these resources that Keïta constructs a fascinating narrative over the course of three minutes. In the end, minimalism is not necessarily evident in immanent features (the population of onsets alone would undermine such a suggestion); minimalism instead invites a perceptual attitude.

Conclusion

I have tried to demonstrate a core minimalism at the heart of the African compositional mode. While the full geo-cultural extent of African minimalism remains to be established definitively, a preliminary map based on the handful of examples that we have discussed in this chapter would include areas in Uganda, Rwanda, Mozambique, South Africa, Angola, the DRC in particular, the Central African Republic, the Gambia, Niger, Togo, the Cote d'Ivoire, Nigeria, and Ghana. Deriving from a simple but essential procedure of repetition (in the domains of pitch, rhythm, and timbre), minimalism is distributed across a variety of forms and genres, and attracts a host of values and metaphors.

Speaking of "African minimalism" and "Western minimalism" is of course a simplification. By now, Western minimalism has assumed myriad forms. For example—and choosing more or less at random—Nik Bartsch's brand of minimalism brings bebop jazz, funk, and Reichian repetition into the same orbit; the minimalism of Aldo Clementi (1925–2011) is quiet and internally directed; it is not the jolly minimalism sometimes heard in Reich. Not all minimalisms are invested in rhythm; Clementi's works *Hallelujah* (1982) or *Due canonic per flauto in sol, violin e pianoforte* (1994) are sparse in a different sense. And earlier in the twentieth century, the minimalist element in a composer like Webern was of a different order, restricted to clock-time brevity but saturated with dense and concentrated "content." Scholars of

Western minimalism have accordingly made many distinctions to account for these diverse tendencies. By contrast, there is as yet no comparable set of distinctions to characterize the African idioms. Which is why my task here has been to suggest that the designation "African minimalism" can be useful for African musicology. I may well have under-complicated both Western and African minimalism in the process of staging such advocacy, but certain acts of under-complication are forced on us by the constraints of pedagogy. In any case, as long as it is understood that some of the grosser distinctions between minimalisms cannot account for every last nuance, the danger of misleading the reader is minimized.

In appropriating the label minimalism to describe certain products of the African imagination, I am not unaware of the kinds of charges that have been leveled against minimal music—that it is sterile, static, boring, infantile, and going nowhere. Critics enamored of the trajectories of eighteenth and nineteenth century tonal music, with their archetypal plots of managed desire followed by immediate or delayed fulfillment, sometimes have trouble reconciling themselves to alternative trajectories. But as we have seen, there are other, less stylized ways of staging temporality. African minimalism's way, with its underlying groove, its recognition of simultaneous doing, its non-negotiable human (as opposed to mechanical) presence, its disruption of an us-versus-them performance arrangement, and its entangled temporalities offers one such way.

There is obviously room for further study of African minimalism. One project might be to compare intra-African streams, following in the manner of Kubik's 1997 conspectus on musical styles, which has made possible a more secure delineation of regional practices.[21] Another would be to extend the comparisons with Western minimalisms by showing how the constraints imposed by dance ultimately install a human presence that is not always in evidence in minimalisms that are not rooted in body movement. (It would explain, for example, why Africans generally do not—indeed cannot—dance to Steve Reich's music!) In these and numerous other instances, we find again and again that while the material resources that enable African minimalism may be modest (two or three pitches, a pair of contrasting timbres, or nuggets of distinctly shaped rhythmic patterns), the ingenuity and creativity displayed by performer-composers are surely of the highest order—maximal rather than minimal.

[21] Gerhard Kubik, "Intra-African Streams of Influence," in *Africa: The Garland Encyclopedia of World Music*, edited by Ruth Stone (New York: Garland, 1997), 293–326.

2

Iconicity in Musical Thought and Expression

At the heart of African expressive behavior is a family of devices that promote varieties of sameness through repetition and imitation. While no single term for them has so far emerged from African language designation, the devices collectively represent a widespread and favorite modality. I will use Charles Sanders Peirce's term *iconicity* to refer to the underlying mode of signification (Peirce 1931–1935).[1] Icons are based on resemblance and analogy. They rely on factual similarity between signifier and signified to do their work, and they belong to a category that Peirce calls *firstness*. They are at once basic and unavoidable in African thought and expression. Like the minimalist impulse that animates forms of creativity (discussed in the previous chapter), the iconic impulse models acts of conceptual transposition across the boundaries of different elements and domains while maintaining their notional equivalence at a certain level of abstraction. This chapter assembles instances of iconicity in the visual and auditive fields as a basic introduction to the phenomenon. I proceed inductively. The aim is thus descriptive rather than theoretical. I will, however, pose a broader philosophical or political question at the end of the chapter: From a composer's point of view, what kind of gift, legacy, constraint, or opportunity is iconicity? Formulating an answer to that question will take us beyond the boundaries of music

[1] Peirce, "*What Is a Sign?*": *Collected Papers of Charles Sanders Peirce*, vol. 2, edited by C. Hartshone and P. Weiss, pp. 281, 285, and 297–302 (Cambridge, MA: Harvard University Press, 1931–1935). Peirce's thought is widely discussed. See, for example, Umberto Eco, "Introduction to a Semiotics of Iconic Signs," *Versus* 2 (1973): 1–15. An illuminating introduction to semiotic concepts is Winfried Nöth's *Handbook of Semiotics* (Bloomington: Indiana University Press, 1995). A helpful introduction to Peircian thought as it might be applied to music is Thomas Turino, "Signs of Imagination, Identity and Experience: A Peircian Semiotic Theory for Music," *Ethnomusicology* 43 (1999): 221–255. The literature on iconicity is surveyed in Irit Meir and Oksana Tkachman, "Iconicity," in *Oxford Bibliographies Online*, accessed July 8, 2021, https://www-oxfordbibliographies-com.ezproxy.princeton.edu/view/document/obo-9780199772810/obo-9780199772810-0182.xml.

On African Music. Kofi Agawu, Oxford University Press. © Oxford University Press 2023.
DOI: 10.1093/oso/9780197664063.003.0002

(narrowly conceived) and prompt us to imagine other patterns of semiotic prioritizing in African creativity.

As elsewhere in this book, many claims in this chapter are tied to specific performances chosen mostly from the traditional repertoire, a repertoire that some of us believe constitutes the backbone of African musical thinking. There are thirteen of them as listed in Figure 2.1. Each citation includes a title (including ad hoc titles given by annotators as distinct from authentic titles given by the originators themselves), ethnic group and/or country of origin, and discographic information. Briefly: item (1) is an example of the

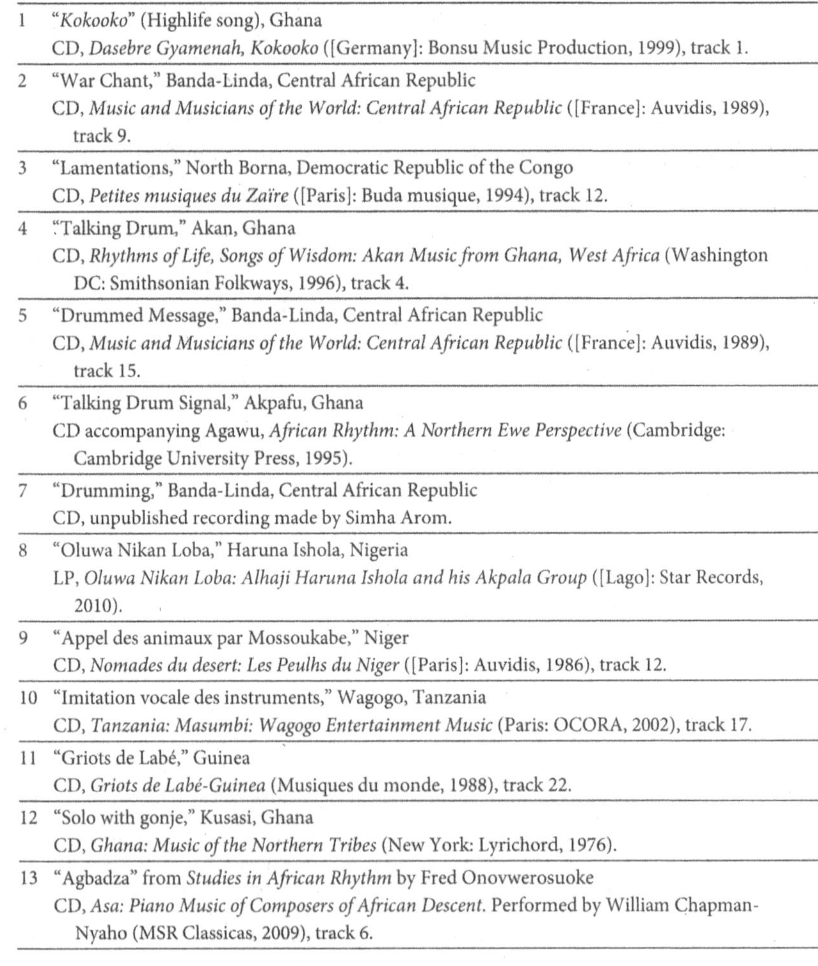

1	"*Kokooko*" (Highlife song), Ghana CD, *Dasebre Gyamenah, Kokooko* ([Germany]: Bonsu Music Production, 1999), track 1.
2	"War Chant," Banda-Linda, Central African Republic CD, *Music and Musicians of the World: Central African Republic* ([France]: Auvidis, 1989), track 9.
3	"Lamentations," North Borna, Democratic Republic of the Congo CD, *Petites musiques du Zaïre* ([Paris]: Buda musique, 1994), track 12.
4	"Talking Drum," Akan, Ghana CD, *Rhythms of Life, Songs of Wisdom: Akan Music from Ghana, West Africa* (Washington DC: Smithsonian Folkways, 1996), track 4.
5	"Drummed Message," Banda-Linda, Central African Republic CD, *Music and Musicians of the World: Central African Republic* ([France]: Auvidis, 1989), track 15.
6	"Talking Drum Signal," Akpafu, Ghana CD accompanying Agawu, *African Rhythm: A Northern Ewe Perspective* (Cambridge: Cambridge University Press, 1995).
7	"Drumming," Banda-Linda, Central African Republic CD, unpublished recording made by Simha Arom.
8	"Oluwa Nikan Loba," Haruna Ishola, Nigeria LP, *Oluwa Nikan Loba: Alhaji Haruna Ishola and his Akpala Group* ([Lago]: Star Records, 2010).
9	"Appel des animaux par Mossoukabe," Niger CD, *Nomades du desert: Les Peulhs du Niger* ([Paris]: Auvidis, 1986), track 12.
10	"Imitation vocale des instruments," Wagogo, Tanzania CD, *Tanzania: Masumbi: Wagogo Entertainment Music* (Paris: OCORA, 2002), track 17.
11	"Griots de Labé," Guinea CD, *Griots de Labé-Guinea* (Musiques du monde, 1988), track 22.
12	"Solo with gonje," Kusasi, Ghana CD, *Ghana: Music of the Northern Tribes* (New York: Lyrichord, 1976).
13	"Agbadza" from *Studies in African Rhythm* by Fred Onovwerosuoke CD, *Asa: Piano Music of Composers of African Descent*. Performed by William Chapman-Nyaho (MSR Classicas, 2009), track 6.

Figure 2.1 Thirteen examples of iconicity

incorporation of an onomatopoeic word into sung melody; (**2**) is a vocal ensemble's recreation of memories of war; (**3**) is mediated sung-weeping; (**4**), (**5**), (**6**), (**7**), and (**8**) are renditions of speech on various drums; (**9**) is a vocal mimicking of animal sounds; (**10**) is a vocal imitation of instrumental performance; (**11**) is a purely instrumental rendition of a joint vocal/instrumental performance; (**12**) is accompanied song premised on an idealized oneness between sung melody and accompanying melody; and (**13**) is a modern reconstruction of a traditional dance-drum piece for the piano.

Four Preliminary Cases

In 1999, Ghanaian Highlife musician Daasebre Gyamena (1972–2016) came out with a song that impressed many (**1**). Entitled *Kɔkɔɔkɔ*, it is a lover's plea to be let into his loved one's room. "I'm standing behind your door knocking *kɔkɔkɔ*," says he to her; "I have something sweet [*adi dɛdɛɛdɛ*] to tell you." "Wuwu, yeah yeah," he continues in American slang as he crosses over from the Twi language into English, "I can never live without you." Now, the three-syllable word *kɔkɔkɔ* bears three high tones [HHH, not LLL, where H and L denote high and low tones respectively] and signifies knocking on a door. Although the middle syllable is often elongated in speech [*kɔkɔɔkɔ*], reflecting a sound-symbolic influence whereby the elongated syllable adds emphasis, Gyamena's setting retains an equi-durational pattern. My interest here is in the incorporation of a common, indeed inter-ethnic, lexical item into a musical setting in such a way that it retains its referential baggage even while doing ordinary musical work. The word *kɔkɔkɔ* signifies by resemblance, giving rise to a form of *iconicity*.

Consider next this diversion from among the Banda Linda people in the Central African Republic (**2**). Five older men are rehearsing memories of war, complete with literal imitations of rifle shots (using words like *kpo*!, *kpokpokpo*!, and *gidi*!). Their utterances are constrained by a pentatonic structure and by a regular beat that is felt but not externalized by any of the men. Unlike Gyamena's *Kɔkɔɔkɔ*, in which an extramusical element becomes musical without shedding its semantic or referential baggage, the Banda-Linda elders' performance incorporates uninflected iconic effects of spoken language into a musico-poetic structure. In other words, the imitated gunshots, for example, are strictly speaking not part of the musical system. The sort of "compound" texture featured in this performance—a combination of song, poetry, and spoken interjections bearing literal descriptive value—is common throughout Africa, and may be understood as a manifestation of an enduring iconic impulse.

In a similar vein is this scene from a funeral ceremony among the North Borna ethnic group of the Democratic Republic of the Congo (**3**). An entire village is mourning the departure of their chief's son. As often happens in societies ruled by a communal ethos, this public expression of grief is mediated. The specific vehicle is a descending melodic fragment, ending from time to time on something like the pitch C-natural. "Weeping on or toward a C-natural," we might say. The effect of this mediation is to transform first-level (or natural) weeping into a second-level *representation* of weeping. The mode is thus doubly iconic insofar as it combines the thing itself with the thing represented. As far as I can tell, there is no loss of authenticity or emotional sincerity when Congolese weep on C-naturals.

Next is an example of iconicity in the form of speech surrogacy (**4**). In a staged performance (as distinct from an actual, real-life, or in-context rendition) of an Akan text honoring Odɛefoɔ Boa Amponsem, the king of Denkyira, a drummer employs poetic lines to enhance the stature of the king. Had this been an actual performance (typically, a funeral, the celebration of a rite, a durbar, or a state occasion), the drum would speak on its own, and be understood by those versed in this particular drum language. In this didactic version recorded by American ethnomusicologist Roger Vetter in 1996, however, a young woman speaks the lines in Twi while a young man renders each line immediately on a pair of *atumpan* pair drums. It is nowadays not clear how many people attending an event like a funeral or durbar actually understand drum talk—as distinct from merely recognizing the mode of articulation as a form of speaking. I cite it here as a straightforward example of the kind of equivalence basic to iconicity and the demonstration as an instance of simultaneous translation—another popular contemporary practice often encountered in multilingual churches.[2]

[2] While the basic mode of talking drumming—rendering speech on a drum—is widely practiced throughout Africa, there are regional differences stemming from the qualities of individual languages, the nature of the instruments used to produce them, and performance conventions. Examples 4–8 in Figure 2.1 provide further illustration of speech surrogacy. For a brief introduction, see my *The African Imagination in Music*, pp. 127–135, where I also cite several specialized studies.

Icon-Index-Symbol

These are but four little manifestations of a phenomenon that is widespread in many world cultures. In C. S. Peirce's universal algebra of sign equations, the icon belongs to a trichotomy of signifying modes comprising icon-index-symbol. All three stress different qualities. *Icons* are based on firstness and likeness, on similarity between the sign vehicle and its object, as we find in photographs, paintings, portraits, algebraic formulas, diagrams, metaphor, and ideographs (these are Peirce's own examples). *Indices* exemplify secondness and are based on contiguity between sign vehicle and object (as when smoke indexes fire, or a hole in a window indexes a gunshot). And in the case of symbols, a form of thirdness, there is an "imputed character" that links sign vehicle and denotatum. These categories are obviously not watertight, nor are they mutually exclusive. Indeed, the signs they model often function in conjunction with one another to produce various hybrid forms, such as iconic indices, symbolic icons, indexical symbols, and so on. Strictly speaking, there are no pure icons, pure symbols, or pure indices; all icons, symbols, and indices admit of a degree of contamination.[3]

If we now think through the four examples we just heard using Peirce's categories, we might observe the following signifying tendencies. Recurrences of the word *Kɔkɔkɔ* in Gyamena's *Kɔkɔɔkɔ* exhibit a form of iconicity. Sung rather than spoken, the rendition crosses a systemic border between speech and song. The word is imported from ordinary language to depict its normative function—signifying a knock on the door—but because this is song rather than speech, the enunciation of *Kɔkɔkɔ* is subject to other constraints, notably the melodic and scalar constraints upon which this particular song is built. No one doubts the resemblance between the sung *kɔkɔkɔ* and its (imagined) spoken form, but because the two domains—the domain of speech and the domain of song—are notionally distinct, we can describe the resemblance as a form of iconicity.

There is an additional semiotic dimension here. The singer's entreaty to his lover to open the door for him presumably compels a response from his addressee. In that sense, the entreaty acquires an indexical quality because

[3] On "mixed" signification, see Roman Jakobson, "Language in Relation to Other Communication Systems," in *Selected Writings*, vol. 2, pp. 697–708 (The Hague: Mouton, 1971).

the signs function contiguously. Similarly, while our Banda-Linda elders are engaged in a form of iconic signaling—by enacting the sounds of rifles using sung pitches and rhythms—a parallel symbolic dimension is activated for some listeners by what is after all a "historical" performance, a recollection of the sounds of war from the past. And the weeping mourners from the Democratic Republic of the Congo exemplify indexicality to the extent that singing triggers weeping; at the same time, the relationship between sung weeping and unsung weeping is one of resemblance, a form of iconicity. In short, these signs signify in overlapping ways, even if we need to separate them for analytical purposes.

The semiosphere we know as contemporary Africa is marked by a vibrant trade in signs and symbols. Whether this exceeds the putative global norm is a question I'm not prepared to answer, although it is often remarked how deeply *symbols* penetrate African cultural expression. In the performing arts, rampant acts of communication animate practically every performance, and each act is invariably made possible by an exchange of signs. The semiotic dimensions of the African musical arts are readily observed. Thus, dancers react to signals from drummers, while dancers in turn sometimes inspire drummers to play certain patterns. Singers manipulate the signs of language (text) and melody to affect their hearers. Instrumentalists play on the semiotic competence of their listeners. And composers and orators routinely deploy codes designated for decoding. A comprehensive review of all modes of signification would be a mammoth undertaking, as is obvious from the sprawling legacy of Peirce himself, especially from the huge secondary literature his work has engendered. For the more modest purposes at hand, let us, by way of contrast, acknowledge a few instances of visual iconicity before returning to auditive iconicity.

Visual Iconicity

Visual iconicity is manifest in the diverse products of the African artistic imagination such as paintings, photographs, portraits, carvings, textiles, masks, and religious icons, among many others. While auditive iconicity is perceptible in the realm of hearing, visual iconicity is associated with the realm of seeing. The presumed priority accorded the visual dimension within the hierarchy of the senses makes visual iconicity readily apprehensible, perhaps more readily apprehensible than auditive iconicity.

We have room for just one set of examples, so-called *fantasy coffins*.[4] Made in shapes that reflect or project particular identities (real or imagined), fantasy coffins can take the form of tools (hammer), books (the Bible), objects (shoes, beer bottles, soda bottles), animals (elephants), birds (hens), or even body parts (a polished uterus). When the accomplished Anlo-Ewe drummer, Godwin Agbeli, died in 1998, he was seen off in a coffin shaped like the great *atimewu* drum of which he was an acknowledged virtuoso-exponent.[5] (Not to be morbid, but I have often wondered how some musicologists or music theorists would choose to make the journey: in a coffin shaped like a fortepiano or bassoon; in one shaped like a book, say the first edition of Schenker's *Der freie Satz* or the *Liber Usualis*; or in one cast as a recent issue of the flagship journal, *Journal of the American Musicological Society*?) The wanton exercising of an iconic impulse that motivates the making of fantasy coffins does not always leave a great deal to the imagination: a coffin in the shape of a hammer is a carpenter's resting place; one shaped like a Mercedes Benz car sees off an affluent man; another made in the image of the Bible is preferred by a devout Christian; and one shaped like a uterus stands for a devoted mother. Although the choice of coffin type is sometimes made by the now-deceased while still living, many choices in fact represent the fantasies and desires of those tasked with burying the dead. And deploying an iconic mode in designing the vehicle ensures ready comprehensibility.

It bears repeating that although we're focusing here on iconic signs, other sign processes are simultaneously at work. Take the case of a wooden coffin shaped like a Mercedes Benz car. The most basic condition for iconic signification is satisfied by the reproduction of features from one material domain (metal) to another (wood). This brand of car is also indexical of wealth—it makes us think of the deceased as wealthy. The question of wealth in turn arises because, at this historical moment within this particular African culture, Mercedes Benz cars are symbols of affluence. We thus have a combination of iconic-indexical-symbolic functions active within the single practice of using fantasy coffins.

This particular manifestation of the iconic mode does not represent the height of semiotic imagining in Africa for the simple reason that it is manifest,

[4] For an introduction, see Thierry Secretan, *Going into Darkness: Fantastic Coffins from Africa* (London: Thames and Hudson, 1995).

[5] Godwin Agbeli is featured on the cover of David Locke's *Drum Kpegisu: A War Drum of the Ewe* (Tempe, AZ: White Cliffs Media Company, 1992). His teaching is frequently acknowledged by Locke; see, for example, his *Drum Gahu: An Introduction to African Rhythm* (Tempe, AZ: White Cliffs Media Company, 1987).

obvious, and unambiguous. I will return to this point at the end of the chapter, but it is worth conceding that more nuanced ways of manipulating signs in other modalities exist. So while iconic signs are immediately accessible and often ubiquitous, their worth as tools for artistic creation is variable.

Fantasy coffins are not, of course, the only forms of visual iconicity. Other prominent forms include the lively critiques of political authority disseminated through cartoon journalism (in Cameroon and Nigeria, for example) and various message-bearing fabrics worn by families or members of various groups and associations at funerals, anniversaries, festivals, durbars, and so on.[6] Visual art is an obvious site for the cultivation of iconicity in part because of the ostensible social prioritization of what is *seen* over what is *heard*.[7]

Auditive Iconicity

Auditive iconicity takes two principal forms, iconicity of language (which we have not discussed so far) and musical iconicity (which we have introduced, but will discuss in more detail in the next section of the chapter).

One of Ferdinand de Saussure's influential insights into language is that of arbitrariness, according to which the relationship between signifier and signified is characterized as arbitrary, conventional, or unmotivated. To rehearse a canonical example: the word *dog* refers to the animal dog not because the letters d-o-g have any demonstrable dog-like qualities but because you and I agree that when we speak English we will use this particular three-letter sequence of consonant-vowel-consonant to depict that four-legged animal that some people keep as pets, exploit emotionally, and include in their wills—or treat as a source of protein. Some linguists have countered Saussure's premise

[6] See Achille Mbembe, "The 'Thing' and Its Double in Cameroonian Cartoons," in *Readings in African Popular Culture*, edited by Karin Barber, pp. 151–163 (Bloomington: Indiana University Press, 1997). For a sampling of Africa's political cartoons, visit the website founded by Teju Olaniyan http://africacartoons.com/about/ (accessed August 2017). See also Olaniyan, "Cartooning Nigerian Anticolonial Nationalism," in *Images and Empires: Visuality in Colonial and Postcolonial Africa*, edited by P. S. Landau and D. D. Kaspin, pp. 124–140 (Berkeley: University of California Press, 2002).

[7] In her search for an "indigenous Anlo sensorium" (*Culture and Senses: Bodily Ways of Knowing in an African Community* [Berkeley: University of California Press, 2002]), Kathryn Linn Geurts challenges a number of received ideas about the way the senses are prioritized in different cultures. An important study showing the place of the visual in Ewe performance is Daniel Avorgbedor, "The Place of the Visual in Constructing and Extending Affect and Meaning in Ewe Performance Traditions with Attention to *Dufozi*: Some Theoretical and Methodological Implications." Paper read at the international symposium, *African Music in the 21st Century—An Iconic Turn?* (Mainz, 2009).

by pointing out that iconic traces may be found in such things as the order in which words are arranged in a sentence to mirror a sequence of historical events, or to depict distances between objects. Arbitrariness between signifier and signified now seems less secure as a premise.

In her 1990 presidential address to the Semiotic Society of America, American linguist Linda Waugh argued that the English lexicon may in fact be more iconic than had previously been granted.[8] The evidence she adduced included *onomatopoeic iconicity* (as heard in words like wheeze, knock, splash, crash, garble, grumble, giggle, fizzle, chuckle, cackle, babble) and *sound-symbolic associations*, themselves a form of iconicity (examples include the association of front and higher pitched vowels with smallness and brightness, and back and lower-pitched ones with largeness or darkness.) No African language data appear in Waugh's study, but the attempt "to take the con out of iconicity" can be easily strengthened by data from African language studies. Two dimensions in particular may be cited, and it is no accident that they embody fundamental links with music: first is the widespread use of ideophones; and second is the existence of speech tones. Both phenomena exhibit an underlying iconic mode.

Ideophones, according to linguist Mark Dingemanse, are "marked words that vividly depict sensory perception."[9] They have been called different things by different scholars: *Lautbilder* or picture words (Westermann), vocal images (Levy-Bruhl), *mots expressifs* (Grammont), and echoisms (Smith).[10] Anyone who has acquired language in a milieu in which ideophones abound will have an intuitive understanding of them, even if it takes some conscious thought to isolate examples and analyze their workings. The basic insight stems from a postulated parallelism between form and meaning. The process by which ideophones come to be marked (as distinct from unmarked) may be characterized as pushing language toward the condition of music. This is because ideophones are often sonically distinct; indeed, we might even say that they manifest an excess of sonic value. Simple ways to achieve this "excess" include the use of reduplication, the elongation of vowels, and marked registral placement. In Ewe, *wole gbudugbudu wɔm* means "they are causing tumult," *tsitotsito* depicts thoroughness, while *knkenkenken* conveys

[8] Linda Waugh, "Let's Take the Con Out of Iconicity: Constraints on Iconicity in the Lexicon," *American Journal of Semiotics* 9 (1992): 7–48.

[9] Mark Dingemanse, *The Meaning and Use of Ideophones in Siwu* (PhD dissertation, Radboud University/Max Planck Institute for Psycholinguistics, Nijmegen, 2011), 25.

[10] Dingemanse, "The Meaning and Use of Ideophones in Siwu," 21.

completeness. In Siwu, Dingemanse cites the following ideophones as being in regular use in the early 2000s: *kananaa* (silent), *fututu* (pure white), *nyɛkɛnyɛkɛ* (sweet), *gbogboro* (tough), *dɛkpɛrɛɛ* (fine grained), *kɛkei* (small). Words like this appear in riddles, children's game songs, folk tales, funeral dirges, greetings, and of course everyday conversation. Of the various enabling features, reduplication is pertinent because it activates an iconic horizon through contiguous repetition, bringing sounding language closer to the condition of music—music being a phenomenon saturated by repetition. Put differently, ideophones may be said to inflect language away from language by letting sound do the work of sense-making, not in the conventional ways associated with the signification of a word like *dog*, but in motivated ways whereby an increase in rhythmic activity generates meaning.

The use of ideophones is not always regarded as a sign of sophistication in language use. Conventional critiques hold that their use is childish, that they play a minor or merely occasional role in the overall language system, and that they are not organically linked to the rest of language. Their widespread occurrence in a number of world languages, however, suggests a willing investment in the kinds of expressive work that ideophones do in speech.

Understanding ideophones as forms of iconicity is appropriate because the depiction of sensory data that Dingemanse postulates as basic to ideophones is literal: a long vowel depicts silence by impeding novelty; tumult is conveyed by a noisy reduplication; a closed and registrally high vowel depicts smallness, and so on. Iconicity in turn reinforces the intersection between the domains of language and of music.[11]

Another well-known phenomenon that is even more readily conceptualized as "musical" in a tone language is the phenomenon of speech tones. As is well known, tone is phonemic in a tone language, which means that the meanings of lexical items are tied to a relational tonal scheme such as LMH (Low, Mid, High). In order to retain their semantic validity outside the realm of speech, speech tones typically exert an iconic hold on musical tones. Thus parallelism between melodic contour and the contour of speech tones would seem to preserve the semantic meanings of the words. And yet, because music (or song) is a categorically different semiotic system (no matter how many properties their internal elements share), the influence of speech tones on melody cannot always

[11] On other aspects of ideophone iconicity (such as imagic iconicity, diagrammatic iconicity, Gestalt iconicity, and relative iconicity), see Dingemanse, "The Meaning and Use of Ideophones in Siwu," 163–188. The inference that ideophones model a *musical* rather than a merely sonic dimension is mine, not Dingemanse's.

be a matter of giving priority to speech tones; sometimes constraints that may be regarded as *purely musical* are at work.[12]

If the parallelism between speech tone contour and melodic contour is recast in terms of an iconic imperative, then we can say that song manifests varying degrees of iconic fidelity. Or, formulated from a composer's point of view, a central challenge in the composition of song in a tone language is to determine the degree of resistance to the iconic imperative needed to achieve one's compositional goals. Many native-speaker composers often seem unwilling to set aside the iconic imperative of spoken language when they invent not only melodies but entire polyphonic textures. (In this respect, it seems that composers of African popular music are more willing to ignore or resist the iconic imperative than composers of certain traditional genres.) This is not because communication is threatened when melody departs from the proto-melody of language, as is often claimed. The issue is deeper, I think, and impinges on the psychical security provided by the relational world of speech tone. To some composers, tone languages are like sacred cows. They embody a certain will-to-iconicity, in effect, a will-to-truth. To violate them willfully in composing threatens to undermine the compositional subject's very linguistic and spiritual essence. While violations are not ultimately avoidable, they must be understood as departures from an ideal, as occasional features, as options dictated by purely musical forces. Iconicity (or parallelism) remains the ideal.

Anyone who has ever wondered about the relative paucity of strophic song (not a strophic impulse) in Africa's traditional heritage will find a partial answer in the influence exerted by tone languages on melodic construction. The arrival of Protestant missionaries in West Africa from the 1840s on initiated a quite extraordinary regime in which African converts were placed under strophic arrest, so to speak, made to utter "untruths" Sunday after Sunday by singing hymns (and later, under the influence of school music, a whole slew of English folk songs in strophic form) in which different sets of words with different tone schemes were sung to the same tune. It is not that occasional departure from the prescriptions of speech tones

[12] See also Laura McPherson, "The Talking Balafon of the Sambla: Grammatical Principles and Documentary Implications," *Anthropological Linguistics* 60 (2019): 255–294; and Stephen Morey and Jürgen Schöpf, "Tone in Speech and Singing: A Field Experiment to Research Their Relation in Endangered Languages of North East India," *Language Documentation and Description* 10 (2012): 37–60.

was unheard of; it was rather that the sheer scale of the missionary licensing was massive, sometimes total, and this has had damaging repercussions on the will-to-iconicity prescribed by indigenous languages. In semiotic terms, it was as if the more natural iconic constraint posed by speech tones (and presumably practiced for generations) was ignored or placed under erasure. The effects of this semiotic confusion are, I would argue, still very much with us.

Auditive Iconicity: Further Examples

At the beginning of this chapter, I cited four performances (of highlife, musico-poetic entertainment, crying in tune, and talking drumming) to introduce the sorts of phenomena that might be analyzed under the umbrella of iconicity. To these may be added five more to expand the scope while reinforcing some of the attributes mentioned previously (refer back to Figure 2.1).

The first is a Wodaabe Peul imitating animal sounds with his voice (**9**). We might describe this as unmediated auditive iconicity, framed not as function but as play. Framing this performance as play in turn suppresses the indexical value of the performance. Second is a performance from the Wagogo of Tanzania in which a male vocal quartet is imitating the playing of instruments (**10**). In behaving like instruments, voices strive to achieve a form of firstness. They have to forgo semantic valency, produce sounds in a high falsetto voice, and labor under a demanding rhythmic regime. The voices are not called upon to translate, adapt, or otherwise domesticate the instrumental idiom, but rather to render it as faithfully as the singers can, to remain at a first level of iconicity. The result is an overall strain in the profile of the performance—a "double articulation" of singing and (imagined) playing of the same musical material.

Third is a strikingly similar form of mimicry, this time from Guinea, in which an ensemble of flutes imitates a griot performance (**11**). A groove is first activated, as if imitating the sound of the traditional accompanying instrument, a kora or perhaps even a guitar. Then one of the flutes intones the griot's part, soaring into a high register to deliver a message. This performance is further proof that African musical ideas sometimes float free of their timbral encasing. Fourth is a gonje or one-stringed fiddle performance in which the played and sung strive to achieve a degree of sameness (**12**). Singing and playing the same thing speaks to the exercise of an iconic impulse. Fifth and finally is a piano étude by Nigerian composer Fred Onovwerosuoke (b.1960) based on a popular traditional Ewe dance, *Agbadza* (**13**). Onovwerosuoke has in effect translated a dance-drumming polyrhythmic texture (made up of a bell, rattle, support drums and lead drum) into a two-handed piano texture, making adjustments as needed for the new medium. The bell pattern (a recurring 2-2-1-2-2-2-1 figure) is entrusted to the right hand as an ostinato; support drum is given to a figure in the middle of the texture. Then lying low in the left hand is the lead drum part. We may well be broaching the upper limits of iconicity with this example insofar as it is, on the one hand, an original, art-music composition and at the same time a recreation of a traditional dance.

Also iconic are the structural homologies that are said to link social structure to musical structure. For example, some have suggested that Aka polyphony reproduces the egalitarian character of Aka social interaction by denying the principle of hierarchy in the way the constituent voices of a vocal ensemble are arranged; or that the principle of call-and-response models hierarchic social arrangements featuring a king (or chief, or big man) and his subordinates; or that, according to Meki Nzewi, the rhythmic formation known as cross rhythm (3:2) may be conceptualized as a strategic denial of coincidence—be it in the form of a non-consummation of a love relationship, or in the form of objects approaching each other in space but failing to make contact.[13]

The will to oneness that lies at the core of iconicity is familiar to musicians practicing in all traditions. We might say that this is simply where musicians live. In an early study of iconic relations in music, David Osmond Smith reminded us that iconicity may well be synonymous with the essential procedure of music.[14] According to him, "music has extensively developed the manipulation of what might be termed intramusical formal analogy, which is to say the establishment of thematic material and its subsequent variation and development." Osmond Smith's examples are taken from the music of J. S. Bach, but they could just as easily have come from any number of

[13] Meki Nzewi, *African Music: Theoretical Content and Creative Continuum: The Culture-Exponent's Definitions* (Olderhausen, Germany: Institut für populärer Musik, 1997), 39.

[14] David Osmond Smith, "Iconic Relations within Formal Transformation," in *Actes du 1er congress international de sémiotique musicale/Proceedings of the 1st International Congress on Semiotics of Music*, Belgrade 1973, edited by Gino Stefani, pp. 45–55 (Pesaro: Centro di Iniziativa Culturale, 1975). See also Ben Curry, "Resituating the Icon: David Osmond-Smith's Contribution to Music Semiotics," *Twentieth Century Music* 9 (2012): 177–200.

African repertories, including the ones cited in this chapter. Acts of copying, imitating, and repeating promote not just intra-musical formal analogy but inter-musical formal analogy; they also promote formal analogy between expressive systems. The domain of iconicity is potentially boundless.

Beyond Iconicity

Immediacy, equivalence, resemblance, overtness, mimicry, firstness, and so on: these are the main qualities associated with iconicity. Our examples have ranged from the literal to the metaphorical, from the direct to the mediated; and they have come from the Central African Republic, the Democratic Republic of Congo, Ghana, Niger, Tanzania, Guinea, and Nigeria.

But why dwell on something as elementary as iconicity, with its replicas, echoes, and simulacra? Surely African music signifies in more subtle ways. My goal all along has been to describe, not to celebrate iconicity. Rather than merely aestheticizing iconicity, we might consider both what it enables and what it inhibits in the way of creativity.

An anecdote may be helpful here. The story is told of one of President Kwame Nkrumah's ministers who—shall we say—had a rather strained relationship with idiomatic English. Asked to introduce speakers on a panel at a public function, he sat in the center, three speakers to his right, three others to his left. Starting with the one farthest from him on the right and working his way toward the center, he began: "On my extreeeeeeeeeeeeeeme [very long] right is Mr. Kwakye"; then, "on my extreeeeeme [long] right is Mr. Boateng"; and finally, "on my 'extrim' [extremely short] right is Mr. Owusu." [General laughter].

What was going on? The minister's problem was a deficiency in manipulating certain symbols. He did not know the meaning of the word *extreme*, so he compensated for this by employing a form of iconicity—using vowel length to represent physical distance. This is an ingenious solution, of course, and it is one that may well appeal to those who see such follies in purely aesthetic terms, who will call this poetry rather than error, who, hungry for ironies and difference, and never angry about the outrageously biased positioning of language in global competition, search for text-making opportunities at such sites. Krobo Edusei, who was otherwise a very skilled politician, should have spent more time in English classes so that the word *extreme* would not be made to take on a sound-symbolic quality that belied its actual meaning. It might be argued that the minister was only availing himself of what Tucker Childs calls "a common type of universal iconicity . . . associated with expressive lengthening or (unlimited) reduplication"[15]; or maybe he was being ironic. But why deny him the mastery that would enable him to produce ironies based on choice rather than on a lack?

The qualities we associate with iconism show it to be immediate, requiring no mediation, natural, self-evident, infantile, even true. Which is why, on one level, many artists (including composers and writers) routinely commit strategic acts of violence against iconicity in the name of artistic creativity and experimentation. They do so by resisting first-level truths, by inviting mediation, and by investing in symbols. Symbols, for example, require interpretation, they are based in cultural knowledge available only to some, and they can be imposed on others. They proffer secret knowledge, and can even be deceiving. The symbolic realm is closed, whereas the iconic realm is relatively open. If it is true that the iconic mode is dominant in African cultural expression, if we are in some sense trapped in iconism because of our tone languages, our talking drums, and our ideophones, then what might be called the African problem is in part a semiotic problem.

As far as I know, the "African problem" has never been formulated as a specifically semiotic problem, but if there's any merit at all to that characterization, it should suggest that study of cultural codes—in particular music, dance, and language—is a pre-requisite for adequate understanding of society. It implies, too, that we need to look beyond the longstanding romance with various facets of iconicity if we are to come to terms with the challenge of modernity and its aftermath. The trappings of tone languages, for example, which have posed innumerable problems for honest composers, need to be interrogated; reticence about violating them needs to be overcome. In other words, the reassuring alliances made possible by iconicity need now to be replaced by rougher, less beautiful constellations in order to enhance creativity. Indeed, we are already seeing some of that in contemporary artistic projects that engage with traditional resources without according them an a priori reverential status. It should be emphasized that from a historical point of view, the iconic impulse in African cultures has always existed alongside other impulses. Religious discourses, for example, are heavily invested in symbolism, and have shown the sources of a different kind of power, while

[15] Tucker G. Childs, "African Ideophones," in *Sound Symbolism*, edited by Leanne Hinton, Johanna Nichols, and John J. Ohala, p. 193 (Cambridge, UK: Cambridge University Press, 1994).

musical forms that refuse the facile incorporation of uninflected linguistic elements already provide the foundations for a critique of iconicity. So we have everything in place within these self-same African cultures to domesticate the iconic imperative and encourage creativity under other semiotic regimes. A beautiful thing, iconicity, but it is time to go beyond it.

3

Tonality as a Colonizing Force in Africa

> The modern musical world is not really imaginable without the musical results of colonialism.
>
> —Bruno Nettl

> Colonial administrators and their allies, the European missionaries, condemned everything African in culture—African names, music, dance, art, religion, marriage, the system of inheritance.
>
> —Adu Boahen

> Colonial education was a series of limitations inside other limitations.
>
> —Walter Rodney

> [The] ideological premises [of colonial education] obliged its agents to have recourse to texts, images, and other modes of discourse and representation that devalue the humanity of their dark-skinned wards, as parts of the effort to establish the cultural and moral authority of the colonizing race.
>
> —Abiola Irele[1]

Tonality, understood as a hierarchically organized system of pitch relations animated by semitonal desire, accompanied Europe's ostensibly civilizing mission to Africa from the 1840s onward.[2] Stabilized earlier

[1] Bruno Nettl, "Colonialism," *Grove Music Online*, accessed June 15, 2021; A. Adu Boahen, *African Perspectives on Colonialism* (Baltimore, MD: Johns Hopkins University Press, 1987), 107; Walter Rodney, *How Europe Underdeveloped Africa* (London: Bogle-L'Ouverture, 1972), 264; and Abiola Irele, *The African Imagination: Literature in Africa and the Black Diaspora* (Oxford, UK: Oxford University Press, 2001), viii.

[2] I extend here the discussion "Tonal Harmony as Colonizing Force," begun on pages 8–10 of my book *Representing African Music: Postcolonial Notes, Queries, Positions* (New York: Routledge, 2003). In keeping with its origins as a talk, the argument here is partly inscribed in the recorded examples cited in this essay and listed in the discography. Readers are encouraged to consult the recordings while reading the text.

On African Music. Kofi Agawu, Oxford University Press. © Oxford University Press 2023.
DOI: 10.1093/oso/9780197664063.003.0003

in the works of composers like Corelli, Bach, Handel, Vivaldi, and their contemporaries, tonality is typically expressed by a key-defining impulse. When we speak of a symphony "in G minor" or a sonata "in F major" or a concerto in "B-flat major," we are acknowledging the existence of a ruling tonic-dominant polarity as well as degrees of relatedness with and among the remaining members of the work's triadic universe. Different theorists explain the process differently. The expression of a sense of key may involve cadential punctuation of varying strengths, temporary departures from "home" for purposes of contrast and also to enhance—or indeed intensify—the desire for return, or a multileveled unfolding of the tonic triad as both linear and vertical configurations. These differences notwithstanding, many would be inclined to agree with Brian Hyer that "tonality is perhaps best conceptualized as a *tertium quid* that integrates melody, harmony and metre into a single nexus."[3] It has been the most influential system of pitch organization in Western Europe since the early eighteenth century.[4]

That such a central and resilient resource played a role in the network of exchanges and impositions that defined European colonialism in Africa should come as no surprise. Church music, choral anthems, and light music for dancing and entertainment—all of them tonal—enhanced or even defined civic and religious life in communities in Sierra Leone, Ghana, Togo, Nigeria, Uganda, Kenya, Zambia, Tanzania, Malawi, and South Africa, among other places. A ready example and perhaps *the* iconic marker of the kind of tonal thinking exported to Africa is the Protestant Christian hymn. Examples 3.1 and 3.2 show the familiar hymn "My Jesus, I Love Thee, I Know Thou Art Mine" along with its importation into the Ewe hymnal ("Nye Yesu, Melɔ̃a Wo, Be Tɔnye Nenye").[5] The extraordinary popularity of hymns like

[3] Brian Hyer, "Tonality," in *The Cambridge History of Western Music Theory*, edited by Thomas Christensen, p. 735 (Cambridge, UK: Cambridge University Press, 2006).

[4] For a useful guide to the literature on tonality, see Thomas Christensen, "Tonality," in *Oxford Bibliographies Online*, accessed June 15, 2021 https://www-oxfordbibliographies-com.ezproxy.princeton.edu/view/document/obo-9780199757824/obo-9780199757824-0252.xml. A study of tonality's enabling mechanisms seen through geometrical lenses and exemplified in a wide range of repertory is Dmitri Tymoczko, *A Geometry of Music: Harmony and Counterpoint in the Extended Common Practice* (New York: Oxford University Press, 2011).

[5] This hymn was composed in 1876 by the American Baptist preacher Adoniram Judson Gordon (1836–1895) to words by William Ralph Robertson. The version quoted in Example 3.1 is reproduced from Hymnary.org. For a recording, see *More Than 50 Most Loved Hymns* (Hollywood, CA: Liberty Records, 2004), CD 1, track 16. It appears as #409 in the Ewe hymnbook *Nyanyui Hame Hadzigbalẽ Gã*, 5th ed., p. 484 (Maharashtra, India: Evangelical Presbyterian Church, Ghana, and Eglise Evangélique Presbytérienne du Togo, 2002). For a comprehensive study of music in the E. P. Church, see Divine Gbagbo, *Recreation, Rites, and Rulership: Postcolonial Christianity in Ewe Music of Ghana* (PhD dissertation, Ohio University, 2021).

Example 3.1 Hymn "My Jesus, I Love Thee" by A. J. Gordon (1876)

My Je - sus, I love___ thee, I know thou art mine; for thee all the
fol - lies of sin I re - sign. My gra - cious Re - deem - er, my
Sav - ior art thou;___ if ev - er I loved_ thee, my Je - sus, 'tis now.

this and hymn-based compositions throughout Africa stems from both their message and music. Hymns carry messages about Christian living; they comfort those in distress, reinforce ties with an all-powerful God, and offer enticing glimpses of the better life that awaits the faithful in the hereafter. Vehicles for delivery of these messages include simple poetic forms (typically quatrains featuring end rhymes), vivid imagery, and memorable or quotable lines. Hymn tunes are conveniently placed within the normal registers of male and female voices so that they can be easily learned and remembered by congregations. Typically diatonic, hymn phrases are arranged with a clear expressive profile (*aaba* in the case of "My Jesus I Love Thee," where *a* is a presentational phrase that returns to perform a recapitulatory and closing function, and *b* is the contrasting and at the same time intensifying phrase). They are harmonized using the primary chords of the tonal system (tonics, dominants, and subdominants, or their functional substitutes), cadence frequently, and thus display only modest trajectories of tonal thought.

Leaving aside the religious message, this collection of attributes frequently entails a series of reversals from indigenous African expression, musical as

Example 3.2 Ewe version of "My Jesus, I Love Thee" (2002)

well as linguistic. Hymns introduced by Protestant missionaries in the nineteenth century typically came in a standardized four-part texture (SATB) that no African group had ever used before. They were clothed in a prosody that few Africans would have recognized, including poetic meters with syllabic counts like 8.7.8.7 (as in the lyrics of "The King of Love My Shepherd Is" or "Love Divine, All Loves Excelling") and 11.11.11.11 (as in the lyrics "My Jesus I Love Thee, I Know Thou art Mine" or "Immortal, Invisible God Only Wise"), and they displayed a rhyme scheme that is difficult to achieve in indigenous tone languages. Finally, in domesticating hymns whose texts were originally in German or English for local consumption, melodies often disregarded the natural declamation of indigenous singing, imposed a regime of regular and symmetrical periodicity, and rode roughshod over the intonational contours prescribed by speech tones.[6]

[6] For a valuable introduction to hymns—their history, texts, religious function, reception, and aesthetics—see *An Annotated Anthology of Hymns*, edited by J. R. Watson (Oxford, UK: Oxford University Press, 2002). An early discussion of African hymnody appears in A. M. Jones, *African Hymnody in Christian Worship: A Contribution to the History of Its Development*, Mambo Occasional

All of this amounts to musical violence of a very high order, a violence whose psychic and psychological impacts remain to be properly explored. To be sure, the collective practices associated with the African reception of the Protestant hymn served both colonizer (the encountering society) and colonized (the encountered society) alike. For the colonizer, they were a means of exerting power and control over native populations by making them speak a tonal language that they had no chance of mastering. (The European tonal language of which hymns were a part underwent various forms of chromatic enrichment in the course of the nineteenth century, but few of these "progressive" developments reached African musicians operating within a hymn economy.) Limited and limiting, the language of hymns, with its reassuring cadences and refusal of tonal adventure, would prove alluring, have a sedative effect, and keep Africans trapped in a prison house of diatonic tonality. For the colonized, on the other hand, hymn singing was a passport to a new and better life; it was a way of "speaking" a new language, one that was moreover introduced by self-announced enlightened Europeans; it promised access to some precious accoutrements of modernity and eventually a place in heaven.

Hymn-based tonality has by now spread throughout Africa, encompassing a wide variety of musical forms and genres. In urban popular music from highlife to hiplife, afrobeat to *soukouss*, and *mbaqanga* to *benga*, chord progressions are often anchored by a tonic-dominant polarity.[7] In the realm of art music, itself another (direct) response to the European heritage, and one in which tonal experimentation is normal, black African composers have generally preferred the relative security of closed tonal forms to the uncertainties and insecurities of post-tonal expression.[8]

Papers (Gwelo, Rhodesia: Mambo, 1976); and in Lazarus Ekwueme, "African Music in Christian Liturgy: The Igbo Experiment," *African Music* 5 (1973–1974): 12–33. See also Roberta King, Jean Ngoya Kidula, James R. Krabill, and Thomas A. Oduro, *Music in the Life of the African Church* (Waco, TX: Baylor University Press, 2008). For an important recent study of the mission-based reception of European tone systems in Africa, including modal as well as tonal usages, see Anna Maria Busse Berger, "Spreading the Gospel of *Singbewegung*: An Ethnomusicologist Missionary in Tanganyika of the 1930s," *Journal of the American Musicological Society* 66, no. 2 (2013): 475–522. See also the author's *The Search for Medieval Music in Africa and Germany, 1891–1961* (Chicago: University of Chicago Press, 2020).

[7] For helpful insights into the reception of tonal harmony by highlife musicians, see David Coplan, "Go to My Town, Cape Coast! The Social History of Ghanaian Highlife," in *Eight Urban Musical Cultures*, edited by Bruno Nettl, pp. 96–114 (Urbana: University of Illinois Press, 1978). In refining the claim that I–IV–V progressions rule in African popular music, one might note the use of modality and pentatonicism in repertories such as "King" Sunny Ade's jùjú and Fela Kuti's afrobeat.

[8] By "European heritage" I mean, essentially, Handel and a bit of Bach; some Mozart, Beethoven, Chopin, and Mendelssohn; a little Brahms; and plenty of Gilbert and Sullivan. The preference

Understanding the *why* of these developments would entail looking into a complex of factors: some of them material and economic, some political, some educational, and all mediated by the movement of global capital, for it appears that tonality has always followed the movement of global capital.[9] Indeed, as Nettl notes in one of the epigraphs to this essay, one can hardly imagine the modern musical world "without the musical results of colonialism." But the exportation and importation of tonality are topics too big to be dealt with adequately in a short chapter like this. What I would like to do, instead, is paint a stark portrait of African tonal thinking before and after contact with Europe as a step toward future theorization of the dynamics of musical colonization. We know that colonial assaults on Africa through spoken language (French, English, and Portuguese, principally) and religious expression (Islam and Christianity, principally) have already claimed tens of millions of casualties. Relatively little has been said about parallel developments in the area of musical colonization, however. One reason is ontological: the variety of music's modes of existence, including its essence as a performed art, the centrality of its aesthetic function, and the complex trajectories of transmission, influence, and ownership all present challenges to arguments suggesting a denial of sovereignty or the domination of individual or group consciousness in the sonic realm.

Another reason is institutional: the discipline that traditionally houses research on African music is ethnomusicology, but ethnomusicology itself is a child of colonialism, a discipline rich in colonial filiation and affiliation. As one of its leading practitioners concedes, "Colonialism and its cultural outcroppings have been a major and, indeed, indispensable factor in the development of ethnomusicology (at least as practiced in North America and Western Europe)."[10] Another warns that "where ethnomusicology loses sight of its complex and thorny historical complicity with colonialism, it reproduces its myths."[11] Ethnomusicology's richly diverse research programs are yet to give pride of place to a systematic interrogation of the effects on African psyches of having to speak a foreign or European tonal language. Embrace of such

for tonality is mainly statistical, however. A few composers—Akin Euba, Joshua Uzoigwe, Bode Omojola, and Gyimah Labi—have experimented with atonal or post-tonal resources.

[9] I owe this observation to the music theorist Brian Hyer, whose remark in the course of a roundtable discussion during the Tonality in Perspective conference at King's College London in March 2008 I am recalling here. See also Hyer, "Tonality."

[10] Nettl, "Colonialism."

[11] Martin Stokes, "John Blacking and Ethnomusicology," in *The Queen's Thinkers: Essays on the Intellectual Heritage of a University*, edited by David N. Livingstone and Alvin Jackson, pp. 168–169 (Belfast: Blackstaff, 2008).

projects would demand both a practical and political commitment; it would also entail an honest critique of the very foundations of the discipline. This is not to suggest that no voices have ever been raised in opposition to Western tonal influence in Africa. A. M. Jones, himself a missionary, devoted a chapter to what he called neofolk elements in his groundbreaking book *Studies in African Music*, while Michelle Kisliuk has recently sided with the BaAka pygmies against the missionary efforts of the Grace Brethren Church in the Central African Republic.[12] And the literature on Southern African music (by Veit Erlmann, Christine Lucia, and Martin Scherzinger, among many others) includes helpful discussions of Africans' consumption of Western tonal products and systems, including the diatonically biased learning system associated with tonic solfa.[13] It is fair to say, however, that there is simply no equivalent in Africanist ethnomusicology to Frantz Fanon's *Black Skin, White Masks*; Albert Memmi's *The Colonizer and the Colonized*; or Walter Rodney's *How Europe Underdeveloped Africa*—all works that address the forms, content, and, especially, psychological impact of colonial-imperial influence in Africa.[14] Indeed, nowadays, the sometimes uncritical appropriation of

[12] A. M. Jones, *Studies in African Music*, 2 vols. (Oxford, UK: Oxford University Press, 1959); Michelle Kisliuk, *Seize the Dance! BaAka Musical Life and the Ethnography of Performance* (New York: Oxford University Press, 1998).

[13] See Veit Erlmann, *Music, Modernity and the Global Imagination: South Africa and the West* (Oxford, UK: Oxford University Press, 1999); Christine Lucia, "Back to the Future? Idioms of 'Displaced Time' in South African Composition," in *Composing Apartheid: Music for and against Apartheid*, edited by Grant Olwage, pp. 11–34 (Johannesburg: Wits University Press, 2008); and Martin Scherzinger, "Negotiating the Music Theory/African Music Nexus: A Political Critique of Ethnomusicological Anti-Formalism and a Strategic Analysis of the Harmonic Patterning of the Shona Mbira Song 'Nyamaropa,'" *Perspectives of New Music* 39 (2001): 5–118. On tonic solfa specifically, see Robin Stevens and Eric Akrofi, "Tonic Sol-fa in South Africa—A Case of Endogenous Musical Practice," in *Australian Association for Research in Music Education: Proceedings of the XXVIth Annual Conference, 25–28 September 2004*, Southern Cross University, Tweed-Gold Coast Campus, New South Wales, Australia, September 25–28, 2004 (Clayton, Victoria: Australian Association for Research in Music Education, 2004), 301–314.

[14] See Frantz Fanon, *Black Skin: White Masks*, translated by Charles Lam Markmann (1952; repr., London: MacGibbon and Kee, 1968); Albert Memmi, *The Colonizer and the Colonized*, translated by Howard Greenfield (Boston: Beacon, 1965); and Rodney, *How Europe Underdeveloped Africa*. The literature on the effects of colonialism in Africa is obviously too large to be meaningfully referenced in a single note. Among writings with a philosophical orientation, I might mention Paulin Hountondji, *African Philosophy: Myth and Reality*, translated by Henry Evans with Jonathan Rée (Bloomington: Indiana University Press, 1996); Kwasi Wiredu, *Cultural Particulars and Universals: An African Perspective* (Bloomington: Indiana University Press, 1996); V. Y. Mudimbe, *The Invention of Africa: Gnosis, Philosophy, and the Order of Knowledge* (Bloomington: Indiana University Press, 1988); and Olufemi Taiwo, *How Colonialism Preempted Modernity in Africa* (Bloomington: Indiana University Press, 2010). Several of the essays gathered in *A Companion to African Philosophy*, edited by Kwasi Wiredu (Oxford, UK: Blackwell, 2004), deal with the colonial influence. From the perspective of social theory, see Achille Mbembe's *On the Postcolony* (Berkeley: University of California Press, 2001). For a variety of literary perspectives, see Olakunle George, *Relocating Agency: Modernity and African Letters* (Albany: State University of New York Press, 2003); Irele, *The African Imagination*;

tropes of hybridity—uncritical insofar as they pass over in silence the losses, indignities, and humiliation suffered by people who are forced to speak other people's musical languages instead of their own—together with a principled resistance to essentialism have effectively muted discussion of *transformations in consciousness* wrought by the tonal forms exported to Africa.[15]

I have assembled a few recorded performances to lay bare the sonic environments that might support the argument that tonality has functioned as a colonizing force in Africa. I will address these in three stages. First, by means of a simple show-and-tell strategy, I acknowledge a few obvious traces of tonality (citing examples from South Africa and Ghana). Second, stepping back from the present, I draw attention to salient features of the (imagined) sound of pre-colonial Africa, the African soundscape before tonality arrived (these examples are from Gabon, Ghana, the Central African Republic, and the Republic of Benin). Third, returning to the present, I consider three imaginative responses to European tonality, attempting—indirectly—to answer the question, "What does it mean to compose under a tonal regime?" (These last examples are from Nigeria and Ghana.) It should be emphasized that for every one of the aural texts cited here, there are literally hundreds of others that essay similar tonal courses. So, although geo-cultural reference is, for the sake of convenience, limited to six African countries (Nigeria, the Central African Republic, South Africa, Gabon, Benin, and Ghana), a much larger set of examples could easily have been cited from both live performances and recordings.

Finally, I recognize that colonialism is too complex and profound a historical phenomenon to be reduced to a few local signs, and it cannot be analyzed by means of hasty or knee-jerk reactions. Nevertheless, if—as I believe—we are a long way from restoring sovereignty to Africans in the spheres of politics, language, religion, and music, then there may be some point to making a programmatic and symbolic argument.

Traces of Tonality in African Music

Ladysmith Black Mambazo, an all-male a cappella group from South Africa, has over the years produced a popular repertory that labors under tonal rule.

and Gaurav Desai, *Subject to Colonialism: African Self-fashioning and the Colonial Library* (Durham, NC: Duke University Press, 2001).

[15] On the colonization of consciousness, see Jean Comaroff and John Comaroff, *Of Revelation and Revolution: Christianity, Colonialism and Consciousness in South Africa* (Chicago: University of Chicago Press, 1991).

Collectively, Ladysmith's tonal experience is wide and varied, ranging from hymnlike original compositions through the folk-inflected harmonies of Paul Simon's *Graceland* to the sometimes chromatic harmonies of Mozart's "Ave verum corpus."[16] The beginning of their song "Paulina" will serve as an example.[17] Here are the opening lines, each of which finishes on tonic harmony:

> Paulina, Paulina, somebody's crying for you.
> You, Paulina, somebody's crying for you.
> Paulina, why did you leave him alone?
> Now, he asked me to call you
> I looked for you all over.
> You were nowhere to be found.
> Please, Pauline, come back to him
> He loves you, he wants to marry you
> Get away from those who want to touch-touch and kiss-kiss
> Thereafter they leave you alone.

What kind of tonal thinking is on display here? We never leave the home key; the sound of the tonic predominates, and the interstices are weighted toward the subdominant rather than the dominant. The absence of half cadences, important agents for the arousal of tonal desire, confers on the song as a whole a somewhat flat trajectory. Indeed, repeating harmonic cycles (I–IV–I) are made to bear various semantic weights in the expression of text. The same tonic freight accompanies questions ("Why did you leave him alone?"), statements ("You were nowhere to be found"), entreaties ("Please, Paulina, come back to him"), and warnings ("Get away from those who want to touch-touch and kiss-kiss"). This apparent lack of alignment between semantic sense and tonal meaning is, however, not an exception but rather the rule in the global aesthetics of song. Ladysmith's way of enriching the tonal palette is to invoke a not-so-distant pentatonic horizon and to hint at the microtonal realm through the use of glissandi on phrases like "*call* you" and "he *loves* you." There are no large trajectories of tonal thought here, just repetitions of a single progression. What keeps listeners engaged, however, is the asymmetry that results from the additive

[16] For a sampling of Ladysmith's tonal experiences, see the CD *No Boundaries: Ladysmith with the English Chamber Orchestra* (Cleveland, OH: Heads Up International, 2004).
[17] *Best of Ladysmith Black Mambazo* ([US]: Shanachie Entertainment, 1992), track 14.

patterning of harmonic cycles. This pedal-like function serves to channel a Christian-tinged message about what boys do to girls. A simple diatonic base rules throughout.[18]

A second example of the reception of tonal harmony comes from the brass-band tradition found throughout the continent and also in diasporic communities in Bolivia, Peru, Suriname, and Jamaica. Brass bands are associated with Protestant churches, police and military bands, and various community entertainment groups. A good example is a "highlife hymn" recorded by the Peace Brass Band from Ghana.[19]

The harmonic palette here is a little more varied than Ladysmith's. Within a basic diatonic framework, the Peace Brass Band incorporates deceptive as well as perfect cadences; the phrase discourse proceeds in two- and four-bar blocks. What may sound like infelicities in voice leading result from the use of both the flattened and natural seventh scale degree in the approach to the final cadence. The former is used as part of a descending line, while the natural seventh occurs within an ascending motion. These cross-relations are not aberrations, however; they are uninflected elements in the song's polyphonic system.

The influence of foreign musical procedures is most evident in the realm of voice leading. Each member of the Peace Brass Band has presumably grown up speaking a musical language in which parallelism rules in multipart expression. Here, however, under the constraints of a hymnlike texture, they attempt to speak a harmonic language that not only forbids certain parallels (like seconds, fourths, and fifths) but also abandons even permitted parallels (like thirds) in the approach to cadences. And so the musicians find themselves caught between opposing impulses. The situation is perhaps analogous to the kinds of error we make when speaking a foreign language. But whereas in linguistic grammar they are simply called errors, in musical language they are endowed with poetry or are said to be "interesting" or—worse—"different." Aestheticizing other people's errors is apparently a favorite colonialist pastime.

[18] A comprehensive study of Ladysmith is included in Veit Erlmann's study of *isicathamiya* in *Nightsong: Performance, Power and Practice in South Africa* (Chicago: University of Chicago Press, 1996). See also his *Music, Modernity and the Global Imagination.* In a lively review of this book, Martin Scherzinger takes issue with some of Erlmann's analytical claims pertaining to tonal orientation in ways that are pertinent to the discussion of tonal understanding in this essay. See Scherzinger, "Review of *Music, Modernity and the Global Imagination: South Africa and the West*," *Journal of the Royal Musical Association* 126 (2001): 117–141.

[19] *Frozen Brass: Africa and Latin America*, CD (Leiden: Pan, 1993), track 2.

This highlife hymn is ontologically conceivable only since the early 1900s, only as a product of colonial-missionary influence in West Africa (Ghana, Sierra Leone, Togo, Côte d'Ivoire, Nigeria). Although bands of wind instruments played throughout the precolonial era—we will encounter an example from the Central African Republic later on—none of them utilized functional harmony, or the kind of cadential phraseology we heard in the Peace Brass Band's performance, or indeed a consistently hierarchic separation between a treble and a functional bass voice and two inner voices (SATB). What is of interest from the point of view of a postcolonial critique is the apparent ease with which African musicians seem to surrender aspects of their native musical languages; it would seem that as soon as they were offered a taste of hymnlike cadences and phraseology, they were prepared to give up a part of their tonal-harmonic birthright. (The question *why* African musicians seem uneager to resist in the tonal-harmonic realm but not apparently—or at least not to the same extent—in the area of rhythmic behavior is an interesting one. Some would say that indigenous harmonic systems are not as strong as the invading European ones, but that argument is weakened by the fact that the imposition of tonal rule was always accompanied by various forms of material, political, and religious control.)

These are only two brief examples of tonal production enabled by colonialism. I could have cited many more: national anthems of various countries, scores of compositions produced under the rule of tonic solfa, music designed for praise in charismatic churches; arrangements of folk music for voice and piano, original choral anthems and masses for school and church choirs, and so on. But the point is made, I think, namely, that certain forms of tonal imagining and expressing became possible only after exposure to European tonal harmony. To the Bible and the gun (again following Basil Davidson), we can now add diatonic tonality as an instrument of colonial domination.

The question surely arises: what were Africans doing (tonally or harmonically) before the Europeans came along?

African Tonal Thinking in the Pre-European Era

It should come as no surprise that African tonal thinking took many forms before Europeans arrived. We catch a glimpse of this plurality in A. M. Jones's *Studies of African Music* (1959), one of the key texts in the history of analysis of African music. On the basis of field research in Zambia and close listening to then-available recordings, Jones was able to partition a large portion of the continent according to the intervals preferred by individual ethnic groups in polyphonic performance. A fold-out, color-coded map inserted into the second of his two-volume treatise differentiates between groups according to whether they sing in parallel thirds, sixths, fourths, fifths, unisons, or octaves. The so-called 8-5-4 groups, for example, are the pentatonic groups, while those that use thirds and sixths belong to a heptatonic category. Although Jones's early taxonomy now stands in need of a sizeable supplement to take account of research done in the last half century, it was possible, already in 1959, to observe the heterogeneous nature of African polyphonic choices. More recently, Gerhard Kubik has assembled a conspectus of African polyphonic behaviors, with emphasis on eastern, central, and southern parts of the continent. He quotes from various written accounts, studies the procedures used especially by the San and the pygmies (who are noted for their distinctive polyphonic style of singing), and describes some of the most important techniques, emphasizing the existence of different sound ideals and especially of the ingenuity with which parts are negotiated.[20] A brisk review of these resources and associated procedures is impossible given the size of the corpus, so I will simply highlight one particular resource, the so-called anhemitonic pentatonic scale (roughly equivalent to the black keys of the piano), one of the most characteristic and widespread tonal constructs found on the African continent, but also common in other world music cultures. I will later add a piece of drumming to complete the account of tonal expression originating in the pre-European era.[21]

[20] Gerhard Kubik, "Multipart Singing in Sub-Saharan Africa: Remote and Recent Histories Unravelled," in *Papers Presented at the Symposium on Ethnomusicology: Number 13 University of Zululand 1995 and at the Symposium Number 14 Rhodes University 1996*, edited by Andrew Tracey, pp. 85–97 (Grahamstown, South Africa: International Library of African Music, 1997). See also his earlier essay, "African Tone Systems: A Reassessment," *Yearbook for Traditional Music* 17 (1985): 31–63.

[21] One point of clarification regarding methodology: I'm not trying to construct a genealogical argument here, a literal "before-and-after" scenario. In other words, I do not, for example, trace a single ethnic group's tonal thinking from its precolonial state to its colonial and postcolonial phases. This periodization is, in any case, the colonizer's, and it almost certainly subtends interests, values, and desires that are antithetical to those of the colonized. I'm depending rather on strategically displaced attributions in order to enhance the potential for cross-ethnic generalization. The disadvantage in proceeding in this manner is that what might have been a temporally intact historical narrative dissolves into a series of speculations and affiliations. The advantage, however, is that it allows readers with different African referents to plug their particular variables into the framework outlined here. This "contrapuntal" approach is not yet normative for Africanist ethnomusicology, but it seems to me more promising than approaches that accept the strictures of conventional history and ethnography and thus decline the invitation to indulge in certain kinds of intertextual imagining.

A five-voice performance by Bibayak pygmies from Gabon provides a good example of pentatonic usage.[22] Each singer has internalized the pentatonic horizon and sings her individual part against that horizon, assured that articulating one or two notes—that is, a subset of the five-note collection—is enough to guarantee the integrity of the resultant pentatonic texture. There are no long-term trajectories in this mode of play, no phrase-generated expectations, no authentic cadences, no archetypal urges of managed desire and its fulfillment. There is only presentness, the repetition of notes and groups of notes into patterns organized around a palpable pulse. The form emerges additively from an accumulation of nows, a kind of moment form. The aesthetic is minimalistic, and the tonal resource is accepted and treated with reverence, not manipulated with the dubious ethics associated with individual cleverness. If modern artistic production were being guided by this pentatonic practice, it would explore the openness of resultant sounds; give priority to intervals of seconds, fourths, and fifths; embrace a nonteleological temporality; and prefer an egalitarian texture to a hierarchic one. This is, of course, not a prescription for what composers *should* do but a thought experiment about what they *would* do if they were following certain cultural or communal imperatives.

Pygmies are not the only exponents of pentatonicism in Africa. Closer to my own home are the Southern Ewe of Ghana, some of whose vocal music is based on this scale. A good source is a recording of music from Dzodze made by the American ethnomusicologist James Burns.[23] The verbal message in one song is directed at a beautiful young woman: "Do not bluff, young woman, do not bluff, beautiful one; the day you die, termites will be in the ground." As in the Bibayak pygmy example, the pentatonic serves throughout as a source of pitches, but the Anlo-Ewe style is different. For one thing, the initial call-response pattern signals a kind of hierarchic organization that the more egalitarian pygmies generally avoid. Each melodic part avails itself of the scale or part thereof, but the voices do not proceed mechanically in parallel. From the singers' point of view, this Southern Ewe performing practice privileges linearity over verticality. Sonorities are incidental except at ends of phrases (where

For a cogent advocacy and exemplification of contrapuntal reading, see Brent Hayes Edwards, "The Sound of Anti-Colonialism," in *Audible Empire: Music, Global Politics, Critique*, edited by Olaniyan and Radano, pp. 269–291 (Durham, NC: Duke University Press, 2016).

[22] Recorded on the CD *Gabon: Music of the Bibayak Pygmies: Epic Cantors* (France: Ocora, 2001), track 2.

[23] See the CD *Ewe Drumming from Ghana: The Soup Which Is Sweet Draws the Chairs Closer* (London, Topic Records, 2005).

they attain purity in the form of unisons or octaves), and they are based on the purposeful *melodic* use of the pentatonic, although the polyphonic outcome is known in advance given the referential collection. In other words, if each singer stays within the pentatonic orbit, then every two-note, three-note, four-note, or five-note resultant will conform to the source set. The pentatonic thus constitutes a kind of sound field, a *complexe sonore* subjected to various forms of articulation—syllable-based articulation by the pygmies (who use vocables but not words) and word-based articulation by the Anlo-Ewe.

The pentatonic is not, of course, manifest solely in vocal repertories; instrumental music for horns, trumpets, and xylophones often features a pentatonic referent. A vivid example may be cited from the repertory of a horn orchestra from the Banda ethnic group of the Central African Republic, recorded (and later analyzed) by Simha Arom.[24] Incidentally, this is one of the African repertoires that fascinated György Ligeti in the early 1980s and about which he writes in the preface to the English translation of Arom's magnum opus, *African Polyphony and Polyrhythm*.[25]

The recording features eighteen horns, each playing a single note. The whole is based on an anhemitonic pentatonic scale (in descending order): G-E-D-C-A-(G). The hocket technique so beloved of such ensembles is on display here. No individual part is meaningful without the others, and this is because only the resultant produces the desired Ur-melody. Strictly speaking, there is no hierarchy here, no treble versus bass. Although the instruments are assigned different registers such that the total ensemble range encompasses two and a half octaves, contrapuntal priority does not reside in any pair of parts. Again, this is music of precolonial origins, owing nothing to Europe and everything to black Africa.

Consider, finally, a snippet from a different kind of music of pre-European origins: *dùndún* drumming from among the Yoruba of Benin.[26] These

[24] Excerpted on the CD accompanying Monique Brandily's *Introduction aux musiques africaines* (Paris: Cité de la Musique; Arles: Actes Sud, 1997), track 21.

[25] Simha Arom, *African Polyphony and Polyrhythm: Musical Structure and Methodology*, trans. Martin Thom, Barbara Tuckett, and Raymond Boyd (1985; repr., Cambridge, UK: Cambridge University Press, 1991). For a thorough exposition of Ligeti's African affinities, see Martin Scherzinger, "György Ligeti and the Aka Pygmies Project," *Contemporary Music Review* 25 (2006): 227–62. In listening to the Bibayak pygmy excerpt, please take account of a margin of tolerance in the relational tuning of the horns so that the core pentatonic collection C-D-E-G-A is not replaced by a chromatic variant.

[26] *Yoruba Drums from Benin, West Africa* (Washington, DC: Smithsonian/Folkways, 1996), track 12, "Esikesi." Two major scholarly studies of the dynamics of Yoruba drumming are Akin Euba, *Yoruba Drumming: The Dùndún Tradition* (Beirut, Lebanon: African Studies Series, 1990); and Amanda Villepastour, *Ancient Text Messages of the Yorùbá Bàtá Drum: Cracking the Code*, SOAS Musicology Series (Surrey, UK: Ashgate, 2010).

so-called hourglass drums are noted for their ability to mimic the inflexions of spoken language and, in the process, explore a wide tonal spectrum. The dùndún both talks and mimics talking, that is, a given drummer may drum in the speech mode without actually saying anything. While some parts of the musical utterance are oriented toward indefinite rather than definite pitch, we can just about infer a distant pentatonic horizon in this recording. Although nowadays the dùndún, in the hands of an expert such as the Yoruba master drummer Adebisi Adeleke, sings everything from "Amazing Grace" to "God Save the Queen," its tonal potential is more closely aligned with the complex tonality of (in this case) spoken Yoruba. Such a language-based or language-derived tonality offers a rich resource for African composers, one that boasts an expressive and historical depth different from that available from the imported hymn-based tonality associated with Ladysmith or the Peace Brass Band.

We would obviously need more than five brief examples to characterize precolonial African tonal thinking comprehensively, but I believe that these examples are paradigmatic and thus adequate to the task of introducing the imagined sound of precolonial Africa. (I speak of them as "imagined" because the specific recordings cited here were made in the last half century, so they postdate the actual precolonial period, but this says nothing about the stability of the traditional institutions that sponsor these performing practices and repertories.) It should perhaps be emphasized that the techniques and scalar resources enshrined in these excerpts are not necessarily unique to Africa—pentatonicism, for example, may well be universal, occurring as it does in Africa, Asia, Indonesia, and in various corners of Europe—but that they were in use in Africa until functional harmony came along and decisively transformed the musical soundscape. Now, functional harmony did not cover every inch of musical surface on the continent, only some of it, notably the coastal regions, urban locations, places with schools (including mission schools), and, of course, churches. But quantity may be deceptive here, for these are privileged symbolic sites for interpreting African modernity.

Composing under a Tonal Regime

What, finally, did colonization make possible, and how has the challenge of postcolonial creativity been handled in specific reference to tonal thinking? Once again, there are dozens of models on which one might frame an answer, but I will confine discussion to two categories of music: art music by the Nigerian composer Joshua Uzoigwe (1946–2005), and popular or neotraditional music by Wulomei, a 1970s Ghanaian band.

The peculiar alchemy of an indigenous complex of tonal, rhythmic, and timbral resources inflected or transformed by functional tonality has not lent itself to straightforward theoretical formulation. Regarding compositional practice and aesthetic choice, two options seem to have been favored. First is a simple grafting of one tonal system on to another; the effect here is one of strategic indifference to the foreign source, a mode of coexistence (sometimes peaceful, sometimes fraught). Second is an inflection or transformation of the traditional African input, or its translation into a modern, postcolonial economy, drawing on consciously crafted procedures, some of them borrowed from Europe, others abstracted from indigenous idioms; the whole, however, is arranged in conformity with the ethical and aesthetical imperatives of indigenous creativity. Although these strategies—separate existence versus interpenetration (and there are several others, of course, as well as differing degrees of enactment)—are not always localized in a single work, they nevertheless offer useful vantage points for critical interpretation.[27]

Among Uzoigwe's works is a set of four Igbo songs for voice and piano, composed in 1973.[28] Although the melodies originate from folk song, they have been done up in ways that distance them from those origins—"defamiliarized," we might say after the Russian formalists. The first of the set, "Eriri Ngeringe" (meaning "a riddle") is based on the following text composed by Uzoigwe himself (the original is in Igbo):

Let it be, let it be
Let be the thin thread
The thin thread
That lengthened the snake's tail
The thin thread
That caused the bird to balance in the air.

[27] Nigerian composer and scholar Akin Euba has given a great deal of thought to the creative choices available to the modern African composer. See, for example, *Essays on Music in Africa 2: Intercultural Perspective* (Lagos: Elékóto Music Centre, 1989). Also of interest is Geoffrey Poole, "Black-White-Rainbow: A Personal View on What African Music Means to the Contemporary Western Composer," in *Composing the Music of Africa: Composition, Interpretation and Realisation*, edited by Malcolm Floyd, pp. 295–334 (Aldershot, UK: Ashgate, 1999).

[28] For a concise introduction to Uzoigwe's music, see Godwin Sadoh, "Intercultural Creativity in Joshua Uzoigwe's Music," *Africa: Journal of the International African Institute* 74 (2004): 633–661.

Shown in Example 3.3 are bars 1–11 followed in Example 3.4 by a harmonic ostinato that supports the singer's narrative (first heard in bars 2–3). The latter is heard both at this pitch level and in transposition up a perfect fourth. In light of the tonic solfa placed above the staff notation in his

Example 3.3 Bars 1–11 of Joshua Uzoigwe's "Eriri ngeringe" from *Four Igbo Songs* (1973)

Example 3.4 Five-chord ostinato deployed in "Eriri ngeringe"

original manuscript, Uzoigwe apparently heard this progression in D minor (ending with a Picardy third). Such melodic-harmonic cycles are common in the traditional music that the composer knew, so he may simply have been "speaking" naturally. At the same time, the careful arrangement of parts in this five-chord cycle betrays a European influence, perhaps the influence of hymn playing at the keyboard.

It is legitimate, I believe, to speak of a transformation of whatever Uzoigwe borrowed from Europe, because he has not allowed himself to be submerged entirely in that tonal world. The specific act of tonal resistance is the simple one of anchoring the expression in folk material, material with its own modal center, which Uzoigwe enriches without violating. The sung melody (not shown in the figure) is familiar and yet has been made strange in this nontraditional arrangement for voice and piano. And the singer's style is beholden to the presentational forms of the lied or even opera. The harmonic progression is framed by dissonances; indeed, the closing D^7 sonority, although normatively unstable, is deployed in a terminal position, thus endowing the ostinato with a more mobile feel. Because the top voice in the figure is entirely diatonic, it contrasts with the other voices, each of which contains at least one chromatic pitch. Some listeners will moreover hear something of the sound of drums in the percussive style of piano playing. This music too is not conceivable except as a product of the colonial-missionary encounter, but unlike the more or less passive acquiescence that we might read into the music of Ladysmith or the Peace Brass Band, Uzoigwe's "Eriri Ngeringe" displays an element of struggle and thus announces an ideological stance. The hybridity of Uzoigwe's song is marked; it is an earned hybridity, perhaps a hard-won one, not a default outcome or one that represents a flabby coexistence of antithetical elements.

Composing under a tonal regime may be further illustrated by the third of Uzoigwe's "Talking Drums," a set of piano pieces composed in 1991.[29] Modeled on a traditional Igbo dance, "Egwu Amala," this composition immediately creates a vibrant atmosphere based on forward-driving rhythms and a tonal arrangement that, while not diatonic, charts an

[29] All three are recorded on the CD *Senku: Piano Music by Composers of African Descent* (S.I.: Musicians Showcase Recordings, 2003). The published score of "Egwu Amala" is included in *Piano Music of Africa and the African Diaspora*, edited by William Chapman Nyaho (New York: Oxford University Press, 2009). For an appraisal of this first-ever anthology of piano music by black composers, see Chapter 4.

evolving centricity.[30] Uzoigwe anchors the work in an African sound field by using the unusual meter of $\frac{19}{8}$, a meter that is said to be the indigenously felt meter by performers of the original dance. He invokes a communal performance style by deploying a call-response gesture in the manner of a refrain throughout, and he devises an approach to pitch organization in which pentatonic elements are incorporated into a more complex chromatic texture.

Tonal thinking in "Egwu Amala" is more sophisticated than that which we heard in Ladysmith's "Paulina" or in the highlife hymn. There is more obvious compositional labor here than anything the pygmies do. Uzoigwe's harmonies are paper harmonies, harmonies conceived through acts of inscription. They are, at least for this composer, a most productive site for resisting tonality's colonizing tendencies. Notable is the fact that Uzoigwe, perhaps unusually among composers of his generation, was never a passive recipient of a European tonal legacy; rather, he sought to reinscribe everything under an African sign. At least that seemed to be the intention.

My final musical example is from the repertoire of a Ghanaian band active in the 1970s known as Wulomei ("priests" in the Ga language). Theirs is popular music; some would describe it as neotraditional (analogous to neoclassic or neofolk). The song "Soyama" (meaning boat or ship) is a fine example of Wulomei's style.[31] Immediately noticeable from the first sounds is the animating dance beat. This is at once functional music and an invitation to contemplative behavior. Featured are a guitar, various bells and drums, and two female lead voices. The main narrative is presented in the introduction and the first two melodic verses. In the introduction, a clave time line underlies the solo guitar's rhythmic paraphrase of the melody that is about to be sung. The first verse features the two singers in alternation (four bars each); then, in the second, the voices proceed in a mixture of parallel thirds and fifths (four bars each). There is a critical moment at the end of each verse, where a cadence on B-flat is sounded. In some ways, this is the linchpin of the song, the key to understanding the colonial element inscribed in "Soyama."

The bundle of attributes that conveys the African essence of "Soyama" includes a self-satisfied, almost flirtatious beat that both invites and at the

[30] For an ethnographic study, see Sister Marie Agatha Ozah, *Égwú Àmàlà: Women in Traditional Performing Arts in Ogbaruland* (PhD diss., University of Pittsburgh, 2008).

[31] See the CD *Legendary Wulomei* (Sam Records, 2000), track 14. Already in 1978, David Coplan drew attention to Wulomei's artistry in an essay on highlife music, "Go to My Town, Cape Coast!" A comprehensive recent study of Wulomei is Gavin Webb, *The Wulomei Ga Folk Group: A Contribution towards Urban Ethnomusicology* (PhD diss., University of Ghana, Legon, 2012).

same time discourages dancing, a series of bell ejaculations that regularly punctuate the otherwise untroubled duple meter, the linguistic message ("He is waving a hand at me," says she about her lover), and the drum commentary in speech mode that seems to emanate uncannily from a subterranean world. This last advances the rhythmic narrative, expands the registral limits by opening up the lowest registers, and assumes a meta-musical function in directing the performance as a whole. Regarding the tonal imagination on display, the chantlike melody itself is modal, and the collection of pitch classes and their intervallic disposition suggest the Phrygian mode. In its initial chantlike appearance, where it is heard in a gentle rhythmic elaboration by the guitar, the mode is clear and the melody proceeds almost exclusively in parallel thirds. When the singers give up the guitarist's rubato and perform the melody in a relatively strict rhythm (verse 1), we hear a series of short-long dominant-chord punctuations played by the guitar. These seem blissfully oblivious to anything else that might be going on. Their persistence sets up an expectation for resolution. (In semiotic terms, we might say that they are charged indexical signs.) Confirmation of their meaning comes at the end of the eight-bar verse where they acquire their object in the form of a I chord. Talk about "desire" as a defining feature of tonality.

Notable in "Soyama" are the ways in which the composers (the songwriter Saka Acquaye and the lead drummer Nii Ashitey) have managed, as it were, to resist the colonizing force of tonality by using it and at the same time undermining it—placing it under erasure, we might say. A large-scale dominant-to-tonic progression is present, but it no longer has the uncontested status of a controlling background. To the extent that there is a background, it is a more complex configuration that incorporates the Phrygian elements as well as the pitched but nontonal sounds of bells and drums. Put in stark binary terms for rhetorical purposes, we might say that the guitar comes from the outside but plays insider-inflected music. Singing in parallel thirds and fifths comes partly from the inside: this is the traditional African way, but whereas singing in thirds dovetails with the European way, Europeans typically interrupt the stream of thirds in order to cadence satisfactorily. Singing in parallel fifths is *not* the European way, at least not according to the specific tonal models exported to Africa in the nineteenth century. The net effect of the tonal procedures of "Soyama" is of an imaginative recasting of African and European elements. The colonizing force is contained. Semitone tonality (as heard in hymns) is acknowledged but it does not rule; it is incorporated as one element in a constellation. All told, this is African music of some imagination, a music that, as critique perhaps, signals what it might mean to relativize and contextualize the primitive tonal resources with which European missionaries and colonial administrators colonized African consciousness. Relatively simple and transparent, Wulomei's "Soyama" is nevertheless significant and productively paradoxical music whose structure inscribes affirmation as well as resistance.

Conclusion

Historians of Africa have not been restrained in their assessments of the colonial period. Basil Davidson described "the arrival of Europeans [since the early sixteenth century]" as "the greatest calamity in [Africa's] history."[32] For Adu Boahen, "the colonial era [1880–1970] will go down in history as a period of wasted opportunities, of ruthless exploitation of the resources of Africa, and on balance of the underdevelopment and humiliation of the peoples of Africa."[33] And Walter Rodney saw in colonial education only "a series of limitations inside other limitations."[34] Similar sentiments have been expressed by political and social theorists, linguists, and language planners. An analogous critique by scholars of African music has, however, not been as audible. Are musicologists perhaps too enamored of the aesthetic, reveling in the ostensible otherworldliness or "nonlinguisticity" of music to confront the political and ideological work it does? Is daily practice in Africanist ethnomusicology long on description and short on evaluation? If so, a reordering of priorities would be in order, for I believe we can affirm one aspect of the historians' claim on the basis of our own reflections on tonal routines: Europe underdeveloped Africa tonally by creating the conditions of possibility for inaction (or limited action) in the realms of creation (or *poiesis*) and reception (or *esthesis*).

There is reason to be skeptical of the argument presented here, however. It could be said, for example, that the churches, schools, community centers, and dance halls in which tonality animates music-making are so firmly established as sites of African modernity that any claim that the musical forms they sponsor are derivative, or that they betray a colonization of consciousness,

[32] Basil Davidson, *Africa: A Voyage of Discovery* [video recording], Program 5: "The Bible and the Gun" (Chicago: Home Vision Select, 1984).

[33] Boahen, *African Perspectives*, 109.

[34] Rodney, *How Europe Underdeveloped Africa*, 264.

seems entirely beside the point. So what if the national anthems that channel pride—symbolically speaking—in many independent African nations are deeply marked by European harmony and phraseology? Why does it matter that many popular songs use a musical language beholden to the primary chords of European tonality, and who cares if vast portions of music in Christian worship are riffs on the limited tonal trajectories enshrined in nineteenth-century European hymns? Even if they were produced in the course of culture contact, have they not been assimilated as naturalized *African* modes of expression?

Assimilated without losses? In the rush to embrace a borderless global aesthetics, or to celebrate hybridity and pluralism, we may have turned a blind eye to the violence that attends certain forms of sanctioned coexistence. We may have ignored the deficits that have accrued to those who have been forced to give up their native musical languages and speak others'. Tonality, let us not forget, is a complex resource, a nexus of freighted options presented to various African communities under a number of political, economic, and religious imperatives. If the analogy with language is valid, if composing is akin to speaking a language, then, for some Africans, composing tonally at certain historical moments was like speaking a foreign language—complete with new regimes of syntax, grammar, and intonation—distinct from their (musical) mother-tongue. Even in instances where the colonized attained a measure of fluency in using the colonizer's language, an immediate and practical outcome was almost always the gradual loss of a heritage language.

More tragically perhaps, we have overlooked or undervalued the creative potential of a number of musical resources, resources that have been consigned to the margins at various schools of music since tonality took center stage as the desired modern language. Various uses of nontempered scales, the possibilities opened up by overtone singing, echo-chamber effects associated with water drumming, subtle explorations of the boundaries between speech and song (in funeral laments and dirges, and in weeping songs and epic recitation), and the achievement of closure not through stepwise motion or a juvenile slowing down but by the use of melodic leaps and the injection of rhythmic life all constitute a rich set of stylistic opportunities for the modern composer. We await an African-originated resistance to the easy victories that tonal harmony has won on the continent since the 1840s.

4

African Pianism and the Challenge of Art Music

In 2009, Oxford University Press published a five-volume anthology of piano music of Africa and the African diaspora edited by Ghanaian pianist and scholar William Chapman Nyaho.[1] This unprecedented and potentially eye-opening event went by largely unnoticed. There were no book-signing ceremonies in Accra, Berlin, Lagos, or London, no celebratory broadcasts on NPR, the BBC, or VOA, and no recitals in Carnegie Hall or Wigmore Hall. Although notice of its publication appeared in the journal *Ethnomusicology*, it was decidedly low key.[2] Only a few educators and music lovers, among them members of piano teachers' guilds, some of them looking for new, perhaps exotic, or at least different repertoire to adorn rather than replace the old canon, heard strains of the anthology's sound worlds from Nyaho's live demonstrations at their meetings.

How could this publication have gone unnoticed? How, indeed, have the controllers of discourse on African music been able to downplay the historical fact that black Africans since at least the middle of the nineteenth century have routinely composed sonatas, études, suites, and any number of arrangements of folk songs and negro spirituals, as well as operas, cantatas, choral anthems, and symphonies?

Ours is a busy world. Events come and go, registering differentially on our radar screens. Our dispositions and expectations differ; our choices are manifold. Colonialism came and went, leaving its traces on politics and culture, but no one, it appears, has been waiting for a Mozart or Beethoven to emerge from the African continent. Saul Bellow famously gave voice to this prejudice: "When the Zulus produce their Tolstoy we will read him." And with that facile encapsulation of race-based superiority, our historical oppressors

[1] William Chapman Nyaho, ed., *Piano Music of Africa and the African Diaspora* (New York: Oxford University Press, 2009).

[2] Caroline Rae, "Review of *Piano Music of Africa and the African Diaspora, Vols. 1–3, ed.* William Chapman Nyaho," *Ethnomusicology* 53 (2009): 146–151.

On African Music. Kofi Agawu, Oxford University Press. © Oxford University Press 2023.
DOI: 10.1093/oso/9780197664063.003.0004

are absolved from looking out for the kind of music enshrined in Nyaho's anthology. "When the Ewes produce their Bartók," they might say, "we will listen to him."

Art, Popular, and Traditional Music

There are other reasons for the neglect of African art music. If African music as a notional whole is framed within a tripartite model consisting of traditional, popular, and art music, then art music is the least prominent of the three. By this is meant art music's relatively limited visibility in village and city, whatever its symbolic potency. Whereas traditional music is tied to ritual and to social and entertainment functions that form the fabric of daily musical life, and whereas popular music, given its media-aided mode of circulation, has become unavoidable in urban and increasingly rural locations, art music in its modern guise as the performance of composed (written) scores for nonparticipating audiences reaches only small audiences. This poor showing is partly due to the recent histories of African nations, to political, economic, and social factors impinging on the training of musicians, to the availability of patronage, and to audience reception. Another factor is the nature of the relationship between art and traditional music, on one hand, and art and popular music on the other.[3]

"African music" was once indexed primarily through its traditional layer, in particular its drumming traditions, which seemed to hold a special fascination for (mostly foreign) observers from the fifteenth century on. Never mind that song rather than drumming was and remains the predominant mode of expression, never mind that the continent's billion-plus people represent a diversity of musical cultures whose cumulative richness is dramatically undermined each time we reduce "African music" to "African drumming" (on the jembe, no less!), and never mind that what is expressed on drums (and, for that matter, on many other African instruments) is so thoroughly infused with the sound and sense of various indigenous languages that those champions of drumming who routinely ignore its linguistic bases aren't really getting it. True, traditional music boasts a long and deep

[3] On the conditions of possibility for African art music, see Abiola Irele, "Is African Music Possible?," *Transition* 61 (1993): 56–71, and Martin Scherzinger, "Art Music in a Cross-Cultural Context: The Case of Africa," in *The Cambridge History of Twentieth-Century Music*, edited by Nicolas Cook and Anthony Pople, pp. 584–613 (Cambridge, UK: Cambridge University Press, 2004).

history—partly real, partly fanciful—with a different sound world from popular music. And yes, the elaborate and sophisticated structural procedures of traditional music performed solo or in ensemble on horns, xylophones, voices, and drums have become better understood only in recent times, thanks to dedicated efforts of scholars like Simha Arom, Gerhard Kubik, Paul Berliner, David Locke, Willie Anku, Godfried Toussaint, and Martin Scherzinger, among others, who have examined the musical patterns closely.[4] Soon, however, the priority enjoyed by traditional music had to contend with an emerging new music. Just as the modern African novel emerged in the twentieth century out of a vast and varied oral literature and in response to a network of outside stimuli comprising secular and religious literatures aimed at a new literate class, so African art music began to be cultivated in the new institutions that missionization and colonialism brought.[5]

The high value placed on African traditional music by ethnographers often overlooked the fact that its potentialities are best revealed not by gathering and confining samples of the music to sound archives and museums, but by probing the music compositionally, engaging it through creative violation, perhaps. It is impossible to overestimate the quality and quantity of the kinds of knowledge that are produced by self-consciously manipulating traditional music's materials and procedures. Unfortunately, though perhaps not surprisingly, ethnomusicologists, to whom we might look for guidance about forms of creativity in traditional societies, have shown little interest in such music-on-music exploration. This task has been left to African scholar-composers like Kwabena Nketia (1921–2019), Akin Euba (1935–2020), Bode Omojola (b.1958), Ayo Oluranti, and their followers.[6]

[4] Simha Arom, *African Polyphony and Polyrhythm*; Gerhard Kubik, *Theory of African Music*, Vols. 1 and 2. Paul Berliner, *The Soul of Mbira: Music and the Traditions of the Shona People of Zimbabwe* (Berkeley: University of California Press, 1978); Berliner, *The Art of Mbira: Musical Inheritance and Legacy* (Chicago: University of Chicago Press, 2020); David Locke, *Drum Gahu: An Introduction to African Rhythm* (Tempe, AZ: White Cliffs Media, 1998); Willie Anku, *Structural Set Analysis of African Music 1: Adowa* (Legon, Ghana: Soundstage Production, 2002); Anku, *Structural Set Analysis of African Music 2: Bawa* (Legon, Ghana: Soundstage Production, 2002 .Godfried Toussaint, *The Geometry of Musical Rhythm: What Makes a "Good" Rhythm Good?* (Boca Raton, FL: CRC Press, 2013); and Martin Scherzinger, "Negotiating the Music-Theory/African Music Nexus: A Political Critique of Ethnomusicological Anti-Formalism and a Strategic Analysis of the Harmonic Patterning of the Shona Mbira Song *Nyamaropa*," *Perspectives of New Music* 39 (2001): 5–118.

[5] The broad impact of colonialism on African music is discussed in Agawu, *Representing African Music*, 1–22.

[6] A list of works up to 1982 is included in Euba, *Modern African Music: A Catalogue of Selected Archival Materials at Iwalewa-Haus, University of Bayreuth, Germany* (Bayreuth: Iwalewa-Haus, 1993). See also Godwin Sadoh, "African Musicology: A Bibliographical Guide to Nigerian Art Music (1927–2009)," *Notes* 66 (2010), 485–502.

Compositional Probing

There are many examples of compositional probing from traditions around the world, and they all represent avenues to enriched knowledge.[7] Hungarian composer Béla Bartók comes most readily to mind as a role model for African composers in general. Among his achievements are exemplary fieldwork in Eastern Europe and North Africa, a large body of folk songs meticulously transcribed, and, best of all, a body of original compositions that range in content from the merest inflection of a folk tune by endowing it with an accompaniment that seems already derived from the tune itself, through learned manipulations of and additions to such tunes in the context of art music, to the most intricate and subtle incorporation of the aura of folk music into the most decidedly anti-folk environment of the string quartet, art music's most intellectual genre.

No wonder that Akin Euba, one of Africa's leading art music composers, described himself as a *disciple* of Bartók. Euba's notion of "creative ethnomusicology" emphasizes the connection between field research and individual composition. For him, the highest goal of research into traditional music at this time in history should be to inspire original composition—paper-based musical composition by Africans.[8]

A number of composers have grappled with "folk" heritages of various sorts, among them Liszt, Dvorak, Moussorgsky, Kodály, Mahler, Vaughan-Williams, Berio, and Britten. So what I have described as Bartókian, which also lies at the heart of the challenges for composing African art music, is indeed widespread, some would even say normal. There is, moreover, a sub-tradition of intercontinental musical encounters marked by the appropriation of not just any folk music but African music specifically. Because "African music" in this economy is always already folk music, it becomes a site of distant authenticity to which Euro-American composers can turn for

[7] See for example, Yayoi Uno Everett and Frederick Lau (eds.), *Locating East Asia in Western Art Music* (Middletown, CT: Wesleyan University Press, 2004); Michael Tenzer, "José Maceda and the Paradoxes of Modern Composition in Southeast Asia," *Ethnomusicology* 47 (2003): 93–120; Melanie Plesch, "Decentring Topic Theory: Musical Topics and Rhetorics of Identity in Latin American Art Music," *Portuguese Journal of Musicology / Revista Portuguesa de Musicologia* 4 (2017), 27–32; and Plesch, "The West and the Rest: Some Reflections on Ex-Centric Art Musics" (Unpublished keynote address to the workshop, *Musicology or Ethnomusicology? Discussing Disciplinary Boundaries in Non-Western Art Music*. Cambridge University, Faculty of Music, March 22, 2019).

[8] On creative ethnomusicology, see Euba, *Essays on Music in Africa 2: Intercultural Perspectives* (Elekoto and Bayreuth: Iwalewa-Haus, 1989), 121–123. For one exemplary application, see Omojola, *The Music of Fela Sowande: Encounters, African Identity and Creative Ethnomusicology* (Point Richmond: MRI Press, 2009).

musical and spiritual renewal. American minimalist Steve Reich's encounter with African music is a case in point. Reich studied Ghanaian drumming and made ample use of polyrhythmic textures and African bell patterns in numerous compositions.[9] Critics are divided on the significance of this aspect of his achievement. On the positive side are those who see in such a turn to others' music a way of rejuvenating an exhausted, if not dying, Western tradition. Such critics sense a dissolution of boundaries and an expansion of the soundscape resulting from the new proximity of previously distant territories and creative strategies. On the negative side are, first, those who cannot abide the ineradicable asymmetries of power entailed in the appropriation of third-world music by first-world composers and, second, those who, at a purely aesthetic level, sense in the outcome of such encounters an inorganic collage of sound worlds different in kind from the more normative products of postmodern pastiche, play, and quotation on account of the geo-cultural provenance of their constitutive materials.

Ultimately, history will position Reich's appropriation as it sees fit, but for now we can benefit from the aural light that his experimentation has shed on the nature of things like African bell patterns. To my ear, the function of time lines (in particular, the so-called standard pattern consisting of seven strokes spread out with maximal evenness across a span of twelve eighth-notes[10]) in works like *Clapping Music, Electric Counterpoint*, or *Music for Pieces of Wood* differs significantly from their function in *Agbadza* and *Gahu*, two of the traditional (Ewe) dances that Reich studied in Ghana, and which he subsequently described using Jones-style transcriptions.[11] Reich's usages do not *sound* African partly because the environment in which the pattern appears is different. His investment in pulse-based repetition undermines the metrical hierarchies of Agbadza's and Gahu's periodic cycles. It effectively erases, or at least mutes, the danceable aura normally invoked by their time lines. From an African perspective, Reich's music seems enclosed in quotation marks.

All this jibes with the composer's stated intention to imitate structure rather than sound; procedure and technique rather than material content. The difference can be subtle, however, but the point remains that by seeking

[9] Reich describes his visit to Ghana in *Writings on Music, 1965–2000* (New York: Oxford University Press, 2002), 55–61.

[10] For a detailed treatment of the "standard pattern," see Agawu, "Structural Analysis of Cultural Analysis? Competing Perspectives on the 'Standard Pattern' of West African Rhythm," *Journal of the American Musicological Society* 59 (2006), 1–46.

[11] Reich, *Writings on Music*, 60–62.

a creative rather than documentary engagement with African sources, Reich has made a significant contribution not only to our understanding of (his own) new music but, more significantly, to our perception of the structural potentialities and associations of specific African rhythmic patterns and textural arrangements.

Equally enlightening on the subject of Euro-American appropriations of African music is the case of Ligeti, whose professed fascination with certain African repertories is well known. The resulting creative acts reveal a complex, less mimetic relation between source and original composition. In a detailed enquiry into Ligeti's sources, Martin Scherzinger shows that the composer's fascination with Africa runs deeper than what might be casually inferred from the frequently quoted statement posted as a foreword to the English translation of Arom's magnum opus, *African Polyphony and Polyrhythm* (1991).[12] Telling inscriptions in the margins of the composer's sketches suggest a curiosity about Zimbabwean mbira music, Ugandan amadinda xylophone repertory, and Ghanaian Gyil xylophone music, among many others. Ligeti also studied extensively a broad range of music from Central, Eastern and Southern Africa, thanks to the ethnographic and analytical writings of Arom, Kubik, Dauer, Simon, and others. Whether one senses a gap of similar magnitude between intention and realization (as one does in the case of Reich), or whether Ligeti's more abstract mode of appropriation ultimately erases any real traces of Africa from his music, thus aligning compositional credo with actual achievement, will require more discussion than is possible here. Ligeti's encounter with various African repertories helps clarify the nature of multiplicity and simultaneity, and in the process conveys some of the compositional potential of African materials. He helps us to look to the future, to see possibilities that lie hidden within ostensibly "ordinary" elements.[13]

Like other composers of their generation seeking enlightenment and inspiration from non-Western music, Ligeti and Reich engaged African traditional music. In recent decades, however, "African music" as a construction has been accessed through the proliferating diversities of urban popular music: Afrobeat, Bikutsi, Fuji, Highlife, Hiplife, Juju, Mbalax, Makossa,

[12] See Scherzinger, "Györgi Ligeti and the Aka Pygmies Project," *Contemporary Music Review* 25 (2006): 227–262 and Ligeti, "Foreword" in Arom, *African Polyphony and Polyrhythm*, xvii–xviii.

[13] For further exploration of Ligeti and Reich's engagements with African music drawing on earlier studies by Stephen Taylor and Martin Scherzinger, see my "Rethinking Ligeti's (and Reich's) African Affiliations," *A Tribute to György Ligeti in his Native Transylvania*, edited by Bianca Ţiplea Temeş and Kofi Agawu, pp. 103–129 (MediaMusica: Cluj-Napoca, Romania, 2020).

Mbaqanqa, Soukous, Taarab, and others too numerous to mention. Erstwhile charges that popular music is derivative or beholden to mimicry are nowadays easily refuted, at least programmatically, and despite ongoing questions of motivation and power in the production of popular music—for example, whose notion of hybridity legitimizes a given song or repertory?—the sheer phenomenal presence of its collective repertories, like that of traditional music in its original performing spaces, puts art music to shame.

Significantly, scholarship on popular music has not privileged its structural elements, the naked note-by-note relations formed according to conventions of syntax. Popular music is cited for its open quality, its pragmatic appropriation of elements without concern for their geo-cultural provenance, and its immediate appeal and hence potential to forge unities across boundaries. There are no equivalents in African popular music studies of the transcriptions *in extenso* and detailed technical discussion of rhythm, melody, and polyphony found, for example, in the writings of Jones, Arom, Rouget, Locke, Berliner, and Fernando on traditional music.[14] What we find instead are consumer reactions, discussions of technological enablers, and, perhaps most importantly for those curious about material content, interpretations of meaning guided by culture and politics and indexed not so much through sound but through sung words. Words provide access to the genre's worldliness. Popular music seizes the attention of cosmopolitan audiences, transcends ethnic, regional, and even national boundaries, and re-contextualizes the ritual and intellectual bases of traditional music by rendering them, in effect, marginal to the overall effect of a given performance. Whereas broadcasting ethnic-bound traditional music to an ethnically diverse urban population severely taxes producers because they have to find ways of appealing to regional or local radio audiences, popular music invites the listener/dancer through its groove and harmonic conventionality to an enjoyable encounter that thrives on a certain number of fulfilled expectations.

Unlike African traditional music, popular music has not yet become a major source of ideas and procedures for composers of art music, although West African composers like Sowande, Euba, Nketia, and Amu have

[14] A. M. Jones, *Studies in African Music*, 2 vols. (Oxford, UK: Oxford University Press, 1959); Arom, *African Polyphony and Polyrhythm*; Gilbert Rouget, *Un roi Africain et sa musique de cour: Chants et danses du palais à Porto-Novo sous le régne de Gbèfa* (Paris: CNRS Editions, 1996); Nathalie Fernando, *Polyphonies du Nord-Cameroun* (Paris: Peeters/SELAF, 2011); Locke, *Drum Gahu*; Berliner, *The Art of Mbira*.

occasionally incorporated highlife rhythms into their compositions. This suggests an affinity between traditional music and art music that does not exist between popular music and art music. And so, although popular and art music stand as reciprocal historical responses to Europe, although they are both urban phenomena, and although the "charge" of hybridity could be leveled against them equally, they are also radically different in attracting different clienteles and enlisting different sources of creativity. The fact that part of the potential audience for Nyaho's anthology has been siphoned off by devotees of the less elitist popular music may further explain why its publication did not make headlines.

Piano Music of Africa and the African Diaspora

In terms of the anthology itself, *Piano Music of Africa and the African Diaspora* has a strongly symbolic value. It displays a range of African creativity in the written rather than aural/oral sphere. It provides students of the piano anywhere with a hitherto marginalized repertory that includes work by Egyptian composers Halim El-Dabh, Riad Abdel-Gawad, and Gamal Abdel-Rahim; Nigerian composers Akin Euba, Christian Onyeji, and Joshua Uzoigwe; Ghanaian composers Gyimah Labi, J. H. Kwabena Nketia, and Robert Kwami; South African composers Martin Scherzinger, Bongani Ndodana-Breen, and Isak Roux; Sudanese composer Ali Osman; Congolese composer Bangambula Vindu; and African-British composer Samuel Coleridge-Taylor, not to mention composers of the African diaspora located in Britain, Jamaica, Brazil, Cuba, Haiti, Guadeloupe, Dominican Republic, Canada, and the United States. Piano recital programs may now be diversified so as to place an El-Dabh next to Chopin, a Labi next to Bartók, and an Uzoigwe next to Ligeti.

An anthology of new music should impress us in precisely that way: it should be new. By "new" I do not mean merely unprecedented; it must also possess a certain cutting-edge quality. As the first ever published anthology of this kind and on this scale, *Piano Music of Africa and the African Diaspora* meets the former criterion. How it negotiates the latter criterion, however, is a little more complicated. Certainly, all the music collected here dates from the twentieth century and the majority of the composers represented are still living. But to determine whether expectations regarding autonomy and subjectivity, for example, are met, demands a larger context for analysis, including a review of the earliest attempts to compose art music in the nineteenth century. We would also need to take into account previous studies, starting with Olabode Omojola's 1995 pioneering study, Akin Euba's reflections on the tradition in his dual roles as participant and observer, and essays by, among others, Martin Scherzinger, Bode Omojola, Joshua Uzoigwe, Godwin Sadoh, Paul Konye, George Dor, Christine Lucia, Chris Van Rhym, and Grace Talabi.[15] Since it is obviously not possible to undertake that larger exercise within this chapter, I will turn to the question of a composer's heritage, remark on a few salient features of music included in Nyaho's anthology composed by two composer-scholars, Nketia and Uzoigwe, and then dig deeper into one particular composition, Nketia's *Volta Fantasy* (1967), to observe at close hand the lineaments of African pianism.

Heritage

The African composer's heritage is typically multiple rather than singular. Influences come from outside and inside, from Europe and Africa. But while a composer's upbringing may include exposure to various sorts of traditional and popular music, the moment of inscription or the moment in which the compositional faculty is exercised is often decisively shaped by an aspect of European art-music practice. Crucial in this respect is the challenge of constructing a tonal horizon, for it appears that the choice for many composers is between easy acceptance of a European tonal resource (including common-practice tonality, chromaticism, or in a few experimental

[15] Omojola, *Nigerian Art Music, with an Introductory Study of Ghanaian Art Music* (Ibadan: Institut Francais de Recherche, 1995); Omojola, "Contemporary Art Music in Nigeria: An Introductory Note on the Works of Ayo Bankole," *Africa* 64 (1994), 533–543; Euba, *Essays on Music in Africa 2*; Scherzinger, "Art Music in a Cross-Cultural Context"; Uzoigwe, *Akin Euba: An Introduction to the Life and Music of a Nigerian Composer* (Bayreuth: E. Breitinger, University of Bayreuth, 1992); Sadoh, "Intercultural Creativity in Joshua Uzoigwe's Music," *Africa* 74 (2004): 633–661; Paul Konye, *African Art Music: Political, Social, and Cultural Factors Behind Its Development and Practice in Nigeria* (New York: Edwin Mellen Press, 2007; and George Dor, "Uses of Indigenous Music Genres in Ghanaian Choral Art Music: Perspectives from the Works of Amu, Blege, and Dor," *Ethnomusicology* 49 (2005): 441–475; Christine Lucia, "'Yet None with Truer Fervour Sing': Coronation Song and the (De)colonization of African Choral Composition," *African Music: Journal of the International Library of African Music* 10 (2017): 23–44; Chris van Rhyn, *Towards a Mapping of the Marginal: Readings of Art Songs by Nigerian, Ghanaian, Egyptian and South African Composers* (PhD diss., Stellenbosch University, 2013); and Grace Talabi, A *Study of the Music and Social Meaning of Selected Choral Works from Dayo Oyedun's Cantata* (PhD diss., Stellenbosch University, 2020). See also *Composers Under the Tree of God: Art-Music in Ghana*, a film by Hanne Kaisik-Aumüller and Uli Aumüller (Berlin: Bavarian TV, 1995).

cases, twelve-tone technique) and a(n impossible) resisting of that resource, complete with the ideological baggage that it carries.

Consider the experience of Ghanaian and Nigerian composers. For many of them, the first exposure to notated music is in the form of Protestant hymns or short pieces by European composers from the eighteenth and nineteenth centuries. Many have accepted the limits set by the kinds of cadence and phraseology prescribed by the hymn, as we saw in the previous chapter. This monumental influence is not confined to the domain of music but includes religious belief and formal education as well. We might even go so far as to say that the language of the hymn was part of the cultural capital that postcolonial subjects strove to acquire.

Had the Protestant hegemony been offset by exposure to, say, twentieth-century art music, including that of the European avant-garde (a tradition which, by definition, lies at a certain cutting edge), this tonal heritage would have taken an entirely different form. A familiarity with so-called World Music, too, would almost certainly have affected the tonal imagination of composers. Claims about a new globalized musical economy may soon offer hope of everyone having equal access to the world's repositories of music, but those who occupy the margins for various reasons know better than to order their lives according to the promise of a dream. For now, we must contend with the fact that a largely Protestant tonal legacy continues to dominate the musical consciousness of many budding composers.[16]

The other side of the African composer's heritage comprises the indigenous legacy in all its magnificent diversity. "Africa" must be understood in the broadest possible terms, and its influence may include actual materials, procedures, and performance practices. Acquiring the elements of this heritage would seem to follow a natural path for composers born into the tradition, but the process proves to be a complex one. For some composers, the moment of acquisition comes later in life when, quite self-consciously, they turn to the systematic study of traditional music in reaction to a lopsided educational system that used to assign greater value to knowledge of Schumann and Brahms than to knowledge of Akan funeral dirges or Yoruba dùndún drumming. There is, moreover, no easy formula for determining the

[16] Emphasis on Protestant musical influences should not obscure the wider soundscape of mission-based musical influences in Africa. See for example, Anna Maria Busse Berger, "Spreading the Gospel of Singbewegung: An Ethnomusicologist Missionary in Tanganyika of the 1930s," *Journal of the American Musicological Society* 66 (2013): 475–522 and Jann Passler, "Sacred Music in the African Missions: Gregorian Chant, Cantiques, and Indigenous Expression," *Atti del Congresso Internazionale di Musica Sacra* (Rome: Libreria Editrice Vaticana, 2013), 1287–1309.

ultimate shape that the indigenous influences assume within an individual composer's psyche. Depending upon the intensity and integrity of the exposure, the composer may acquire a groove-oriented metrical attitude, a store of modal melodies, a syllabic approach to word-setting, a network of distinctly shaped and timbre-specific rhythmic patterns (including time-line patterns), and modes of simultaneous doing (or harmony) that preserve a heterogeneous sound ideal.[17]

One task for future scholars of African art music will be to reconstruct the sonic backdrop to individual creative acts. In his study of Akin Euba's music and philosophy, Uzoigwe postulates a "cultural triangle" comprising European, African, and Yoruba elements. The distinction between a generalized "African" field helps to distinguish the generically African from the specifically Yoruba. Similarly, in Omojola's portrait of "the manifold profile of Sowande's work," Yoruba beliefs and musical practices interact with European classical music and—perhaps most significantly—African diasporic music in one and the same consciousness. These two studies could serve as models for revealing the complex and contradictory backgrounds of African composers, and for sharpening our perception of the challenges involved in developing a distinctly postcolonial creative voice.[18]

Nketia

Consider the example of Ghanaian Kwabena Nketia (1921–2019). Although better known as a scholar, Nketia was immensely active as a composer. During his student days at Akropong Training College in the 1930s, he studied the piano and harmonium and was exposed to hymns and excerpts from simple classics by Mozart, Mendelssohn, Beethoven, and any number of minor nineteenth-century European composers. The sonic make-up of many composers of Nketia's generation is revealingly portrayed in a document of limited circulation, the so-called *Seminary Tunes* assembled by the Basel mission in 1907. Today's student can study this anthology with great profit because it contains canonical as well as noncanonical music by composers great and small.[19] At Akropong, Nketia also encountered an emerging choral

[17] See Olly Wilson, "The Significance of the Relationship Between Afro-American Music and West African Music," *Black Perspective in Music* 2 (1974): 3–22.

[18] See Uzoigwe, *Akin Euba: An Introduction*, and Omojola, *The Music of Fela Sowande*.

[19] *Seminary Tunes* (Akropong, Ghana: Basel Mission, 1907).

style in the music of Dr. Ephraim Amu (1899–1995), now recognized as the father of Ghanaian art music, especially in its choral variety. Earlier, growing up in Mampong-Ashanti, Nketia was already quite steeped in the traditions of his village, including a magnificent dirge-singing tradition one of whose leading exponents was none other than a woman Nketia refers to as his grandmother. Later, as a student of linguistics in London in the 1940s, Nketia soaked up other influences in the English capital, ranging from European high art music through jazz to music from other parts of Africa. Meanwhile, his love for languages and his linguistic training deepened his sensitivity to the contours and rhythms of speech, preparing his expertise in the setting of texts and, paradoxically perhaps, stimulating his interest in composing purely instrumental or non-texted music in the 1950s and 1960s.[20]

What came out in the way of autonomous original composition was a diverse output, some of it conventional in nature (like the choral compositions influenced by Amu's style) and some of it experimental (like the "Bolga Sonata" for violin and piano of 1958, or the "Cow Lane Sextet" from 1959). Along the way, Nketia helped to stabilize certain genres (like the art song), enrich the repertory of African pianism, and, more generally, show the vast potential in the composition of pure instrumental music for various ensembles. I often hear in Nketia's music a fresh melodic flavor that I associate generically with Akan song.[21] This immediately stamps his work with a certain authentic flavor. The seams of phrase construction are sometimes exposed, and the tonal resource, which originates in the language of hymns and simple classics, is often taken at face value, although Nketia's output includes experimental works that gnaw at the tonal limits enshrined in his models or inflect that tonal sense with a delicate modality that may well have its origins in indigenous music. A metrical home is also often taken as given, while the energy in the rhythmic realm is concentrated in speech-like modes of enunciation and in quotations of (segments of) familiar rhythmic patterns, including time-line patterns.

Nyaho's anthology includes two of Nketia's compositions. "Builsa Work Song," composed in 1968, is a charming "recreation" (the composer's word)

[20] Nketia tells his own story in *The Creative Potential of African Art Music in Ghana: A Personal Testimony* (Companion Booklet to ICAMD CD Recordings, Accra, Ghana: Afram Publications, 2004 and in *Reinstating Traditional Music in Contemporary Context* (Akropong-Akuapem, Ghana: Regnum Africa Publications, 2016).

[21] Two good places to study the melodic style of Akan music are Nketia, *Folk Songs of Ghana* (London: Oxford University Press, 1963), and Kwasi Ampene, *Female Song Tradition and the Akan of Ghana: The Creative Process in Nnwonkoro* (Aldershot, UK: Ashgate, 2005).

of an indigenous work song from among the Builsa people. The "Volta Fantasy" is a bold work in the key of A minor that makes central use of the standard pattern in an otherwise fragmented texture. (I will have more to say about it shortly). "Builsa Work Song" (see Example 4.1) begins with a snappy iambic rhythm that, together with its long-short retrograde companion, generates a dance groove through repetition. The large-scale form consists of a three-fold presentation of the main tune framed by an initial exclamation that returns as an ending.

Example 4.1 Kwabena Nketia's "Builsa Work Song" (1948)

Example 4.1 Continued

In contrast, trajectories of musical thought are relatively modest, often spread over two or three bars. The main melody is always present, its tail echoed within each presentational phrase. Most subtle is the distribution of rhetorical weight so that closure is achieved not in the last bar of a phrase but in the penultimate bar (the last of the first eight-bar phrase, for example, is silent.) The origins of this cadential mannerism might be traced to any number of "traditional" vocal genres, including the very dirges that the composer absorbed as a young man. Terminal sonorities include bare octaves, thirdless triads, and dissonant trichords. Even though the work's B-centricity is never in doubt, B is made to reckon occasionally with an interfering G-sharp.

Digging Deeper: Nketia's *Volta Fantasy*

Composed in 1967, Nketia's *Volta Fantasy* is one of the best-known of his essays in African pianism. At a moderate tempo (quarter note equals 100) in $\frac{6}{8}$ meter, its 127 bars last less than three minutes in performance. The score is reproduced in Example 4.2 and will be needed for the detailed discussion that follows. My aim is to dig deeper into the language of African pianism

Example 4.2 Kwabena Nketia's "Volta Fantasy" (1967)

by means of a speculative analysis of the work's form and structure. It should be said that, in terms of the actual use of the piano, *Volta Fantasy* lies comfortably on the instrument, boasts no particularly virtuosic passages, and alternates melodic or lyrical fragments with occasional percussive passages.[22]

[22] A performance of *Volta Fantasy* by composer-pianist Eric Moe may be heard on the CD accompanying the book, *Towards an African Pianism: An Anthology of Keyboard Music from Africa and the Diaspora*, edited by Cynthia Kimberlin and Akin Euba, vol. 1, track 5 (Pittsburgh, PA: University of Pittsburgh, 2005). There are at least three YouTube performances by Artis Wodehouse, Harold Richter and Adam Heron. Accessed July 2020.

Example 4.2 Continued

Volta Fantasy is a problematic piece, full of contradictory and antithetical gestures. Introversively, it lacks the organic unity of the composer's "Builsa Worksong"; if anything, the overall impression is of a set of fragments, some associated motivically, others not. There is something of a sleepwalking manner to the narrative—some ideas are introduced and abandoned, some adjacent sections are juxtaposed. An experimental aura thus hovers over the work. It is thus a fantasy in a literal sense. Extroversively, *Volta Fantasy* announces an affiliation with the Volta Region in Ghana, home of most

Example 4.2 Continued

Ewes and origin of what is probably the most famous time-line pattern, the so-called *standard pattern* [2-2-1-2-2-2-1] alluded to in the opening bars then heard as an ostinato starting in bar 28. This pattern invokes the Southern Ewe Agbadza dance and it is used along with prominently articulated intervals of seconds, fourths, and octaves, all of them characteristic of Anlo-Ewe music. But the work is neither a portrayal of Agbadza (as in Fred Onovwerosuoke's 2007 étude for piano, *Agbadza,* discussed in the

Example 4.2 Continued

previous chapter[23]) nor a sustained fantasy on the Agbadza bell pattern; rather, among a slew of contrasting gestures and textures, the standard pattern is foregrounded in places, or absorbed into the motivic processes elsewhere. While listeners familiar with Agbadza will immediately recognize its bell pattern in *Volta Fantasy*, the fact that the same pattern is used in other dances not only in West Africa but also in the African diaspora scatters its

[23] For a discussion, see Agawu, *The African Imagination in Music*, 332–333.

referential associations, pointing generically to "dance" while leaving the specifics to individual imaginations and associated intertextual horizons.

If we now ask how Nketia's composition unfolds, we might tell a story like this. *Volta Fantasy* begins with a six-bar phrase arranged as 1 + 1+2 + 2. A bold ascending-octave gesture in iambic rhythm announces A as a potential pitch class of priority. The same gesture is repeated in bar 2, but the rhythm acquires two additional onsets and thus begins to sound like a foretaste of the standard pattern [2-2-1-1]. Bar 3 begins another figure. Two bars long, this figure outlines the full A-minor tonic and hints at the standard pattern in bar 4. Most poignant in this opening phrase are bars 5–6. Marked *piano*, they provide the first hint of genuine melodic-thematic expression in the work. Also two bars long, this idea (which will return periodically) has a modal flavor and finishes with a degree of openness: the melody departs from the particle A–B and A–C and then reverses A–C to C–A, followed by a rest in the second half of bar 6. Here, too, we get a taste of Nketia's harmonic writing, which is oriented toward the plagal domain. Inconclusiveness is further conveyed by the final chord in bar 6—tonic in second inversion rather than in root position. Altogether, the gestures in these opening 6 bars, although distinct, are not readily classified as questions with corresponding answers. There's something tentative about them. In this period of the work's emergence, the listener is encouraged to resist the urge to predict what will happen in both the short term and the long term. While the whiff of the standard pattern and its Ewe affiliation along with the fragment of Akan melody may signal an inter-ethnic or even cosmopolitan drama, making predictions about the work's expressive trajectory would be premature. We simply have to wait and see what the composer does next.

Unusually, perhaps, Nketia follows these six equivocal bars with an exact repeat (bars 7–12). What is the compositional purpose of this repetition? Is it to confirm equivocality as premise, or hint at the flexibilities associated with fantasy as a genre? Or might there be some uncertainty inside the composer's head?

If the repeated six-bar phrase left the listener with a fragmentary aura, the passage that follows, bars 12–27, compounds the uncertainty. Although it is dynamically shaped and reaches something of a climax engineered by register (bars 19–20), the passage effects a developmental manner (12–21) and introduces new material (22–25) before being "rescued" by the fragment of Akan melody previously heard in bars 5–6 and 11–12. Although the melody in bars 26–27 ends this time on a root-position tonic chord, it lacks a clearly delineated bass progression that might reinforce the sense of closure. Other details in the working out of ideas in 12–27 reinforce the speculative aura of the work. For example, a new motive introduced in the second half of bar 15 (C–C–B) and answered in the second half of bar 17 a fourth higher (F–F–E) hints at the learned style, but the imitation encompasses only those three notes, not what follows. The same idea will be heard again in bar 23 (F–F–E in the "alto"), where it functions as an antiphonal response doubled a tenth below. These procedures exemplify a kind of muted polyphony heard throughout *Volta Fantasy*. Its origins lie in Akan group singing, where sporadic elements of imitation often enliven group singing.

Until the rescue effort of bars 26–27, we are left with no clear rationale for the sequence of formal functions experienced in the developmental passage. For one thing, not enough has been "said" to engender development; nor is it clear what the music's overall direction is. Add to this some strange harmonies (bars 24–25, underpinned by a chromatic bass, A–B♭–B, moving in parallel tenths with the alto) and one is left once again with a sense of ambivalence.

It is for these reasons that bar 28 comes with all the force of a beginning, a new beginning perhaps, a structural downbeat. The standard pattern is projected here as a two-bar ostinato, realized as a succession of rising fourths (E–A and F–B). What is the tonal meaning of this new section? Should E be heard initially as a plagal resolution of the preceding A, does it signal a new Phrygian center, or will it acquire a dominant quality and eventually cadence on A?

The introduction of the standard-pattern ostinato in bar 28 brings a clearer sense of purpose and direction. A repeating two-bar unit serves first as a vamp (28–31), then as an accompanying pattern (32–35), then again as a vamp (36–37), but not quite completing this last function before the melodic voice interjects in 37–39. The next four bars (40–43) are also infused by the standard pattern, but the texture changes to a four-part chorale style and the passage ends in bar 43 with a strong Phrygian cadence. We see now that of the various tonal options entertained at the start of this standard-pattern passage (28–43), the Phrygian reading is made good on.

Although it does not have the same dramatic weight of bar 28, bar 44 marks another phrase beginning. This time the standard pattern is registrally split for the right hand and filled in by the "silent" eighth notes of the original pattern. This well-profiled passage is parsed evenly into 2+2+2+2 bars, where the first pair of 2s is identical while the second pair, although almost identical rhythmically, is underpinned by heavy bass motion in octaves (D–C–B–E in bars 48–49, then, as if repeating, G–F♯–E but declining to leap to a low B or A as might be imagined if the previous contour was being literally followed in bars 50–51). While the entire passage from bar 28 suggests a marked beginning and projects a sense of unity by virtue of the ostinato, there are melodic outliers here and there, as in bars 32–35, or even the left hand of bars 48–51).

Beginnings are normally followed by continuations before reaching endings, so if, in taking stock, we think of bars 1–27 as the work's introduction, bars 28–51 as the proper beginning, then we would expect some sort of continuation that makes good on the premises announced so far. Nketia continues, however, with a strange six-bar passage (52–57), strange because it is not obviously related to anything we've heard up until now. Is this a new theme, perhaps? Materially, it consists of arpeggio figures ascending in the left hand and descending in the right hand, and although associations can be made easily with previous arpeggios (bars 3, 9, 32, 37–38), the connection is not likely to be salient for the listener. As the six-bar passage starting in bar 52 unfolds, however, we come to understand its role as a transition on account of its ascending outer voices: A–B♭–C in the treble against C–D–E♭ in the bass (bars 52, 54 and 56). While the directional element in this passage is readily heard, the harmonic logic is less clear. Are these superimposed triads with different qualities meant to heard as bi-triadic resultants, perhaps?

Clarity and a sense of purpose return with a new, quieter, theme in bar 58. Here is another beginning that has an Akan flavor and may even recall Nketia's melodic manner (as heard, for example, in another solo piano piece, "Libation" [1975]). More immediately, this theme recalls the melodic fragment from near the beginning of the piece (bars 5–6). As we will see, the theme in bar 58 heads a two-phase process, 58–71 and 72–82, leading to a return of the ostinato figure in bar 83. In the first phase, the delicate melody, with its responding staccato bass (58–61), will grow in texture from two to four voices by bar 70, incorporating the earlier fragment in the process (the melodic fragment in bars 5–6 appears in 68–69). In the repetition that marks the beginning of the second phase (bar 72), the pitch class A rather than D accompanies the initial motive (72–73), suggesting for just a moment a plagal response to bars 58–59, but D is soon restored (74–75). A point of culmination is reached with the seven-note fortissimo chords in 78–79. The iambic rhythm of bar 78 stems not only from immediately preceding use (bars 77–78) but from consistent use since the first bar of the piece. Then two bars in bare octaves (85–86) lead to a chorale-style Phrygian cadence in 82. We have heard this Phrygian cadence before (bar 43); indeed, the entire passage from bar 58 contains flashbacks to earlier moments in the work. On the whole, the music since the introduction of the ostinato pattern in bar 28 has been somewhat prismatic. A linear logic is evident largely at more local levels of structure; what predominates gesturally is a network of cross references and associations.

Volta Fantasy's final phase begins in bar 82 with the ostinato figure from 28, now presented in full texture and in an A-minor harmonization. Many listeners will probably hear this as a moment of return, all be it a rhetorically heightened return. Setting aside the tonal adjustment, the material in bars 83–97 is essentially the same as that in 28–43. But as we know, the same materials in different locations can engender different associations. So, whereas the earlier passage had a promissory effect by virtue of its location close to the beginning of the piece, this one invites speculation on its eventual destination, on the possibility of more clearly defined closure. Indeed, the adjustment in bar 98 (which reworks the more straightforward Phrygian cadence of 43) extends the preparation for closure over three bars (98–100). However, as we've learned to expect in this work, nothing is ever predictable.

Although it has gestural affinities with passages we've heard earlier, the passage beginning in bar 101 is one of the strangest in the work. A motive in the left hand is answered by one in the right hand (bars 101–102, reminiscent of 52–57). This antiphonal gesture is immediately abandoned and followed by chorale-like material (103–104) reminiscent of bars 40–43, but it lacks the earlier passage's clear sense of tonal direction—a Phrygian cadence on E. It is also in effect a continuation of the chorale aura that has been hovering over the music since bar 95. While bar 101 seems initially discontinuous (texturally, harmonically, and motivically) from its immediately preceding material, it initiates a four-bar responsorial gesture (2+2, the latter two continuing the chorale texture) that is immediately repeated verbatim (105–108). Something new arrives again in 109—a somber theme reminiscent of one introduced earlier (58) and belonging generically to what I have been calling Akan melody. After three bars, the right hand (bar 112) embarks on a solo voyage, set up by an arpeggiated D-minor chord in the left hand (112). Has there been an enunciatory or even improvisatory urge that has not been allowed to play itself out? The six-bar passage from 109 to 114 suggests that this might be so. A modified and truncated repetition follows in 115–119, recalling for the last time the modally tinged Akan melody that has haunted the work from the beginning. Accompanying voices are enlisted to begin the formal process of closure with a V6–i progression (bar 119). While this progression offers closure in the tonic key, bar 119 is not a moment of strong closure. The task of achieving a full global close is subsequently distributed across the last eight bars. Halting rests demarcate individual gestures in nearly every bar from 119 to the end (the exceptions are 121, 125, and 127). The silences are loud, and we sense that the end is nigh.

Volta Fantasy finishes in A minor. The closing progression in the last three bars is a nominal predominant-dominant-tonic progression. Nketia has chosen a dominant 9th without the third (125, second dotted-quarter beat) and a tonic without the fifth (126–127). And as regards voice leading, the top voice F in bar 125 resolves not to a registrally adjacent E as one might expect but to a C in the top voice of 126–127. The F–C leap of a fourth is, according to George Dor, a characteristic mannerism of Nketia's.[24] Rather than drawing to a culminating, inevitable end, the last nine bars affect a wistful sense of ending. After the evident struggles of the preceding music, the closing A-minor chord seems almost perfunctory, strategically unintegrated with the whole, as if deferring to a conventional imperative. (Debussy's *Petite Suite* exhibits a similar eclecticism.)

A good way to characterize the overall form of *Volta Fantasy* is as circular or rotational form. By this, we mean that the work does not follow a single, linear trajectory from beginning to end, but frequently doubles up on itself, proceeding in waves such that material used earlier is incorporated in later gestures but without a rhythm of predictability. Wagner's *Prelude to Tristan and Isolde* famously uses this type of form, but I have no reason to think that Nketia was seeking to emulate the German composer.[25]

I have called *Volta Fantasy* a problematic piece in part because, although it can be understood within the fantasy traditions associated with the European common practice, it does not sit comfortably within any known African genre. Moreover, its details of part writing, key articulation and sectional organization all possess a range of nonconformist or perhaps interrogative qualities. Different listeners will have different reactions to the work. Some may approach it with few expectations and thus allow themselves to simply be caught up in its jerky rhetoric, some may be inclined

[24] George Dor, "Exploring the Ontology and Application of the 'Nketia Dominant Seventh Chord,'" in *Discourses in African Musicology*, edited by Kwasi Ampene et. al, pp. 350–371 (Ann Arbor: Michigan Publishing, 2015).

[25] Robert P. Morgan, "Circular Form in the *Tristan* Prelude," *Journal of the American Musicological Society* 53 (2000): 69–103.

to dance (imaginatively) to the danceable parts, while others may sing (again silently) in the few singable portions. Works of art are fields of possibility, invitations to contemplative behavior, so it is likely that different listeners will register different kinds of aesthetic valuation. What is most significant in the context of African pianism is establishing critical reference points for evaluating the composer's achievement. Under modernist compositional imperatives, some of the infelicities, strange turns, or odd constructions of this 1967 work may be heard as part of modernism's ordinary language. But the establishment of a language demands a level of consistency that is not to be found in *Volta Fantasy.* Instead, the composer proceeds one step at a time, allowing context to justify its procedures, and claiming the sort of hybridity that, by default, has emerged as the norm of postcolonial musical expression. It remains to be seen whether African pianism can transcend that norm. One thing is certain: *Volta Fantasy* facilitates a discussion of African art music in general and African pianism in particular.[26]

Uzoigwe's "Ukom" and "Egwu Amala"

We may fruitfully compare Nketia's language to that of Joshua Uzoigwe, two of whose compositions, "Ukom" and "Egwu Amala," are included in Nyaho's anthology. Based on an Igbo women's funeral repertory. "Ukom" is a rhythmically aggressive piece, minimalist in its pitch vocabulary (all 182 bars of this $\frac{12}{8}$ piece feature mainly the white notes of an A-pentatonic scale, A-G-E-D-C), and enlivened by snippets of traditional melody (see excerpt from the beginning of the piece in Example 4.3). The composition's generative rhythm is a restless iambic figure that contributes considerable momentum. Something of a dance feel is heard throughout, but the composer's voice is never far away.

In "Egwu Amala," by contrast, Uzoigwe uses a more complex pitch language in which pentatonic elements interact with more complex chromatic material (see Example 4.4 for the opening six bars). The $\frac{19}{8}$ time signature may seem a bit fanciful at first, a "paper meter" perhaps, were it not for the

[26] An important precedent to this effort to make a close reading of a work by Nketia is Nissio Fiagbedzi, "J. H. Kwabena Nketia's Republic Suite: An Analytical Portrait of Movement 1," in *Discourses in African Musicology*, 306–329.

Example 4.3 Bars 1–13 of Joshua Uzoigwe's "Ukom," from *Talking Drums* (1999)

fact that the original Igbo dance from which the composition derives is, according to the composer's ethnographic studies, also in the same meter.[27] Hearing successive groups of 19 may well be a challenge for most listeners, but it need not be a stumbling block in this work because a recurring Call-and-Response gesture confers a larger, rondo-like shape on the piece as a

[27] See Marie Agatha Ozah, "Building Bridges Between Traditional and Western Art Music: A Study of Joshua Uzoigwe's *Egwu Amala*," *Analytical Approaches to Western Music Journal* 3 (2013), accessed June 2021, http://www.aawmjournal.com/articles/2014a.

Example 4.4 Bars 1–8 of Joshua Uzoigwe's "Egwu Amala," from *Talking Drums* (1999)

whole. There is an evident compositional labor here which suggests a degree of compositional autonomy far in excess of anything we observed in Nketia's "Builsa Worksong." This difference may reflect a generational difference (Nketia was born in 1921, Uzoigwe in 1946), it may also represent two different approaches to subjectivity in the composing of African art music.

The contrast between creating a communal space for others to join in, on the one hand, and making individuals sit up and listen, on the other, may well represent one of the enduring challenges facing the African composer. In various poetic guises, this dichotomy, which may be figured as a form of "I-centered" doing as distinct from "We-centered" expression, has haunted many an African composer. The ubiquity of dance gestures, for example, is a sign of victory for communality and unanimity. Similar values promoting social and spiritual bonding are inscribed in the (foreign) practice of hymn singing, thanks to its simple, easily learned tunes, modest tonal trajectories and regular and predictable phraseology; and thanks also to its textual messages laden with assurances and promises of a better life after death. (See the discussion near the beginning of Chapter 3). And yet there are indications that some composers are willing either to leave their communities of origin behind or establish a different set of terms on which they relate to their brethren. If we must compare, we might say that the contents of *Piano Music of Africa and the African Diaspora* seem generally tame, more muted in their exploratory ambitions than avant-garde works by Cage, Boulez, Stockhausen, or Lachenmann.

But there are signs of change. The consistently dissonant ambience of Euba's "Igbá Kerin—Àwon Abàmi Eye" (Supernatural Birds) (see excerpt in Example 4.5) and "Igbà Kìnní—Akèrègbè Baba Emu" (The Gourd Master of the Palm Wine), the rhythmical play and expanded instrumental resources required to perform Ali Osman's "Afro Arab Blues" (the performer is enjoined to "say 'es' and snap [his or her] fingers" throughout) (excerpted

Example 4.5 Bars 1–10 of Akin Euba's "Igbá Kerin—Àwo Abàmi Eye (Supernatural Birds)," from *Four Pictures from Oyo Calabashes* (1964)

Example 4.6 Bars 1–5 of Ali Osman's "Afro Arab Blues" (2005)

in Example 4.6), the discontinuities, improvisatory freedom, and occasional stillness cultivated in Bongani Ndodana-Breen's "Flowers in Sand," and the elemental rhythmic drive and superimposed chords that animate Gyimah Labi's "The Lotus" (excerpted in Example 4.7) suggest that it may not be too long before the two traditions become symbolically indistinguishable.

It is to William Chapman Nyaho's great credit that he has hastened the coming moment in which art music worlds will submit to a different mode

Example 4.7 Bars 200–212 of "The Lotus" from Gyimah Labi's *Dialects-2* (1987, rev. 1994)

of internal differentiation. In bringing together previously scattered works, he has made possible a more focused discussion of the critical and aesthetic issues raised by African pianism. The anthology can also support studies in performing practice, the teaching of music theory, and of course musicological research into musical style. In its richness and diversity, *Piano Music of Africa and the African Diaspora* serves as a salutary reminder that we may have defined the purview of "African music" rather too narrowly. Art music makes a bold incursion into the territory of on-paper creation—a mode previously denied by the collective practices of traditional and popular music. Like other creative artists negotiating the challenges of modernity, African art music composers can place the results of their efforts in a wider cosmopolitan pool of creativity even as they explore what, alas, is the most elusive language of all.

5

Rethinking Music Theory, with African Aid

This chapter originates in a keynote address to the Society for Music Theory in 2015. Aside from eliminating a few personal prefatory remarks, and adding bibliographical references, I have maintained the spoken form of the original and indicated where recorded music was played. My goal was to speak to issues emanating from the quotidian practices of students and colleagues who self-identify as music theorists in the US academy. I recognize that the basic categories deployed here—music, theory, analysis, aid, pedagogy, among others—are subject to wide interpretation around the globe, but on that occasion in St. Louis in November 2015, I took some comfort from knowing that I was addressing members of a relatively small scholarly society who shared similar goals and metalanguages in the production of music-theoretical and music-analytical knowledge.

The Idea of Aid

Between 1960 and 2008, Africa received something like one trillion dollars in aid from Western countries.[1] Some of it was used to provide basic infrastructure (water, electricity, and health), to resuscitate ailing economies, and to provide debt relief so that the cycle of dependency can continue. The dominant form of aid was of course material—goods, cash, loans, expertise, and various economic measures and pressures. While some aid went toward education, relatively little of it was earmarked for enhancing intellectual life on the continent. None of it had music theory in mind.

[1] Dambisa Moyo, "Why Foreign Aid is Hurting Africa," *Wall Street Journal*, March 21, 2009. Moyo's numbers have been disputed by other scholars, some going as low as 500 billion, others as high as 2.6 trillion.

On African Music. Kofi Agawu, Oxford University Press. © Oxford University Press 2023.
DOI: 10.1093/oso/9780197664063.003.0005

There've been vigorous debates about whether aid to Africa is finally a good thing. I won't be getting into those debates here. What I want to suggest to this audience is that music theory could benefit from musico-intellectual aid *from* Africa—speaking both literally and metaphorically. To put it so directly may seem contrary to what we know from history and experience: aid, after all, has typically flowed from richer nations to poorer ones, from the first world to the fourth world, from the North to the South. So my suggestion may be dismissed by those who believe that the collective practices of music theory boast a self-sufficiency that obviates any need for supplementation. Yet, given the current disposition of the world system, given the emergence of new imperialisms masquerading as globalization and internationalization, and given the constraints that these developments are increasingly imposing on academic disciplines, it should not seem unreasonable to suggest that music theory (or at least some corners of music theory) needs rethinking, and that such rethinking take place along the broadest possible lines. My specific suggestion is that foreign aid from Africa can help.

Now, we know that aid typically flows from better-endowed givers to lesser endowed receivers, so it is not intuitively obvious that so-called third- and fourth-world (African) nations can be sources of aid to wealthy nations in Europe and America, except in the most metaphorical senses. But a little reflection on the connotations of *givers* and *receivers* will begin to suggest that, depending on whether we're discussing politics, economics, religion, or culture, the direction of flow of aid may be unpredictable. Let me mention two factors that might support the plausibility of this reversal. First, Jean and John Comaroff argue for "theory from the South," the idea being that theoretical perspectives emerging from the Global South and developed by previously colonized people are increasingly proving effective in explaining new developments in the North, developments that seem to re-enact actions that those in the South are all too familiar with (like fraudulent elections). So, whereas theory was typically thought to have been manufactured in the North and exported to the South, the flow might be usefully conceptualized in reverse.[2]

Another example, older and less literal, is implicit in the thought expounded in 1936 by French ethnographer and composer André Schaeffner in connection with written and oral discourses:

[2] Jean Comaroff and John Comaroff, *Theory from the South: Or, How Euro-America is Evolving Toward Africa* (Boulder, CO: Paradigm Publishers, 2012).

> None of the procedures or properties which we esteem characteristic of music endowed with a writing system [e.g., European music] cannot be found to some extent in music from oral traditions [e.g., African music]. In the final analysis, the difference between these two kinds of music may lie not so much in what one of them has and the other has not, as in what one of them still has and the other no longer has.[3]

Policy-makers following the implications of this premise would thus enjoin their subjects to seek help from the Global South, from those who still have that something that the Global North no longer has.

Schaeffner's point is corroborated by a familiar sight: generations of Europeans rushing to various parts of Africa in search of supplements and alternatives to their own impoverished or damaged lives—spiritual, medical, and cultural practices, and patterns of sociality deeply embedded in human-centeredness. Aid from Africa (in the form of models for a better life) comes to the rescue, serving as a boost, an enrichment, a source of rejuvenation. How this aid is delivered depends on the supporting infrastructure. While the trillion-dollar aid to Africa was mediated by numerous institutions, by policy and contractual agreements constructed under the influence of no small measure of prejudice and partisanship, music studies boast no such elaborate frameworks for the dissemination of aid, except for nascent attempts to establish copyright regulations. I will leave others to supply this missing practical dimension of the argument I will be presenting here.

Now, this is clearly a huge topic that cannot be done full justice in the time at my disposal. So let me simplify my task by framing this talk as an invitation—an invitation to sample some African music (and ideas about it) and to consider whether further engagement might not actually enhance the work that music theorists do. I will proceed in four stages: firstly, I'll briefly say what I mean by "African music" and by "music theory"; then, I'll take pleasure in reminding you of some Western attitudes to non-Western music; thirdly, I will cite a number of core attributes of African music whose study can, I believe, enrich music theory; finally, I'll reflect briefly on a couple of the pedagogical and methodological consequences of embracing African music. Obviously, I will be telling only part of the story, not the whole story. For example, I will not be addressing the reciprocal benefits to the givers of aid.

[3] André Schaeffner, *Origine des instruments de musique: Introduction ethnologie à l'histoire de la musique instrumentale* (Paris: Payot, 1936), 342; quoted in Arom, *African Polyphony and Polyrhythm*, vii.

I will also have to ignore some of the tributaries that flow from my main argument, including possible implementation strategies. So you might want to treat this as a first pass through the terrain, a programmatic announcement that I hope will elicit thought and eventually action.

What Is African Music?

In our best traditions, let me begin by defining my terms.

African music is music conceived, composed, and (often in the first instance) performed by African people. Although the actual word "music" does not occur in many indigenous languages, varieties of sound sculpting bearing choreographic supplements are not merely present in, but are existentially definitional of, African societies. They include repertoires of great historical depth transmitted orally and aurally. A simple and convenient way to think about these repertoires, as we saw in the previous chapter, is to assign each item to one of three classes (a trichotomy always seems unavoidable wherever we theorize or classify!): first, *traditional music*, whose roots lie in ancient Africa, and which has been reinvented periodically such that it always bears traces of its past historical encounters; in my view, this forms the backbone of Africa's musico-intellectual heritage; second, *popular music* of relatively recent provenance (it originates in the 1900s), openly hybrid in its instrumental and idiomatic resources and procedures, and widely disseminated through a variety of modern media; and third, *art music*, which originated over a century and a half ago, and boasts a relatively small but symbolically significant repertory produced by born-in-the-tradition composers who have been trained in Western music and whose creative output is marked at the deepest levels by both African and European music. All three classes of music exist within the same time frame nowadays, but they reach radically different segments of the population.[4]

Allow me to share the briefest of samplings of African traditional music, the backbone of Africa's musico-intellectual heritage. (The recorded excerpts featured here were heard by audience members when this chapter was first given as a talk in 2015. They are listed here to provide a context for readers.

[4] See also Simha Arom, "Intelligence in Traditional Music," in *What is Intelligence?* (Darwin College Lectures 1992), edited by J. Khalfa, pp. 137–160 (Cambridge, UK: Cambridge University Press, 1994). A few of the limitations of the three-fold categorization were discussed in the previous chapter.

Some of them are available on streaming services such as Spotify; others may be found in the holdings of university libraries)[5]:

1) Here's some vocal music by the Peul (Fulani) of Niger, notable for its drone-like continuity. There's no pulse, no obnoxious marking of time, just a collective gesturing toward infinity.
2) Next, from Uganda, is an ensemble of so-called Makondere horn players. This archetypally communal music features stacked ostinatos out of which emerge various melodic patterns, patterns that do not necessarily coincide with what the individual horn players play. The manner is minimalistic and a choreographic supplement central to the African aesthetic is felt by those primed to feel it.
3) From Ghana, here is a brief excerpt from the Pan African Orchestra. An ensemble of iron bells, elephant horns, drums (large and small), bamboo flutes, and hand claps (so-called *corpophones*) essays a polyrhythmic course that is held in place by an ostinato pattern known as a time line.
4) My next example features the talking instrument par excellence, the so-called *dùndún* drum of the Yoruba, heard here in both its speech mode and song or musical mode. This is a variety of African music that compels a consideration of its underlying linguisticity.
5) Turning westward to the French-speaking country of Guinea, here is an ensemble of flutes imitating a griot singing to kora accompaniment. First, we hear a kind of vamp, then one flute soars above the others to deliver praise, like the griot himself. You can see that the iconic modality, so characteristic of expression in art and language, is alive and well in musical practice (see Chapter 2). You can also see that musical ideas are not imprisoned in their original timbres; we may

[5] The six excerpts are taken from the following recordings: 1) "Choeurs des Peuls Wodabé," from the CD *Introduction aux musiques Africaines* by Monique Brandilly (Arles, Citel de la musique: Actes sud, 1997), track 3; 2) "Rwakanembe" [Music of the Nyoro], from the CD *Music of Africa Series: 30 Musical Instruments 4 Flutes and Horns* (Grahamstown: International Library of African Music, n.d.), track 14; 3) "Mmenson," from the CD *Pan-African Orchestra, Opus 1* (New York: Real World, 1995), track 3; 4) Haruna Ishola & His Apala Group, *Oluwa Nikan Loba*, LP (Star Label, 2010); 5) "Griots de Labé," from the CD *Musiques du monde* (France: Playa Sound, 1989) track 22; and 6) "Ame Ngolo," from the CD *Centrafrique: pygmées Aka (Chants de chasse, d'amour et de moquerie)* (Paris: Ocora, 1998), track 5. I have used some of these excerpts in other contexts throughout this book and in other publications of mine, and I have done so mainly for convenience. While I have no ambitions to create a canon of African musics, the *idea of a canon* as a referential body of texts is I believe critical for the institutional practice of African musicology. Canons are always provisional, of course, but without them our attempts to construct knowledge intersubjectively are made just that much more difficult.

therefore speak—at a certain level of abstraction—of the autonomy of those ideas.

6) Finally, and in a more intimate register, here is an Aka pygmy man singing and playing a harp to amuse himself. On display is the grossly undervalued melodic dimension of African music. The use of vocables relieves the singer of responsibility in the semantic realm, allowing him to play with motifs while keeping the tonal sense open until the very end of the excerpt.

For a continent with over 1.3 billion people, divided by our historical oppressors into 55 states, speaking some 2,000 languages, it may seem preposterous to present six brief examples (from Niger, Uganda, Ghana, Nigeria, Guinea, and the Central African Republic) as representative of Black African music. Such synoptic acts are unavoidable, however, wherever one aims to communicate, so I'm sure you'll forgive me for merely being mortal here. But even if you're hearing this music for the first time, you (and I mean *you* as people whose vocation involves daily close, inquisitive listening) have probably already noticed a variety of temporal environments ("how time passes," as Stockhausen put it[6]), an array of timbres, a complex of rhythmic procedures and metrical orientations, pitch collections with different centers, and modes of "linguistic" articulation—the very things that music theorists normally attend to in the repertories they study. So there is potential here for dialogue.

What Is Music Theory?

Let me now deal with the other term in my title, *music theory*: What is music theory, and how has music theory dealt with the non-West in its 1,000-plus-year history?

When faced with a task like this, I often find it helpful to consult a standard dictionary or encyclopedia, where one invariably finds a formulation of sufficient generality to serve simultaneously as a point of departure and as an object of (easy) critique. So here are two sources: Palisca (1980) and Rehding and Rings (2015).

[6] Stockhausen, ". . . How Time Passes," translated by Cornelius Cardew, *Die Reihe* 3 (1957): 10–43.

First, here is Claude Palisca writing in *Grove 5* (1980), the most important English-language music reference work of the time:

> Theory is now understood as principally the study of the structure of music. This can be divided into melody, rhythm, counterpoint, harmony and form, but these elements are difficult to distinguish from each other and to separate from their contexts. At a more fundamental level theory includes considerations of tonal systems, scales, tuning, intervals, consonance, dissonance, durational proportions, and the acoustics of pitch systems. A body of theory exists also about other aspects of music, such as composition, performance, orchestration, ornamentation, improvisation, and electronic sound production. . . . The Western art music tradition is remarkable for the quantity and scope of its theory.[7]

Palisca then proceeds to a magisterial report on theoretical activity from the Hellenic period to the late twentieth century. You've probably all read this, or at least consulted it, especially those of you who've had to pass one of those dreaded PhD qualifying examinations in the history of music theory! I am not concerned today with the specific content of Palisca's article, only with its remarkable scope. I have to admit that it remains a wonder to me how many men and women have labored over the years to produce this vast body of work. Surveys of the fields of theory and analysis confirm the commanding size of this legacy and affirm the depth, vitality, and continuing diversification of theoretical inquiry. So when Palisca says that "the Western art music tradition is remarkable for the quantity and scope of its theory," he is, at least from an Africanist perspective, not exaggerating.[8]

[7] Palisca, "Theory," *Grove Music Online*, accessed July 2020. Incidentally, the years around 1980 were significant years in the history of the Society for Music Theory. The Society itself was founded in 1977, held its first annual meeting in 1978, and began publishing its flagship journal, *Music Theory Spectrum*, in 1979; attacks from the left, spearheaded by Joseph Kerman, were just about to be launched in 1980 with the article, "How We Got into Analysis," *Critical Inquiry* 7 (1980): 311–331. On the formation of the Society, see Allen Forte, "The Founding of the Society for Music Theory," *Music Theory Online* 9 (2003); for a concise history, see Patrick McCreless, "Rethinking Contemporary Music Theory," in *Keeping Score: Music, Disciplinarity, Culture*, edited David Schwarz and Anahid Kassabian, pp. 1–49 (Charlottesville: University of Virginia Press, 1997); and for one among several responses to Kerman's 1980 article, see my "How We Got Out of Analysis and How to Get Back in Again," *Music Analysis* 23 (2004): 267–286. Julian Horton keeps the flame alive in a recent article, "On the Musicological Necessity of Musical Analysis," *Musical Quarterly* 103 (2020): 62–104, accessed July 2021, https://doi-org.ezproxy.princeton.edu/10.1093/musqtl/gdaa005.

[8] For overviews of research activity in the fields of music theory and music analysis, see Palisca, "Theory"; Thomas Christensen, ed., *The Cambridge History of Western Music Theory* (Cambridge, UK: Cambridge University Press, 2006); Ian Bent (rev. Anthony Pople), "Analysis," in *Grove Music Online*; David Damschroder and David Russell Williams, *Music Theory from Zarlino to Schenker: A*

Second, for comparison, let us mention the recent collection conceived and edited by Alex Rehding and Steven Rings. The contributors take a critical look at critical concepts like interval, mode, scale, tonic, timbre, polyphony, rhythm, temporalities, and even music itself. While there is clearly some carry over from the Palisca article, there are many newer things as well, not least the fact of multi-authorship. For my immediate purposes, two features are relevant. First, Rehding and Rings include only one chapter that has significant African content (Martin Scherzinger's on temporalities); second, there is no separate chapter devoted to dance, something that would be unthinkable from an Africanist perspective.[9]

Music theory typically models music composed by members of its societies of origin. The massive legacy of European theory therefore includes music of Italy, Germany, Russia, France, and England, among others. Although these theoretical discourses include occasional or passing references to non-Western musical traditions, the core of music theory has been the core European music and its thinkers, and not just any music but that belonging to the tradition of art music, a tradition that is thought to display a high level of intellection and imagination. Jean-Jacques Rousseau in the eighteenth century, Fétis in the nineteenth, and more concertedly, the so-called comparative musicologists of the twentieth century (Hornbostel, Stumpf, Schneider, Sachs, and others) all had things to say about non-Western music, but they were not necessarily the numerically dominant voices in the broader field of music studies in their day.[10]

Bibliography and Guide (Stuyvesant, NY: Pendragon Press,1990); and David Russell Williams and C. Matthew Balensuela, *Music Theory from Boethius to Zarlino: A Bibliography and Guide* (Stuyvesant, NY: Pendragon Press, 2008). On Schenker, see David Carson Berry, *A Topical Guide to Schenkerian Literature: An Annotated Bibliography with Indices* (Hillsdale, NY: Pendragon Press, 2004)and www.Schenkerdocumentsonline.org. See also *The Oxford Handbook of Critical Concepts in Music Theory*, edited by Alex Rehding and Steven Rings (2015 online; 2020 in print). Acknowledging this vast legacy should not shield it from critique, however. The institutions, policies, and practices that have enabled its production need to be interrogated regularly.

[9] See, however, the *Journal of Music Theory*'s special issue on choreo-musical analysis (*JMT* 65, no. 1 [2021]) for a rare treatment of the subject in a mainstream music theory journal. For a thoughtful review-article of the Rehding-Rings volume, see Andrew J. Chung, "Music Theory Splintered Up, Not Broken Down," *Music Theory Spectrum* 44 (2022): 173–186, which helpfully contextualizes the volume's themes within contemporary critical and philosophical discourses.

[10] On Fétis, see Thomas Christensen, *Stories of Tonality in the Age of François-Joseph Fétis* (Chicago: University of Chicago Press, 2019); on comparative musicologists, see Anna Maria Busse Berger, *The Search for Medieval Music in Africa and Germany, 1891–1961: Scholars, Singers, Missionaries* (Chicago: University of Chicago Press, 2020). See also the updated agenda proposed by Patrick E. Savage and Steven Brown, "Toward a New Comparative Musicology," *AAWM Journal 2* (2013).

In the last two decades, however, American music theory has experienced something of a sea change in selecting objects for study. Armed with sets of data-collecting tools, analytical methods, and technologies for the iconic capture of an array of realities, music theorists, without abandoning the Bachs, Beethovens, Brahmses, or Weberns, have turned to sound production more broadly construed, and taken on eco-musicology, ringtones, protest music, and urban soundscapes, among others. This sweeping expansion of repertory (see, for example, the offerings in the journal *Music Theory Online*, which include papers on African, Indian, and Japanese music alongside studies of hard rock, pop, and jazz), with its implicit gestures toward a socially responsible inclusionism, should not blind us to the attitudes and positions that were once exhibited—and still persist—in theorists' encounters with non-Western music. So let us recall some of these remarks as background to the forthcoming discussion of African music as a nexus of aid mechanisms.

Sordid Moments in Music Theory's Past: Kerman, Tiersot, Schenker, and AAWM

If we now ask, How has music theory dealt with the non-West?, the picture becomes—shall we say—not pretty. Begin your narrative in the eighteenth century, the century on which so much modern thought has located its origins, and you will find that the non-West is either missing, appears sporadically, is endowed with an add-on status, or is cast as inferior or subordinate. (Again, I ask for your indulgence as I speak in very general terms). These and subsequent discourses were produced within particular traditions of knowledge production, they represent bids for different kinds of power, and they emanate from various sorts of pressures and impulses—all too numerous to enumerate here. Although we would not normally require a theory of Western art music to concern itself with non-Western music, the fact remains that some of these theories were being produced at the same time as Europe and America were engaged in various imperial activities around the globe. The aura of the non-West hovers unavoidably over music theory and has done so since at least the eighteenth century.[11]

[11] See, for example, Scherzinger, "Temporalities," in *The Oxford Handbook of Cultural Concepts in Music Theory*, edited Rehding and Rings (2018). If we recall earlier writings on medieval and Arabic theory (including North African offerings), the geo-cultural scope widens considerably.

Discerning coevalness (or denying it) and the related matters of constructing contemporaneity and distilling a zeitgeist are complex tasks, however; they defy the easy causalities that all too often tempt historians to find (or invent) similarity across interpretive domains. So let me not be heard insisting that the history of the development of European music theory be linked willy-nilly to the histories of empire, slavery, or colonialism. No doubt some simultaneous happenings may be motivated by similar or analogous factors while other connections remain to be demonstrated. Let me then sidestep the broader historical question and simply cite four little moments.

First: In his 1984 book, *Contemplating Musicology*, Joseph Kerman confesses that he is "not very interested in non-Western musics."[12] And he finds a surprising ally in Charles Seeger, the face of ethnomusicology himself. According to Kerman, "It was the *idea* of studying all musics that appealed to Seeger, not those musics themselves as subjects for actual study."[13] I'll defer to Taylor Greer and other Seeger experts on whether that is a fair characterization of Seeger,[14] but what interests me is Kerman's response to the question he poses subsequently: Can ethnomusicological methods help musicology? He thinks not, or rather only in a limited way:

> There are really only a limited number of areas—such as oral transmission and concepts of mode—where ethnomusicological research itself can impinge directly on the study of Western music. Western music is just too different from other musics, and its cultural contexts too different from other cultural contexts.[15]

There you have it: Western music is *just too different*, says the leading American musicologist of the 1980s. Of course, we all know that difference is a construction, that the attribution of difference arises from acts of linguistic and metalinguistic intervention, and that, depending on how you choose to construct the world, any two objects (or musics) may be judged different or similar. Kerman does not reach a deep level of introspection on the conditions of possibility for assigning difference. But here's the thing: Even within the traditions of Western music (assuming the possibility of their

[12] Joseph Kerman, *Contemplating Music: Challenges to Musicology* (Cambridge, MA: Harvard University Press, 1986), 162.

[13] Kerman, *Contemplating Music*, 162.

[14] Taylor Greer, *A Question of Balance: Charles Seeger's Philosophy of Music* (Berkeley: University of California Press, 1998).

[15] Kerman, *Contemplating Music*, 174.

isolation), couldn't one say that Boulez is just too different from Machaut, or that Cecil Taylor is just too different from Scott Joplin, or even that, at a certain level of abstraction, Haydn is just too different from Mozart? All depends on a prior horizon, and on the domain and scale on which you wish to erect your construct. Indeed, one person's difference may well be another's sameness.

OK, there's no need for me to turn this into a "Difference 101" lecture. I just wanted to lament the missed opportunity in Kerman's (triumphant) declaration that Western music is "just too different from other musics," a declaration that deprived his readers of an opportunity to interrogate the impulses that impel attributions of difference.

Second: Before Kerman (1985), a figure absolutely central to the activities of this Society also traded in differences. I'm speaking of the greatest music analyst of the twentieth century, Heinrich Schenker.[16] For him, the issue was not one of mere difference but of downright superiority. At a global level, Western music is simply superior to non-Western music; and at more local (intra-European) levels, German music is at the top—superior, that is, to Italian or French music. (If you come from a nation that is not mentioned, then you don't really exist). And of course, art music is superior to folk music.[17]

Third: Schenker was not alone in holding views steeped in judgments about the relative worth of various musics. Here is a French contemporary of his, Julien Tiersot (1857–1936), musicologist, composer, and musical ethnographer, writing in 1905:

> At the end of the nineteenth century, the history of music has made remarkable progress. It will, however, not be complete without including the study of non-European musics in the field, by expanding its sphere of focus. Though quite different in form from those to which our race has been accustomed for centuries, they're no less worthy of our listening attention. That those arts are inferior to ours must be admitted or rather declared upfront. Nothing is more natural than this truth: since Europe has always been the primary cradle of human civilization, it follows, quite simply, that

[16] Christopher Wintle's judgment, widely echoed in the literature on music theory. See his review of Schenker's *Free Composition* in *Times Literary Supplement* 79, no. 4042 (1980), 1046.

[17] See Schenker, *Der Tonwille: Pamphlets in Witness of the Immutable Laws of Music: Offered to a New Generation of Youth*, vol. 1, nos. 1–5 (1921–1923), edited William Drabkin, translated Ian Bent et al. (Oxford, UK: Oxford University Press, 2004).

musical practice there has reached a level of superiority that people from other parts of the world have not been able to match.[18]

A believer in Europe's supremacy, Tiersot says "yes" to the study of non-Western music because it completes the study of our music, but the truth—the "natural truth"—is that ours is superior.

Now, Julien Tiersot was a musical ethnographer and folklorist, so we could say that he knew whereof he spoke when he made reference to "non-European musics." Schenker's interests were very far from ethnography or folklore, however, but this did not stop him from expressing judgments about non-European music. It is important not to attribute fixed positions to Schenker, however, because his views evolved over time and did so in complex ways.[19]

In considering a few of Schenker's assertions, one need look no further than the section on "The question of modes" in chapter 1 of the counterpoint book to see that he doesn't like the "old modes" and doesn't like "exotic scales" either. Today's Westerner, he says, possesses a "harmonic awareness," while the "Oriental" doesn't. So, "How can anyone dare to suggest that we look to musically inferior races and nations (Japanese, Chinese, Arabic, Indian) for allegedly new systems, when in fact they have no systems at all!"[20]

Quoting further from Rothgeb and Thym's translation: "These exotic people still lack diatony, and that is the reason for the irrational character of their music."[21] It is "shameful" that "artists and theorists in our midst (e.g., Saint-Saëns, Busoni, Bellerman, Capellen, A. J. Polak, L. Riemann, and others) can call for a return to the old church modes and exotic scales as a means of expanding our musical horizon."[22] "Why," Schenker asks, "did our great masters live and work, if today their works—built upon usable systems—can be declared regressive in comparison to little Chinese,

[18] Julien Tiersot, *Notes d'ethnographie musicale*, 2 vols. (Paris: Fischbacher, 1905), i, 1; quoted and translated in Sindhumathi Revuluri, "Orientalism and Musical Knowledge: Lessons from Edward Said," *Journal of the Royal Musical Association* 141 (2016): 207.

[19] On Schenker's views of non-European persons and musics, see Philip Ewell, "Music Theory and the White Racial Frame," *Music Theory Online* 26 (2020). The evolution of Schenker's thinking is a point made by Martin Eybl in *Ideologie und Methode: zum ideengeschichtlichen Kontext von Schenkers Musiktheorie* (Tutzing: Schneider, 1995); and by Timothy L. Jackson in "A Preliminary Response to Ewell," *Journal of Schenkerian Studies* 12 (2019): 157–166.

[20] Heinrich Schenker, *Counterpoint: A Translation of Kontrapunt*, vol. 1, translated John Rothgeb and Jürgen Thym, edited John Rothgeb (New York: Schirmer Books, 1987), 28.

[21] Schenker, *Counterpoint*, 22.

[22] Schenker, *Counterpoint*, 21.

Japanese, and Arabic melodies and scales."[23] These developments were signs of a lamentable condition, the "decline of our art."[24]

There's a lot to unpack here, and indeed a number of scholars have undertaken precisely such unpacking (Nicholas Cook, Martin Eybl, Timothy Jackson, and Thomas Christensen, among others). Some might say that attitudes to difference and Western (specifically German) superiority are of their time, and that they are no longer axiomatic or even widespread. Certainly, today's progressives will probably deny holding beliefs like these. But the biases and convictions that lie at the heart of Schenker's assertions are still very much with us. All you have to do is look objectively at hiring practices in the music academy, concert programming, the award of prizes for scholarly work, and the constitution of influential committees, to see that we're not out of the woods yet. One thing that is clear is that the kind of project announced in my title, "Rethinking Music Theory, with African Aid," would have been roundly condemned by Schenker.

I rather doubt that arguments about musical difference can be settled on the basis of evidence alone, for the attribution of difference is sometimes an expression of desire rather than a report on empirical reality. But let me dwell for a moment on the ostensible *polyphonic deficit* which Schenker finds among Others, those others who, according to him, lack "harmonic awareness," and let me suggest that Schenker's remark has been made rather hastily. A number of African groups are known to have developed polyphonic practices independently, without any prior European influence whatsoever. It may be that the topic of polyphony as such does not register as prominently in European discourses on African music, but that hardly implies absence of the phenomenon.

Here are two brief recorded examples.[25] The first is a Southern Ewe song constrained by an anhemitonic pentatonic system. Singers work within a Call-Response framework, even while negotiating the pull of speech tones. Both Call (sometimes doubled, sometimes even tripled) and Response (typically singular but occasionally missing one or two voices) accommodate contrapuntal expression, but notice the pure octaves at phrase endings—points

[23] Schenker, *Counterpoint*, 22.

[24] Schenker, *Counterpoint*, 28.

[25] Again, I have retained the original oral context of presentation of this material throughout the chapter. Readers unfamiliar with the widely anthologized style of Southern Ewe singing mentioned here may wish to consult the recorded material accompanying James Burns' *Female Voices from an Ewe Dance-Drumming Community: Our Music Has Become a Divine Spirit* (Farnham, UK: Ashgate, 2009).

of purity and unanimity, points that restore a homogeneity in response to earlier heterogeneity.[26]

The second example is a Banda-Linda performance by an ensemble of eighteen horns, each of which contributes a single note to the emerging composition.[27] First, a solo horn's "call" is followed by a full-ensemble response (I'll come back to this chord later, when we talk about contrapuntal hearing). This gesture is repeated; then, one by one, from the highest to the lowest-sounding horns, the composition unfolds gradually, constrained by an anhemitonic pentatonic scale and by a pre-existing song model. The ensemble's many voices have individual roles to play, but each voice contributes essentially to a larger resultant sound. This is polyphony via a different route, produced in the absence of writing and under a deep communal imperative. Different, to be sure, but "inferior"?

One final point before I leave Schenker alone: More than one devotee has sought to separate the technical apparatus from the theorist's political views. Whether such decoupling of the technologies of Schenkerism from their ideological encasement is possible, or indeed desirable, is yet another topic I leave to the experts. Here I simply want to acknowledge that a number of theorists of non-Western music have drawn inspiration from Schenker's approach to the analysis of musical structure: Richard Widdess, Jonathan Stock, Steve Larson, Sam Mukherji, Mike Schachter, myself, and numerous others.[28] Their work is invested in the foundational idea that melodic expression, despite design features that respond to idiomatic rhythmic, topical, and stylistic constraints, is animated by structural pitches disposed within a linear framework, and that these anchoring pitches themselves possess their own progeny—through prolongation or diminution, or by durational extension under a variety of rhythmic impulses. This idea or constellation of ideas, associated (at least in the popular imagination) with Schenker, is not without historical precedent; indeed, it is an idea so simple and yet so consequential that it is in all likelihood part of a universal practice. I predict an increased

[26] Burns CD, *Afa Songs* (Unpublished).

[27] "Trompes de Banda," CD, *Introduction aux musiques Africaines* by Monique Brandilly, track 21.

[28] Richard Widdess and Ritwik Sanyal, *Dhrupad: Tradition and Performance in Indian Music* (Aldershot, UK: Ashgate, 2004); Jonathan Stock, "The Application of Schenkerian Analysis to Ethnomusicology: Problems and Possibilities," *Music Analysis* 12 (1993): 215–240; Steve Larson, *Musical Forces: Motion, Metaphor, and Meaning in Music* (Bloomington: Indiana University Press, 2012); Somangshu Mukherji, *Generative Musical Grammar: A Minimalist Approach* (PhD dissertation, Princeton University, 2014); Michael Schachter, "Structural Levels in South Indian Music," *Music Theory Online* 21 (2015); and Agawu, "Variation Procedures in Northern Ewe Song," *Ethnomusicology* 34 (1990), 221–243.

role for linear analysis (Schenkerian, neo-Schenkerian, or otherwise) in the new African ventures that American music theory is about to undertake.

So far, then: Kerman in the 1980s didn't like non-Western music; Schenker in the 1910s and 1920s didn't think much of it. Tiersot thought we needed to know about it even if Western music is unquestionably superior. Here is a fourth and final story, with a happy ending.

Fourth: In March 2010, a small group of theorists, composers, musicologists, and ethnomusicologists gathered in Amherst, Massachusetts, thanks to the vision of Robert Schultz, Lawrence Shuster, and Kalin Kirilov, to explore a variety of analytical approaches to so-called World Music. Over three days, scholars held forth about time and rhythm, about theory and ethno-theory; we saw transcriptions of Indian, Balinese, and African music, and jazz; and there were spirited discussions of various issues, some of them ontological, others having to do with in-piece specifics. Geo-cultural reference was predictably wide: China, Cuba, India, Iran, Japan, Venezuela, Zimbabwe, and so on. Many participants seemed to welcome the opportunity to speak freely about their interest in non-Western music, and to explore this music analytically without feeling that they needed permission from ethnomusicologists, self-appointed custodians of this or that world repertoire. I dare say that the event was cathartic for some participants, and we all left Amherst with a renewed commitment to the study of so-called World Music.

It would be premature, I think, to declare that the Analytical Approaches to World Music (AAWM) movement has permanently reversed the trends and attitudes fostered by the kind of thinking we've just seen in the writings of Tiersot, Schenker, and Kerman, and which is widely echoed in the history of music theory. Nevertheless, it is gratifying to see the AAWM going from strength to strength, hosting a series of international conferences, sponsoring an interest group within the SMT, and perhaps most importantly, publishing an online journal, *AAWM Journal*, an outfit that has already acquired a distinct profile. So, in response to that huge question, How has music theory dealt with the non-West?, the example of AAWM provides some room for optimism.[29]

[29] Since 2011, the *AAWM Journal* has published over sixty articles in sixteen issues, including a single issue (Volume 3.1, 2013) featuring articles on African music. The affiliated interest group has in the meantime convened seven international conferences at Amherst, Vancouver, London, New York, Thessaloniki, Birmingham, and Paris. Recently (2022), the editors have announced the creation of region-specific sub-journals, one of them being *Analytical Approaches to African Music*.

How Can African Music Help?

I come, finally, to my main point: What do music theorists stand to gain from closer engagement with African music? How, in other words, might they benefit from this form of African aid?

I have boiled everything down to just eight platforms, which I now present in general form, without their technical underpinnings:

1. First, we gain an enhanced sense of music's texts and contexts, and an affirmation of the proposition that music is a part of society, not apart from it. By this I do not mean anything straightforwardly functional, as if African music was designed merely to serve some larger social agenda; I'm pointing rather to complex ways in which the musical and the social are mutually imbricated, including bursts of musical autonomy that defy the prescriptions of social action.
2. Second, we are forced to reckon with the precarious status of those sound-producing objects we call musical instruments—the margins of tolerance that frame the perception of pitch, the enhanced timbres, and, perhaps most importantly, the independence of musical thought from its material expression (recall the Guinean music we listened to earlier in which a performance by griots was being imitated by flutes; think also of Wagogo singers imitating the sound of instruments or Anlo brass bands playing Agbadza songs).
3. Third, we develop a renewed appreciation for the close relationship between music and language. Here are four aspects of that relationship: first, the constraints placed on melodic contour by African tone languages; second, the lexical preponderance of proto-musical items we call *ideophones* or picture words (*Lautbilder*, Westermann called them[30]); third, the use of drums not only as speech surrogates (so-called *talking drums*) but as imitators of speech surrogates (as in some performances of 1980s jùjú music); and fourth, the centrality of song and songfulness. Studying African music, be it vocal or instrumental, without some knowledge of the sound and sense of African language, can only produce an impoverished understanding. Perhaps this engagement with African languages will help engineer a long

[30] Mark Dingemanse, *The Meaning and Use of Ideophones in Siwu* (PhD diss., Max Plank Institute for Psycholinguistics, 2010), 21.

overdue linguistic turn in music theory and make good on earlier work by Lerdahl and Jackendoff, Allan Keiler, Aniruddh Patel, Somangshu Mukherji, and others.

4. Fourth, we encounter an extraordinary rhythmic imagination manifest in a variety of ways, of which I'll mention four: first, the interplay between speech rhythm, complete with its asymmetrical periodicities, and metrically confined strict rhythm; second, a body of autonomous rhythmic patterns known as time lines that serve to animate, flavor, and give identity to many a music-dance genre in Africa; third, a remarkably disciplined network of polyrhythmic behaviors that underlines the considerable aesthetic investment in a relational, communal approach to music-making; fourth, ordered and thoroughly engaging melo-rhythmic narratives performed by master drummers (or, more accurately, *mother drummers*—so-named for their procreative potential), narratives that are not mere "improvisations" but rather in-the-moment compositions based on previously internalized and practiced routines.
5. Fifth, we come to admire a melodic imagination built on the potency of small modules that can be extended infinitely into larger shapes, word-borne motifs that are at once language and music, and contours incubated in an oral-aural economy that prescribes lucidity, vitality, and communicative forthrightness, not the introspective indulgence promoted by the leisurely manner of on-paper composing.
6. Sixth, we appreciate a formal imagination animated by variation and embellishment, parataxis, and even moment form; this formal imagination is underpinned by purposeful fragmentation resulting in part from the functional role for music mentioned earlier (see Platform 1 above), and in part from an embrace of incompletion as an aesthetic category—a formal strategy, in short, based on holes rather than wholes.
7. Seventh, we reckon with the polyphonic imagination constrained by an at-least-two ethos expressed in the first instance as a complementary parallelism; nowadays, the polyphonic imagination (illustrated above) is sometimes inflected by harmonic idioms arriving from the West (including those of the Protestant hymn), giving rise to complex configurations in the interplay between tradition and modernity, the inside and the outside.

8. Eighth and finally, we're forced to reckon with the ethics and aesthetics of *appropriation*, with the rampant or even rabid globalization that has rendered African music (or nuggets of African musical ideas) not just audible but well-nigh unavoidable in the metropolitan soundscape.

It bears emphasizing that these platforms, elaborated more fully in my introductory text, *The African Imagination in Music* (2016)[31], can be accessed in other world repertoires; they do not represent uniquely African ways of doing things. Indeed, there are no uniquely African ways of being in the musical world if, by that, one means ways of being that are unduplicated in any other culture, never previously heard of, not shared by others. What the encounter with African music will bring initially is an expansion of music theory's geo-cultural vistas. And for those who stay the course, numerous conceptual, analytical, and ethical issues will soon have to be confronted. This could be an exciting and chastening journey.[32]

I'm going to have to save the composing out of these topics for a later occasion, but I wouldn't be surprised if many of you have already noted points of convergence and begun to imagine future directions. Here are just a few intersections. The issue of music's social embedding may compel a comparative analysis of egalitarian Aka society or supposedly egalitarian Venda society with Riepel's colorful and nonegalitarian assignation of functions to the harmonic universe or "system of keys,"[33] or to McClary's reading of Bach's fifth Brandenburg concerto,[34] or to Taruskin's interpretation of Stravinsky's *Symphonies of Wind Instruments* as a musical modeling of a Russian Panidka service.[35] The problematization in the African context of the distinction between sound-producing objects and musical instruments, a distinction with roots in comparative musicological thought, and renewed claims for

[31] Agawu, *The African Imagination in Music* (Oxford, UK: Oxford University Press, 2016). I should acknowledge—again—that this list conveys only a part of the African musico-intellectual heritage.

[32] Although I did not make this distinction in the keynote version of this chapter, it now seems pertinent to distinguish *music analysis* from *music theory*, and to suggest that, strictly speaking, this chapter is better titled "Rethinking Music Analysis, with African Aid" to acknowledge the interpretive paths opened up for theorists seeking such enrichment. The distinction between theory and analysis was made with particular force by David Lewin in "Behind the Beyond: A Response to Edward T. Cone," *Perspectives of New Music* 7 (1969): 59–69.

[33] Discussed in Ratner, *Classic Music: Expression, Form and Style*, 48.

[34] Susan McClary, "The Blasphemy of Talking Politics during Bach Year," in *Music and Society: The Politics of Composition, Performance and Reception*, edited Richard Leppert and Susan McClary (Cambridge, UK: Cambridge University Press, 1987), 13–62.

[35] Richard Taruskin, *Stravinsky and the Russian Traditions*, vol. 2 (1996; rpt. Berkeley: University of California Press, 2016), 488–89.

timbre's importance (see, for example, Andile Khumalo's article on "African spectralism"[36]) will find resonance in the fresh re-conceptualizations of the agency of musical instruments by Eliot Bates and Emily Dolan.[37] My own fantasy for a linguistic turn in music theory may take some clues from Aaron Carter-Ényì's empirical and ethnographic studies of Nigerian music and from the increasing attention to the sound of language in hip-hop and other popular music.[38] There is already a considerable investment in rhythm studies, but rather than study phenomena, compositions, or indeed styles in isolation, a comparative framework might bring greater insight. Pieter van den Toorn's recent reflections on Stravinsky's *Rite of Spring* highlights similar processes of stratification in Ewe Gahu music, thus setting into relief similarities as well as differences between orally conceived music and music from a written tradition.[39] And the generative path pursued by Michael Tenzer in linking *Hindewhu* (from the Central African Republic) and *Nyamaropa* (from Zimbabwe) will encourage many more speculative efforts along these lines; for African music research, Tenzer's derivational approach may boost the hitherto fragile desire to treat individual compositions as confluences of melodic forces.[40] Form has been a mainstay of Western theory and analysis, but not of African music studies. If, however, the entry point into Western forms is redefined to privilege holes rather than wholes, we stand a chance of puncturing the holistic certainties normatively prescribed by *Formenlehre* and restoring some of the precariousness surrounding our experience of form. The ostensible improvisation of polyphonic textures in many African cultures may direct theorists to similar polyphonic thinking writ large in some corners of the jazz repertoires. And finally, theorists may be enjoined to confront the ethical issues raised by the appropriation of

[36] Andile Khumalo, "Reading for 'African Spectralism' in Latozi Mphahleni's 'Modokali,'" *SAMUS: South African Music Studies* 38 (2018): 137–158.

[37] Eliot Bates, "The Social Life of Musical Instruments," *Ethnomusicology* 56 (2012): 363–395; Emily Dolan, *The Orchestral Revolution: Haydn and the Technologies of Timbre* (Cambridge, UK: Cambridge University Press, 2013).

[38] Aaron Carter-Enyi, *Contour Levels: An Abstraction of Pitch Space Based on African Tone Systems* (PhD dissertation, Ohio State University, 2016); Kyle Adams, "Aspects of the Music/Text Relationship in Rap," *Music Theory Online* 14 (2008). The linguistic turn may indeed be here already, judging from the numerous studies of text-music relations that have appeared in the last decade or two. But it awaits a naming ceremony that will enhance its institutional imprimatur.

[39] Pieter C. van den Toorn, "The *Rite of Spring* Briefly Revisited: Thoughts on Stravinsky's Stratifications, the Psychology of Meter, and African Polyrhythm," *Music Theory Spectrum* 39 (2017): 158–181.

[40] Michael Tenzer, "Transforming African Musical Cycles," *Music Theory Spectrum* 39 (2017): 139–157.

others' music, and not to restrict inquiry into the mechanics of appropriation to its aesthetical aspects. The possibilities are many.

On Pedagogy: Transcription and Contrapuntal Reading

Further composing out of the dynamics of African aid to music theory will have to wait for a future date, but I'd like to close on a pedagogical note by highlighting just two of the many quotidian practices that the encounter with African music will foster: first, establishing our unanalyzed texts through transcription; and second, developing contrapuntal readings of pieces. The first has practical advantages in getting to know music from the inside, it can claim a degree of objectivity, and it carries symbolic capital. The second taps into a slew of memories and competencies that speak to the realities of our sonic environments. If these two recommendations seem to promote slightly contradictory values, the contradiction is only on the surface; both are in fact complementary and ultimately indispensable.

First: Many of us take for granted the analyzable scores we work with. All we have to do is visit IMSLP and locate whichever score we need. With African music, we don't for the most part have pre-existing scores to work with (unless, of course, we're working in the art music realm). What we have, in addition to audio and video recordings, are oral texts residing in the memories of performers and their audiences. It is the analyst's task to create his or her own usable score for analysis.

It is surely no longer worth asking in this day and age whether it is a good idea to make a written score of an African composition. If we paid attention to the long history of attempts to reduce the sounds of non-Western music in general to notation, and if we observed the rampant experimentation that characterizes the African chapter of this history, including the many roads not taken, we would derive much insight into musical ontology. Careless arguments suggesting that compositions conceived in orality cannot be properly or completely represented, say, in staff notation are foolish distractions that serve no useful purpose. Even the most casual attention to the role that such representations play in scholarly discourse will confirm that if the thing is not written down, it has little chance of competing for power with those things that are written down. I'm taking a pragmatic rather than idealistic stance here based on my reading of the power structures in the academy. Transcriptions are means to ends, and without slighting the long and complex history of attempts to render sounds as decodable signs, we can say that the basic act of border crossing entailed in making a transcription stimulates thought and enhances musical appreciation.

Some of you are well acquainted with the joys of transcription but let me share an anecdote. I occasionally teach a graduate course in transcription. Although Africa features centrally in it, I also assign other music for exercises, including recordings of music for which we already have scores. The last time I taught the course, I included an Ivorian lament, improvisations by Ravi Shankar and Ali Akbar Khan (thanks to my former student Christopher Matthay, who took over this part of the course), a Central African lullaby, a Gabonese folk song, music by Stravinsky and Bartók, and performances by Herbie Hancock, Marion Williams, and Christina Aguilera. Crazy, I know.

Students complained about the weekly exercises, mostly about how time-consuming they were. One student told me that she spent twenty-six hours on the assignments for a particular week—as if that was a big deal. Some even tried to resist the entire exercise on philosophical grounds, but I ignored them. This was a seminar for doers, not talkers. Months after the ordeal, I overheard some students saying how much they had benefited from the process of creating these texts from scratch, how they had learned to distinguish the intended from the fortuitous, the composition itself from a specific performance of it. New intimacies had been created. The process for some had fostered cooperation between eye, ear, and imagination, and this in turn served not only as a pathway to understanding musical idioms old and new, familiar or unfamiliar, but as supplements to ear-training and engaged listening.

I actually think that all music theory curricula should include mandatory courses in hands-on transcription. And if instructors incorporate at least two African items within each reiteration of the course, our collective efforts will contribute to making a small part of the African legacy available in writing. Such availability will in turn improve the level of debate about the organizing principles of African music and, paradoxically perhaps, heighten awareness of the strengths and limitations of scorism.[41]

Second: Music theory's embrace of African music is likely also to affect the way we interpret music, in particular the intertextual worlds that we construct as horizons for our analyses. We might more actively cultivate the

[41] For a cogent, pedagogically oriented statement about the benefits of transcription, see Michael Tenzer, "In Honor of What We Can't Groove to Yet," in *College Music Curricula for a New Century*, edited by Robin Moore, pp. 169–190 (Oxford, UK: Oxford University Press, 2017).

practice of *contrapuntal reading*: reading across repertories in order to unveil unsuspected convergences or easily overlooked dependencies among the production processes of musics of diverse provenance. Stemming in part from his infatuation with J. S. Bach's counterpoint, it was Edward Said who introduced the term to encourage interpreters of metropolitan texts to factor into their interpretation the enabling roles of often far-flung but indispensable structures (e.g., reading Jane Austen's *Mansfield Park* with some awareness of the Antiguan sugar plantations owned by the protagonists, the Bertram family). The concept has been put to good use by literary scholars, among them Brent Edwards and Kathryn Lachmann.[42]

In the limited way in which I'm appropriating Said's term here (by occluding the political contexts of production and focusing for now on the resonances among musical materials), reading an African composition contrapuntally may still take many forms, depending on the scope of the analyst's horizon. I might say, for example, along with Nigerian composer Fela Sowande, the father of Nigerian art music, that a passage in Igbo *Atilogwu* music reminds me of a passage in Sibelius's Second Symphony, without batting an eyelid or fearing the reproach of self-appointed guardians of our authenticity.[43] True, folk music from eastern Nigeria and art music from Finland are far from each other, their material histories different on the surface, and yet, at least to Sowande's ears, these two musics shared certain compelling sub-surface rhythms. Contrapuntal reading is a transgressive act that often unveils convergences where we might be tempted to deny their prospect. Rather than keep our musical memories compartmentalized based on externally imposed geo-cultural politics, we should work toward the dissolution of boundaries so that the kind of observation made by Sowande does not seem far-fetched, fanciful, or inappropriate. Indeed, in view of the ways in which many of us are being sonically programmed today, contrapuntal reading is bound to play a natural role in our interpretive practices in coming years.

I realize that the kind of comparison Sowande makes is anathema to some in the ethnomusicological community. How can you compare high art to ostensibly folk music?, they will ask. Well, why not, especially if the terms of

[42] Edward Said, *Culture and Imperialism* (New York: Vintage Books, 1994); Brent Edwards, "The Sound of Anticolonialism," in *Audible Empire: Music, Global Politics, Critique*, edited by Ronald Radano and Tejumola Olaniyan, pp. 269–291 (Durham, NC: Duke University Press, 2016); Kathryn Lachmann *Borrowed Forms: The Music and Ethics of Transnational Fiction* (Liverpool, UK: Liverpool University Press, 2014).

[43] Reported by F. Abiola Irele, "Editorial: The Landscape of African Music," *Research in African Literatures* 32 (2001): 1–2.

comparison have been set up correctly? How can you compare music that is the product of written labor to music cultivated within the peculiar dynamics of orality? Again, Why not? And how can you compare the music of peasants in the African rainforest with the music of European bourgeoisie? But why not?

Not that such comparisons are unheard of in the history of thought about World Music. For example, German comparative musicologists from a century ago regularly traded in such comparisons, although a number of them worked more at the level of whole systems than within the particularities produced by hermeneutic or close reading of individual compositions. And in 1982, Klaus Wachsmann, one of the most discerning Africanists, gave the Charles Seeger lecture to the Society for Ethnomusicology in which he put into circulation the following items: African music and discourse about it, Beethoven's op. 131, Ravel's *Bolero,* and Shakespeare's *Hamlet*, including *The Tongo Hamlet*, a Ghanaian version of Shakespeare's play written by Ghanaian playwright Joe de Graft. Late in life, Wachsmann felt at liberty to draw parallels and analogies where disciplinary allegiances had previously forbidden or discouraged such actions.[44]

There is perhaps no more urgent task for music theory than to restore the comparativist impulse, juxtapose world traditions in order to reveal underlying affinities, and in general, facilitate acts of border crossing that are our passport to the future.

I thought I'd end by juxtaposing four pairs of sound worlds which have no a priori historical affinities, but which a contrapuntal reading might enjoin us not to discard. First, here are the Nigerien Fulani once more [recorded example].[45] Now compare that sense of infinite extension with the following from Penderecki's *Stabat Mater*: [recorded example].[46] Second, here are our Banda-Linda horn players once again [recorded example].[47] This time, notice the simple sequence of gestures whereby a "small" sound, a kind of shrill "call," is followed by a "big" chord featuring the entire ensemble, a kind of "response." Now compare that to the opening of Stravinsky's *Symphonies of Wind Instruments* (1920) [recorded example]. Third, compare this moment of clapping in a Pentecostal church in Accra with Steve Reich's well known *Clapping Music* (1972) [recorded example]. Fourth and finally, compare

44 Wachsmann, "The Changeability of Musical Experience," *Ethnomusicology* 26 (1982): 197–215.

45 "Choeurs des Peuls Wodabé," from the CD *Introduction aux musiques Africaines* by Monique Brandilly, track 3.

46 Krzysztof Penderecki, "Stabat Mater," on the CD *Music of our Century* (Mainz: Wergo, 1988), track 9.

47 "Trompes de Banda," CD *Introduction aux musiques Africaines* by Monique Brandilly, track 21.

the sound produced by this Angolan boy's vibrating leaf with the "water moments" in John Cage's *Water Music* (1952) [recorded example].

These sonic intersections may seem trivial or accidental, especially when heard outside their fuller contexts, but what they convey is a lesson in the power of framing: the same sounds—produced incidentally in Africa at a fraction of the cost, and tagged as the spontaneous effusions of a community whose members are denied an autonomous subjectivity—are framed in Euro-America as instances of learned, serious art music composed by master musicians in full control of their creative powers. The far-reaching affinities between what is in reality a large reservoir of African sounds, musical as well as nonmusical, and those of a heterogeneous European avant-garde, are thus undervalued, their potential for a more global dialogue muted.

I rather doubt that simply pointing to shared local environments will persuade anyone that the parallels run deep. Indeed, massive European investments in the rhetorics of sophistication, complexity, and a strategic opacity in the finished work, all of them held up as signs of refinement and advance, will not allow an easy acceptance of the kinds of affinities that I am drawing attention to. Europe's self-image depends crucially on maintaining a differential narrative.

Ladies and gentlemen: There is a lot more to say about what music theorists stand to gain from engaging with Black African music. My own list begins with insights into performance, liberation from certain crippling forms of ostensible exactitude, and a renewed and perhaps more earnest encounter with various forms of embodiment. Alas, time is not on our side.

One final thought: The ideas of some of the twentieth century's most influential thinkers have been shaped in important and fundamental ways by encounters with Others, by acts of border-crossing, in life and also in work. I'm thinking—randomly—of philosophers like Sartre, Derrida, Althusser, or post-colonial theorists like Fanon, Said, Spivak, and Homi Bhabha; or African thinkers like Mudimbe, Appiah, Irele, and Mbembe. There may be a lesson in this for all of us.

I said at the beginning that this was going to be an invitation, an invitation to rethink music theory with African aid, and in the process rethink "the exteriority of Africa, its displacement from the Euromodern" on musical terrain.[48] I wonder now at the end whether that invitation has not evolved into an ethical imperative?

[48] Jean Comaroff and John Comaroff, *Theory from the South* (2012), 3.

6
Against Ethno-Theory

Nattiez's Ambivalence

In his 1990 monograph, *Music and Discourse: Towards a Semiology of Music*, Jean-Jacques Nattiez welcomed "a new interest in 'ethno-theories'" as "one of the great virtues of ethnomusicology's anthropological orientation." By their very existence, ethno-theories, defined as "conceptions that indigenous peoples form of their own music," suggest that "the 'savage mind' can also operate in the realm of music theory, with a precision that is a bit disturbing for smug Western feelings of superiority."[1] The context in which these statements appear is a broad semiological study of a variety of discourses about music. Nattiez reflects on the very concept of music and the musical work, the nature of musical meaning, and musical analysis in theory and practice. Along the way, he invokes writers as diverse as Peirce, Ruwet, Lomax, Hanslick, Eco, Ricouer, Molino, Riemann, Schaeffner, and music by Stockhausen, Wagner, the Inuit, the Kaluli, and the Igbo. In other words, Nattiez's purview, already in 1990, was "World Music," and it is against this cosmopolitan background that we might interpret his remarks.

Ethno-theories (the plural is hardly avoidable at this level) are typically reported in ethnographically based studies by "Western" scholars of knowledge systems cultivated within cultures of (mainly) primary orality. They purport to show a high level of verbal and conceptual precision in the way that indigenous people think and talk about music. Nattiez lists writings by Feld, Keil, Powers, Sakata, Smith, Stone, Tedlock, and Zemp as the most significant contributions.[2] Although welcoming of this new development,

[1] Jean-Jacques Nattiez, *Music and Discourse: Toward a Semiology of Music*, translated by Carolyn Abbate (Princeton, NJ: Princeton University Press, 1990), 105.

[2] Nattiez, *Music and Discourse*, 186. References are to Steven Feld, *Sound and Sentiment: Birds, Weeping, Poetics, and Song in Kaluli Expression* (Philadelphia: University of Pennsylvania Press, 1982); Charles Keil, *Tiv Song: The Sociology of Art in a Classless Society* (Chicago: University of Chicago Press, 1979); Lorraine Sakata, *Music in the Mind: The Concepts of Music and Musician in Afghanistan* (Kent, OH: Kent State University Press, 1983); Sandra Smith, "The Constituents of Music Ethnotheory: An Example from the Kuna of Panama," in *Ethnotheory*, edited by Maria Herndon, pp. 1–16 (Dorby: Norwood Editions, 1982); Ruth M. Stone, *Let the Inside Be Sweet: The Interpretation

On African Music. Kofi Agawu, Oxford University Press. © Oxford University Press 2023.
DOI: 10.1093/oso/9780197664063.003.0006

Nattiez was also skeptical. On one side was a positive valuation of the *idea of ethno-theory*, responding perhaps to an ethical imperative to respect native conceptualization; on the other side was skepticism about ethno-theory's intellectual cogency, especially when its claims come into conflict with scientific knowledge:

> When an Inuk says that the throat is the point of origin of sound in Katajjaq, but modern articulatory phonetics (Ladefoged) states that there are no guttural sounds as such, I am hard put to imagine what guilt complex about ethnocentricity could allow privileging the informants' illusion above a well-established physiological fact.[3]

The semiologist does not at this point entertain the possibility that the Inuk explanation may be rooted in a self-empowering myth, or that it represents a bid for power in just the same way that the ostensibly scientific explanation proffered by modern linguistics is invested in institutional power. He is concerned only with the fact that musicians around the world can and do give accurate as well as inaccurate information to researchers, and that we should not hesitate to discount what we judge to be inaccurate.

Since Nattiez's remarks appeared, a number of other scholars have negotiated this particular tension in ways that have enriched our understanding of the dynamics of cross-cultural knowledge production. One such scholar is ethnomusicologist Marc Perlman, who in his book *Unplayed Melodies* considers the epistemology of ethno-theory and pursues the limits of theoretical articulation (and disarticulation) manifest in insider and outsider perspectives on Javanese gamelan music.[4] Another is music theorist Lawrence Zbikowski, who opposes "ethno-theory" to "theory" and

of Music Event Among the Kpelle of Liberia (Bloomington: Indiana University Press, 1982); Barbara Tedlock, "Songs of the Zuni Kachina Society: Composition, Rehearsal and Performance," in *Southwestern Indian Ritual Drama*, edited by Charlotte Frisbie, pp. 7–35 (Albuquerque: University of New Mexico Press, 1980); Hugo Zemp, "'Are'are Classification of Musical Types and Instruments," *Ethnomusicology* 22 (1978): 37–67; Hugo Zemp, "Aspects of 'Are'are Musical Theory," *Ethnomusicology* 23 (1979): 6–48.

[3] Nattiez, *Music and Discourse*, 196. Of special relevance to the African context is David W. Ames and Anthony V. King's *A Glossary of Hausa Music and Its Social Contexts* (Evanston, IL: Northwestern University Press, 1971).

[4] Marc Perlman, *Unplayed Melodies: Javanese Gamelan and the Genesis of Music Theory* (Berkeley-London: University of California Press, 2004).

exposes an inevitable asymmetry at the base of this supposed binary. In *Conceptualizing Music*, Zbikowski describes ethno-theory as "a sort of Third World shadow of 'theory.'" Ethno-theory, he declares, is "not a very comfortable concept: 'theory' remains the privileged term."[5]

There is some pussyfooting here, some dragging of feet, and it is precisely this ambivalence that I want to use as point of departure for a critique of ethno-theory in African music studies. I should admit at the outset that although the will-to-invent ethno-theories has been in force in Africanist ethnomusicology since the 1960s, ethno-theory as such is at present only an emerging discourse, not a fully developed one. Two impulses seem to direct the ethno-theoretical project. The first proceeds from a priori notions of difference held by ethnographers. The *assumption* is that other people are intrinsically different; therefore that their way of thinking must be naturally different from ours. The second, alluded to in Nattiez's remarks quoted earlier, proceeds from an ethical stance that wishes to limit "Western" impositions on the non-West by, as it were, granting the subaltern the ability to speak.

While separate in principle, the two motivations frequently converge in practice. What begins as a gesture of respect for others easily morphs into a construction of their alterity based on a historically freighted script that undervalues or even denies what is shared between cultures. Were it common to find ethno-theoretical efforts that terminate in claims of sameness—a demonstration, for example, that Others think and talk just the way we do, even though they use different linguistic expressions—we might retain some faith in the prospect that the outcome of such efforts has not been determined in advance. Alas, the prospects for cultural translatability are not always given priority by the ethno-theorist. The deck is stacked in favor of those who seek and find difference. And it is precisely here, in the making of claims about others' minds, that we encounter some of the most patronizing, demeaning, and racist attitudes in ethnographic writing.[6]

[5] Lawrence M. Zbikowski, *Conceptualizing Music: Cognitive Structure, Theory, and Analysis* (New York: Oxford University Press, 2002), 116.

[6] V. Y. Mudimbe's *The Invention of Africa: Gnosis, Philosophy, and the Order of Knowledge* (Bloomington: Indiana University Press, 1986) incorporates a subtle critique of a broad range of anthropological writing about Africa. For a narrower critique of difference in Africanist ethnomusicology, see my "Contesting Difference," in *Representing African Music: Postcolonial Notes, Queries, Positions*, pp. 151–171 (New York: Routledge, 2003).

Feld's Kaluli Example: Model or One-Off?

Steven Feld's elegant demonstration of an ethno-theory among the Kaluli of Papua New Guinea would be every ethnographer's dream. The Kaluli, we learn, have a well-developed conception of certain musical elements and practices, and these are coded in a metalanguage affiliated with the semantic fields of water, sound, space, and birds. In effect, the Kaluli problematize the boundary between the musical and the extramusical, conceptualizing musical performance as social action and interaction expressed in evocative terms and metaphors. A vivid example is the phrase, *dulugu ganalam*, meaning "lift up over sounding," which Feld describes as "a spatial-acoustic metaphor, a visual image set in sonic form and a sonic form set in visual imagery."[7]

Feld's achievement inspired a number of scholars in the 1980s and later to look in their places of work to see if their theorizing could be enriched by a more determined attempt to reclaim the native cognitive territory. In my own work on the Northern Ewe, I was encouraged to look for signs of an ethno-theoretical discourse, but the results were not encouraging. While I found indigenous terms for genres and musical instruments, and a number of active verbs designed to energize performance, I did not find a sustained reflective discourse capable of supporting fundamental distinctions between the particular and the general, nor did the Northern Ewe invest in technical discussions of form, syntax, or structure. By that I don't mean that notions of form, syntax, and structure do not occur sporadically in Ewe discourse (or, for that matter, in Yoruba, Akan, Igbo, Fon, Kpelle, and other African discourses); I simply mean that, for various socio-cultural reasons, not to mention historical-materialist factors, these notions had never been consolidated into a separate theoretical discourse. For the Ewe, theory appeared to be that which made composition and performance possible, not a body of reflective discourses cultivated by those who have the leisure to indulge in such activity.

A valuable article by Misonu Amu entitled "Glossary of Ewe musical terms" (1997) affirmed my intuition about the priorities displayed in Ewe discourse.[8] The majority of her 245 items are terms for genre or musical

[7] Feld, "'Flow Like a Waterfall': The Metaphors of Kaluli Musical Theory," *Yearbook for Traditional Music* 13 (1981): 22–47.

[8] Misonu Amu, "Glossary of Ewe Musical Terms," *Research Review* (Institute of African Studies, University of Ghana), 13 (1997): 27–45.

instrument; nine are song words, eight depict musicians, and there are sporadic references to form (such as the introductory section of a song or dance), costume, performance site, posture (such as extending one's buttocks), and state of being (such as being possessed). While this "*technical* glossary of Ewe musical terminology" names, it does not necessarily explain. Little in it is truly technical, and little touches the internal organization of the music itself. We can understand now why one prominent writer, in a gesture reminiscent of Nattiez's, decided to cut through the chase and declare that "African taxonomies, while adequate from a social and/or religious perspective, throw no light whatsoever on the systematic structure of *musical techniques* employed" (emphasis in original).[9]

Misonu Amu modeled her glossary on David Ames and Anthony King's influential *Glossary of Hausa Music and its Social Contexts* published in 1971, the first book on a sub-Saharan African society devoted exclusively to terms and concepts that convey the musical worldview of its people. Neither there nor in a subsequent work by ethnomusicologist Lester P. Monts, *An Annotated Glossary of Vai Musical Language and its Social Context* (also modeled on Ames and King's book[10]), does one glimpse the kind of technical vocabulary that might constitute a music theory rather than a "shadow of theory."[11] I consulted other work, notably that of John Blacking, who, in the 1960s and after, made a lot of noise along ethno-theoretical lines, urging us to consider what the Venda think and how they express their thoughts in talk and in acts of musical performance, and not to assume the a priori validity of our own (metropolitan) concepts and vocabulary. But here, too, one found only nibbles; moreover, it was impossible to locate specific communities among the Venda all of whose members possessed a stable body of indigenous knowledge and its attendant metalanguages that they deployed regularly in theoretical talk about music.[12]

Nor was I encouraged by the evidence assembled in writings by Paul van Thiel on the Ankole, Gerhard Kubik on various East and Southern African peoples, Rouget on the Fon, or Jones on the Zambian and Southern Ewe

[9] Simha Arom, *African Polyphony and Polyrhythm: Musical Structure and Methodology*, translated by Martin Thom, Barbara Tuckett and Raymond Boyd (Cambridge, UK: Cambridge University Press, 1991), 215.

[10] Lester P. Monts, *An Annotated Glossary of Vai Musical Language and Its Social Contexts* (Paris: Peeters-SELAF, 1990).

[11] Zbikowski, *Conceptualizing Music*, 116.

[12] See, for example, John Blacking, *Venda Children's Songs: A Study in Ethnomusicological Analysis* (Johannesburg, SA: Witwatersrand University Press, 1967).

of the existence of a native discourse that was also viable as self-standing theory rather than a collection of fragmentary inputs into a possible theory.[13] Similarly, more recent writings by Charry, Ampene, Askew, Euba, and Waterman, while mindful of indigenous expression, have not pointed to thriving ethno-discourse communities.[14] Here and elsewhere, I found, if anything, an implicit rather than explicit discourse, sporadic rather than sustained assertions, mostly confined to individual idiolects rather than broadly distributed across entire communities.

Feld's recent book, *Jazz Cosmopolitanism in Accra, Ghana*, by and large jettisons the ethno-theoretical effort associated with his earlier *Sound and Sentiment*.[15] This is not because the author is any less alert to how his collaborators talk about what they do; on the contrary, Feld reproduced their words at length throughout the book. It is rather because, for these collaborators in the Ghanaian capital, Accra, the English language (inflected, it is true, by a variety of local usages) has become a standard means of communication, even though none of them are native speakers. Feld apparently saw no need to translate their words from "Ghanaian English" into "American English" in order to recover material with ethno-theoretical potential.

So: had Feld simply been lucky to discover a rich ethno-theoretical terrain such as that of the Kaluli in 1982, or had other researchers been looking in the wrong places, or were simply not skilled enough to construct something of comparable cogency? Was it perhaps the case that the Kaluli enjoyed theorizing while the Northern Ewe (or Akan, Fon, or Igbo) couldn't be bothered, preferring simply to make music on the basis of internalized constraints, rather than talk about it after the fact? What accounts for variations in the density of verbal-theoretical discourse in communities

[13] See Paul van Thiel, *Multi-Tribal Music of Ankole: An Ethnomusicological Study Including a Glossary of Musical Terms* (Tervuren: Musée royal de l'Afrique central, 1977); Gerhard Kubik, *Theory of African Music*, vol. 1 (Wilhelmshaven: Florian Noetzel Verlag, 1994); Gerhard Kubik, *Theory of African Music*, vol. 2 (Chicago: University of Chicago Press, 2010); Gilbert Rouget, *Un roi africain et sa musique de cour: chants et danses du palais à Porto-Novo sous le règne de Gbèfa (1948–1976)* (Paris: CNRS Editions, 1996); and A. M. Jones, *Studies in African Music*, 2 vols. (London: Oxford University Press, 1959).

[14] See Eric Charry, *Mande Music: Traditional and Modern Music of the Maninka and Mandinka of Western Africa* (Chicago: University of Chicago Press, 2000); Kwasi Ampene, *Female Song Tradition and the Akan of Ghana: The Creative Process in Nnwonkoro* (Aldershot, UK: Ashgate, 2005); Kelly Askew, *Performing the Nation: Swahili Music and Cultural Politics in Tanzania* (Chicago: University of Chicago Press, 2002); Akin Euba, *Yoruba Drumming: The Dùndún Tradition* (Lagos: Elokoto Music Centre and Bayreuth African Studies Series, 1991); and Christopher Waterman, *Jùjú: A Social History and Ethnography of an African Popular Music*. (Chicago: University of Chicago Press, 1990).

[15] Steven Feld, *Jazz Cosmopolitanism in Accra: Five Musical Years in Ghana* (Durham, NC: Duke University Press, 2012).

throughout the world? And how can the moral imperative to incorporate native understanding be formulated so that it neither forces a discovery of what is not there, nor leaves the researcher feeling that he or she has ignored a potentially illuminating dimension of a community's musico-intellectual life?

A Lesson from Ethnophilosophy

While these early ethno-theoretical projects were unfolding in ethnomusicology in the 1980s, a burgeoning literature on postcoloniality inspired by Edward Said's *Orientalism* was bringing to the fore questions of knowledge ordering and the politics of representation, including the occidental representation of others across a vast historical period.[16] One tributary of this intellectual movement revolved around work in African philosophy and literature, spearheaded by Valentin Mudimbe's *The Invention of Africa*, Paulin Hountondji's *African Philosophy: Myth and Reality*, Kwasi Wiredu's *Philosophy and an African Culture*, Abiola Irele's *The African Imagination: Literature in Africa and the Black Diaspora* (2001), and Kwame Anthony Appiah's *In My Father's House*.[17] I turned to this literature in part to see what analytical methodologies were in use, and how colleagues in the humanities were negotiating the challenges of the prefix "ethno." How were literary scholars, for example, analyzing poems and ritual texts? Were some methods figured as "African," others as "Western"? Could some of the approaches be described as ethno-theoretical? Answers to these questions varied, of course, but it appears that Appiah's strictures on structures notwithstanding,[18] the consensus was to let the outcome determine the value of a given analytical proceeding, rather than prohibit a proceeding because its method was invented in Paris, Montreal, or Berlin rather than in villages far from Lagos, Nairobi, or Accra.

[16] Edward W. Said, *Orientalism* (New York: Vintage Books, 1978).

[17] See Mudimbe, *The Invention of Africa*; Paulin Hountondji, *African Philosophy: Myth and Reality* (Bloomington: Indiana University Press, 1983); Kwasi Wiredu, *Philosophy and an African Culture* (Cambridge, UK: Cambridge University Press, 1980); Abiola Irele, *The African Imagination: Literature in Africa and the Black Diaspora* (New York: Oxford University Press, 2001); and Kwame Anthony Appiah, *In My Father's House: Africa in the Philosophy of Culture* (New York: Oxford University Press, 1992).

[18] Anthony Appiah, "Structures on Strictures: The Prospects for a Structuralist Poetics of African Fiction," in *Black Literature and Literary Theory*, edited by Henry-Louis Gates Jr., pp. 127–150 (New York: Methuen, 1984).

As for ethno-theories, African philosophers were already engaged in a vigorous debate about the related concept of ethnophilosophy. The idea of a collective philosophy attributed to African peoples and said to exhibit a cogency comparable to Western philosophy had been proposed by Placide Tempels in his 1942 book, *Bantu Philosophy*.[19] Tempels reconstructed a Bantu philosophical investment in forces, and this enabled him to contest the enduring prejudice that Africans lacked a philosophy. A Belgian missionary in the then-Belgian Congo, Tempels' aim was to unveil the workings of the African mind not as an end in itself but as a means to an end; and that end was to facilitate the civilizing mission through Christianity. If we can understand better the way native minds work, if we can grasp the bases of their philosophical system, we can civilize them more efficiently with our Christian beliefs—so reasoned Tempels.

Tempels' project was based on a problematic assumption of unanimist belief across Bantu communities, and Hountondji, in particular, has taken exception to the power ploy implicit in referring to Africans always in the plural, denying the role of individual agency, and failing to embrace the ambition to establish an explicit, "scientific" discourse that transcends the local. Again, without rehearsing all aspects of the critique of ethnophilosophy here, we can suggest that there is a certain isomorphism between ethno-theory and ethnophilosophy. Ethno-theory is in that sense a problematic discourse at the moment of birth, for it is founded on a will to a larger cultural difference that mutes its sensitivity to the very foundational *critical* activity that serves as philosophy's condition of possibility. If we model our thinking and writing about African music on postcolonial African philosophers', then ethno-theory will have to be rigorously thought through before it can serve our purposes.

Emerging Ethno-Theories in African Music Studies

The most immediate gesture in the direction of ethno-theory is the invocation of African-language words in an ethnographer's text. Typically, the writer points out absences using locutions like "They do not have a word for music" or "There is no word for rhythm in their language." He or she may also remark on unfamiliar images such as "The song is going down the road" or

[19] Placide Tempels, *Bantu Philosophy* (Paris: Présence africaine, 1959).

"We hear the dance." While all this seems innocent enough, its ultimate goal as a step in the construction of an indigenous theory is dubious.

Consider the use of African-language expressions in three ethnomusicological texts by Nketia, Stone, and Friedson. In Nketia's 1974 classic, *The Music of Africa*, readers will not find very much in the way of African language data associated with conceptual constructs.[20] It would be hasty to conclude, however, that an African point of view is missing from the book. Only a scholar with a keen understanding of the place of music in African culture, including its linguistic expressions and conceptualization, could have assembled many of the observations in *The Music of Africa*. Ethno-theory, on the evidence of this book, is an implicit discourse; it informs the construction of the text, but it is not displayed as a separate discourse. By contrast, Ruth Stone devotes an entire chapter to Kpelle conceptualization in her book, *Let the Inside be Sweet*.[21] Here, African-language data is gathered to support the use of sound symbolism, the naming of genres, and the denotation of performance actions. On first view, one might conclude that Stone's study, by virtue of its surface deployment of African-language concepts, leads the reader to the workings of the African mind more deeply than does Nketia's. But that would be an unfortunate inference. Speakers of other African languages often find Nketia's English formulations resonant with theirs. This suggests that Nketia thought through the native categories and found ways of rendering them paradigmatically in English. Of course, he *does* use African-language data when occasions demand, but he also recognizes the translatability of concepts.

A third approach is found in Steven Friedson's more recent book, *Remains of Ritual*.[22] Here I believe we have reached another limit in the supposed representation of the native mind. The author includes African-language names and concepts on practically every page. But do we really need to know the Ewe words for *door*, *goat*, *soup*, *fence*, and the like, unmarked words in everyday discourse? If so, why not write the entire book in Ewe?

The Ewe words are meant to assure readers that the author is conversant in Ewe, but the extent to which they advance our understanding of Ewe conceptualization is far from guaranteed by such excess. Friedson's project as a whole embraces the production of differences almost as an article of

[20] J. H. Kwabena Nketia, *The Music of Africa* (New York: Norton, 1974).

[21] Stone, *Let the Inside Be Sweet*..

[22] Steven Friedson, *Remains of Ritual: Northern Gods in a Southern Land* (Chicago: University of Chicago Press, 2009).

faith, so it is not surprising that he has gone to such lengths to suggest a degree of semantic opacity where none exists. Professional posturing of this sort leaves untouched larger claims about how Others think because it privileges acts of crass naming over translation. It is striking how distant Friedson's project is from Nketia's or Stone's. If an ethno-theoretical orientation is meant to guide us to how the Ewe (as portrayed by Friedson) or Kpelle (as portrayed by Stone) or Africans in general (as portrayed by Nketia) think, I doubt that we would automatically accord first place to Friedson's book simply because it splashes African-language words across its pages.[23]

When Experts Disagree

We may glimpse a related aspect of the precarious nature of ethno-theoretical construction from the following anecdote about the naming of parts in pygmy polyphony.

1994. In an article entitled "Intelligence in Traditional Music," Simha Arom reports that BaAka people characterize their polyphony as having "four constituent parts: *ngúé wa limbo* ('mother of song'), *mo.tangole* ('that which gives its words'), *o.sese* ('below,' subordinate to mo.tangole), and *di.yei* ('yodeling')."[24] This is precisely the kind of native scheme that facilitates the construction of an ethno-theory. In this Central African Republic oral culture, controllers of discourse about music have apparently developed technically sophisticated terms to designate the constituent parts of a polyphonic texture.

2006. Suzanne Fürniss draws on this framework to analyze Aka polyphony.[25] This is a direct application; there is no tweaking of the framework, no questioning of its status as a pan-Aka scheme.

2009. Revisiting an old debate about the origins of polyphony, Victor Grauer refers in passing to Arom and Fürniss's word *motangole* as "the name

[23] For promising leads into the realms of indigenous knowledge—not to be equated with ethno-theory—see George Worlasi Kwasi Dor, "Exploring Indigenous Interpretive Frameworks in African Music Scholarship: Conceptual Metaphors and Indigenous Ewe Knowledge in the Life and Work of Hesinɔ Vinɔkɔ Akpalu," *Black Music Research Journal* 35, no. 2 (2015): 149–183. doi:10.5406/blacmusiresej.35.2.0149.

[24] Simha Arom, "Intelligence in Traditional Music," in *What Is Intelligence?* (Darwin College Lectures 1992), edited by J. Khalfa, pp. 137–160 (Cambridge, UK: Cambridge University Press, 1994).

[25] Suzanne Fürniss, "Aka Polyphony," in *Analytical Studies in World Music*, edited by Michael Tenzer, pp. 163–204 (New York: Oxford University Press, 2006).

supposedly provided by the Aka themselves for the 'principal voice' of any song" (my emphasis).[26] In search of corroboration, Grauer turns to another expert on Central African music, Michelle Kisliuk, who "spent much time in the field investigating the musical practices of the same Pygmy group studied by Arom and Fürniss, the Aka." His enquiry elicits a surprising response: Kisliuk "denied any knowledge of a fixed four-part scheme as the basis for Pygmy polyphony, as described by Fürniss."[27] Is it really conceivable that Kisliuk, working within the same set of communities, had never come across a nomenclature that supposedly framed discourse by the Aka about their polyphonic practices? Kisliuk is emphatic about her inability to corroborate its provenance:

> When I read an essay by Fürniss in which she asserts that each "voice" has a particular name, and that somehow each voice is a particular and necessary part of a song, I was surprised, as I'd never heard such a systematic description of voice or part by BaAka. This summer [2007] in CAR [Central African Republic] I attempted to verify her findings with people I've known for years, and though my interviews were not widespread, I could not find a single person for whom Fürniss's terms or even idea seemed familiar.[28]

Ethnographers differ in what they seek and find, but the assertions and denials in this little story raise questions about Aka ethno-theory. Was the four-fold scheme perhaps once part of a thriving institutional discourse that has disappeared since it was first reported in 1994? Were the terms known only to a handful of individual Aka? Or did they emerge under a particular regime of interrogation? Might the terms be of prior metropolitan origin? We would obviously need more information to ascertain the truth, but what is significant here is the contradictory nature of the testimonies. The fact that two groups of researchers working with the same people in a relatively compact area in the Central African Republic are unable to agree on the very existence of an ostensibly common set of terms used to describe the organizational framework of pygmy polyphony says a lot not only about their techniques of field investigation, but also their desires for the people they

[26] Victor Grauer, "Concept, Style, and Structure in the Music of the African Pygmies and Bushmen: A Study in Cross-Cultural Analysis," *Ethnomusicology* 53 (2009): 403.
[27] Grauer, "Concept, Style, and Structure," 413.
[28] Michelle Kisluik, email of October 30, 2007; quoted in Grauer, "Concept, Style, and Structure," 414.

study. By these lights, ethno-theories exist precariously; indeed, they sometimes approximate inventions.

Five Reasons to Be Wary of Ethno-Theory

Here, then, by way of summary and an extended conclusion, are five reasons to be wary of ethno-theory. In stating them so directly, I aim to provoke discussion and debate. Ideally, issues of this magnitude and intricacy would be worked through a series of texts and historical circumstances, but limitations of space forbid that. Perhaps, however, a programmatic statement against ethno-theory will help engender that larger discussion.

A first and perhaps paradoxical reason is that ethno-theory appears not to exist. It is an apparition, a hopeful construct rather than a knowable discourse. Often mentioned and desired, it seems not to be located anywhere in particular. Of the nine titles listed by Nattiez in his "short bibliography of ethno-theories," only two deal with Africa, those by Keil and Stone.[29] Keil's 1979 book, *Tiv Song*, scrutinizes the Tiv lexicon and points to the imbrication of individual items in intricate semantic fields, but denomination without a fuller social delineation of the use of these terms and concepts limits their status as theory. Moreover, given that many of the terms are translatable into English, what we are presented with in the book are "Tiv ways of conceptualizing music" and not "uniquely Tiv ways of conceptualizing music." By erasing non-uniqueness, we erase difference and thus undermine the putative ontological basis for the construction of ethno-theory.[30]

It could be argued that even though ethno-theory does not exist now, it might come into being in the future through the cumulative efforts of individual scholars. Ethno-theory may thus be thought of as something of a promissory note, a desirable future discourse. Like heaven, hell, or purgatory, ethno-theory would be a thing for believers rather than non-believers. Unfortunately, the trajectory of discourse since the 1960s does not

[29] Nattiez, *Music and Discourse*, 186; Keil, *Tiv Song*; Stone, *Let the Inside Be Sweet*.

[30] The claim that a term in an African language is untranslatable into a metropolitan language is unintelligible to me. Terms may not have one-word equivalents across languages, but as long as they are understood, they must be capable of rendition in another language, even if the translation is cumbersome. In some ethnographic contexts, it is part of the (ideological) script to maintain a deficit at all costs in negotiating conceptual transfers between languages. The claims of ethno-theory are shaped by this ideological bias.

inspire confidence in such an optimistic projection. The efforts of Blacking, Merriam,[31] Keil, and latterly Kubik serve as useful reminders that native musicians, too, have ways of talking about music, but they have not (yet) inspired a large ethno-theoretical project. Indeed, scholars nowadays seem more interested in broad and comparative approaches involving dialogue with metropolitan theory, rather than ethnically confined approaches aimed at portraying difference from metropolitan theory.

A second reason to reject ethno-theory is that the categorical distinction it presupposes between "African knowledge" and "Western knowledge" is extremely fragile, if not simply false. In 2003, I argued that "beyond local inflections deriving from culture-bound linguistic, historical, and materially inflected expressive preferences, there is ultimately no difference between European knowledge and African knowledge."[32] I fully expected some resistance to that bald statement, but although the book in which it appears received its share of criticism, this particular claim was overlooked by my most uncompromising critics, Veit Erlmann and Louise Meintjes.[33] It is of course possible that the claim was not deemed worthy of a response, but is it also possible that it threatens the very foundations of the ethnomusicological project?

The construction of a fundamental difference between European and African knowledge originated in European thought. Since the eighteenth century at least, the enabling mindset of many ethnographers has been a presumption of difference, not a presumption of sameness. Erlmann indeed gives the title "Resisting sameness" to his review of my book *Representing African Music*. The presumed dichotomy between African and Western knowledge has in turn provided some justification for the search for ethno-theories. Kubik, for example, once lamented the fact that "publications are rare in which African music is described according to the concepts and ideas of the people in the musical cultures concerned."[34] In other words, African music has too often been described without the benefit of its ethno-theories.

[31] Alan P. Merriam, *The Anthropology of Music* (Evanston, IL: Northwestern University Press, 1964).

[32] Agawu, *Representing African Music*, 180.

[33] See Veit Erlmann, "Resisting Sameness—À propos Kofi Agawu's 'Representing African Music,'" *Music Theory Spectrum* 26 (2004): 291–304 and Louise Meintjes, Review of *Representing African Music*, *Journal of the American Musicological Society* 59 (2007): 769–777.

[34] Kubik, "The Emics of African Rhythm," in *Cross Rhythms* 2, edited by Daniel Avorgbedor and Kwesi Yankah, p. 30 (Bloomington, IN: Trickster Press, 1985).

Kubik then adds that African musicologists have been of no help in resolving this matter because of the way they are trained:

> Most African musicologists . . . have had a predominantly Western approach in their studies of African music. . . . As a consequence of Western musical training they often tend to hear African music similarly to a Western observer.[35]

This extraordinary statement, so confident about the power of Western education to wipe out the last trace of African-ness from an African musicologist, denies individual agency and leaves little room for individuals who, precisely because of their "Western" education, are able to interrogate the "Western approach" keenly, not only in words about music but also—and importantly—through deeds in music. Individuals like the Nigerian composer-musicologists Fela Sowande, Meki Nzewi, and Joshua Uzoigwe each endured "Western musical training" but none could be described as having a "predominantly Western approach in their studies of African music." Is it a surprise that such musicians have not been enamored of ethno-theory?

The most vocal advocates of an African approach are—ironically—Westerners who are often familiar with the "Western approach." Their reasons for seeking to jettison the latter in favor of a little African authenticity are not always self-evident, but they are often traceable to a fundamental will-to-difference that animates the anthropological project. The problem is that the putative "African approach" is always already mediated, always already inflected by the "Western" scholar's desire to construct an authentically African way of thinking. Ethno-theorists thus go to great lengths to seek out the "bush African," not the city African. Bush Africans normally do not participate in metropolitan knowledge production except as informants. They supply ideas, words, and phrases, perhaps even offer some explanation, but it is rare to find them dictating the shape of the resulting theory or stabilizing a meta-language. Nor do bush Africans normally read the theories that ostensibly describe their ways of thinking and talking about music.

Indeed, the reception of ethno-theory can reach amusing heights of arrogance when, assured that bush Africans will probably never read what we write, assured that they will never "write back," so to speak, ethno-theorists return to the field with the books and articles they have written

[35] Kubik, "The Emics of African Rhythm," 30.

about indigenous people, read them out loud, and record their responses for incorporation into future publications. "Dialogic editing," as it has been called, rests ostensibly on a dialogue between the ethnographer and his or her field associates.[36] This is surely a dialogue among unequal parties, however, and it points to one of the less savory aspects of the ethno-theoretical project: the downplaying of the huge gaps in material endowment and profound asymmetries of power between researcher and the researched. It is perhaps little wonder that one rarely encounters a list of the benefits that have accrued to African communities on account of ethno-theoretical exploitation. Benefits accrue overwhelmingly to the individual scholar and his or her interpretive community in the metropolis.

The construct "African knowledge," when deployed in an ethno-theoretical context, is meaningless in the absence of clear borders between it and Western knowledge. A favorite move of ethno-theorists is to locate African knowledge in verbal expressions that differ from those commonly found in the ethnographer's culture. Expressions like "The song caught our throats" and "The mother drum stammers" provide the sort of data that ethno-theorists are drawn to. These colorful expressions illuminate the descriptive and naming priorities within specific African communities, but they also facilitate the pursuit of "writerly" ambitions that do not necessarily serve critical-theoretical ends. Ethno-theories after all are texts.

In any case, isolated lexical items do not add up to a theory. What about the context in which a given expression appears? How do terms combine to form a comprehensive statement with predictive power and explanatory capability? How do different speakers use these expressions in analysis? In attempting to answer these questions, one quickly realizes that there are few models in the field of Africanist ethnomusicology. It appears that ethno-theory is simply not localized anywhere. Is ethno-theory then nothing more than a fleeting, intermittent, or decorative set of effects in a field of discourse not otherwise differentiated from other fields of discourse?

A third reason to reject ethno-theory is that, as a concept, it does not appear to be supported by a constitutive opposition that would guarantee its validity. If "theory" is regarded as the opposing term, then ethno-theory would appear marked while theory would be unmarked. Ethno-theory thus boasts a particularity that theory shuns because theory's claims are in principle

[36] Feld, "Dialogic Editing: Interpreting How Kaluli Read *Sound and Sentiment*," *Cultural Anthropology* 2 (1987): 190–210.

generalizable. Purporting to represent the thinking of whole communities, ethno-theory claims the same kind of generality, but it is always already dependent on theory. The two are thus distinct rather than opposed.

We might also ask why we use the term "ethno-theory" when dealing with Kpelle, Vai, Ewe, Luo, Hausa, or Yoruba, but "theory" when dealing with Mozart, Beethoven, Brahms, or Stravinsky. Why are the treatises of Rameau, Koch, Riemann, and Schenker designated as "theory," whereas those promulgated by Stone (on behalf of the Kpelle), Nzewi (on behalf of the Igbo[37]), and Thiel (on behalf of the Ankole) are consigned to the category "ethno-theory"? Insofar as their repertorial purview is geo-culturally confined to Austro-Germanic music, the theories of Riemann and Schenker could be said to constitute the equivalent of ethno-theories. However, in both designation and aspiration, the prefix "ethno" does not accompany such "Western" usages. The repertoires analyzed are said to be "standard," and the explanatory theories are often presented as if they were universally applicable. A will to power is inscribed in such universalist claims, whether they be those of a Schenker or a Riemann, or of their peers and successors who practiced comparative musicology (like Hornbostel and Marius Schneider). "Ethno-theory" and "theory" thus represent different kinds of bid for power.

A fourth factor to consider in evaluating ethno-theory is the sociological fact that African scholars appear not to be especially interested in ethno-theory. If one examines the writings of African scholars like Nketia, Euba, Vidal, Omojola, Uzoigwe, Sanga, and Nzewi, one does not find anywhere a sustained discussion of ethno-theory. Instead, one finds the sporadic influence of indigenous ideas and vocabulary woven into a more general explanatory or theoretical framework. Consider the example of Nketia, who was able to strike a balance between the particular and the general. His little book from 1949, *Akanfo Nnwom bi* [*Some Akan Songs*], a compilation of seventy-five song texts belonging to different genres, including adowa, adenkum, and nnwonkoro, is rich in indigenous ideas about Akan song and performance.[38] (It is yet to be discovered by ethno-theorists.) In his introduction, Nketia explains the origins of various genres, describes performing strategies and performance occasions, and interprets the drum language. Several technical

[37] Meki Nzewi, *Musical Practice and Creativity: An African Traditional Perspective* (Bayreuth, Germany: IWALEWA-Haus, University of Bayreuth, 1991).

[38] J. H. Kwabena Nketia, *Akanfo nwom bi [Akan Songs]* (London: Oxford University Press, 1949).

terms are introduced and explained, so readers seeking African essences will find much to feed that particular fantasy. Nketia did not maintain this stance toward ethno-theory in later writings, however. In *The Music of Africa*, African-language terms and concepts are introduced from time to time, but they are incorporated into a broader, more cosmopolitan theoretical effort. For this African scholar, then, ethno-theory—if that is what it is—has no separate or autonomous existence; it is simply part of an analytical or theoretical effort to understand a given cultural phenomenon.

Nketia's approach has become paradigmatic for a more recent generation of African scholars. Writing about the Akan genre *Nnwonkoro*, for example, Kwasi Ampene reveals vivid terms of indigenous origin for the parts of song, for calling and responding, for beginning and ending, and for making polyphony.[39] These terms are introduced as parts of a larger theoretical effort, not as items in a separatist category designed to capture the ways in which indigenous practitioners think about their music. That is why they appear alongside terms of ostensibly "Western" origin. Although Ampene does not pause to engage the politics of theoretical posturing, it is obvious that he advocates a cosmopolitan approach that incorporates insights from both local and global theory.

Even Meki Nzewi, probably the staunchest advocate among African ethnomusicologists of indigenous perspectives, is finally not invested in ethno-theory. His is a theoretically diversified portfolio assembled pragmatically from a variety of sources. For example, in his 1991 book on musical practice and creativity, he employs a number of Igbo terms for concepts of play and structure, while in *Musical Sense and Meaning* he explains several aspects of Igbo cultural practice with due attention to indigenous conceptions.[40] Thus "mother drum" is opposed to "master drum" (explained in reference to the procreative potential of the mother). Indigenous terms are not gathered into a separate ethno-theory, however, because in Nzewi's thinking no such boundary exists. Theory is always already marked by ethno-theory, just as ethno-theory stakes a claim to theoretical status.

A fifth—and reciprocal—reason to be wary of ethno-theory is the interest shown in it by "Western" scholars. Ethno-theoretical

[39] Ampene, *Female Song Tradition.*

[40] Nzewi, *Musical Practice and Creativity*; Nzewi, *Musical Sense and Musical Meaning: An Indigenous African Perception* (Amsterdam: Rozenberg Publishers, 2010).

constructions are academic discourses designed for consumption in the Western academy. Consider the example of British ethnomusicologist John Blacking. During the 1960s and 1970s, he emerged as one of the most passionate advocates, if not of ethno-theory in name, then of the impulses affiliated with it. In a series of writings starting with his dissertation-turned-book (*Venda Children's Songs*, 1967) through a popular and popularizing study of the nature of human musicality (*How Musical Is Man?*, 1973) to a posthumous collection of reflective essays, *Music, Culture and Experience* (1995), Blacking touts the particularisms of ethno-theory within a broad view of music as social action.[41] We come to know the Venda as a musical people, and to understand their philosophy of music as different from that of Western classical music practitioners. Laboring under an ideology of difference, Blacking sought native understanding of musical process in order to critique Western thought and practice. Ethno-theory guaranteed that the thoughtworld of the Venda would be permanently perceived as separate from that of a Mahler or an Alban Berg. Yet every one of Blacking's characterizations of Venda music-making is available in the metropolis, just as the impulses that motivate Mahler's and Berg's compositional choice are readily relatable to those of the anonymous Venda composers. Blacking's differences were always already fragile.

The appeal of ethno-theory to non-Africans studying Africa stems in part from its promise to uncover and dramatize differences whose production is *the* enabling condition of ethnomusicological work. If I announce, for example, that the Igbo concept of *nkwa*, which some have translated as "music," includes not one but three elements (singing, playing instruments, and dancing), I can immediately distance Igbo conceptions of music from Western conceptions. But one does not have to be an apostle of sameness to see that two of the three elements of Igbo music—singing and the playing of instruments—are shared by Western music from most eras, while the third, dance, is either present or supplementary to a number of prominent genres—minuets, mazurkas, and waltzes. Attempts to keep these worlds apart oftentimes under-report what is shared among cultures. Add to these affinities the previously noted rich prospects for cultural translation and we see why ethno-theory is a problematic discourse.

[41] See Blacking, *Venda Children's Songs*; Blacking, *How Musical Is Man?*; and Blacking, *Music, Culture and Experience: Selected Papers of John Blacking* (Chicago: University of Chicago Press, 1995).

Postscript

When Jean-Jacques Nattiez announced "a new interest in ethno-theories" stemming from the work of anthropologically oriented ethnomusicologists three decades ago, he seemed in principle favorably disposed to them. At the same time, however, he was urging caution about what exactly we choose to embrace in the process of cross-cultural knowledge production.

In this essay, I have stepped to the right of Nattiez to argue against ethno-theory because I believe that ethno-theory is ultimately a confining rather than liberating discourse. A liberating discourse would incorporate all of the ethno-theorist's data into a larger cosmopolitan construct. While no less committed to the specifics of indigenous thinking and expression, such a discourse rejects their ostensible separateness and insists on the dialogical entailments of indigenous categories. Such a discourse is already in evidence in certain areas of rhythm research, including writings by Simha Arom, David Locke, Polo Vallejo, Willie Anku, Godfried Toussaint, Rick Cohn, and Martin Scherzinger.[42] These writings lay bare the workings of the African creative imagination using the sharpest tools irrespective of origin; they incorporate indigenous perspectives not in the form of symbolic displays of informants' words, but by incorporating insights from pedagogy, reception and close analysis into a broader analytical inquiry. The ingenuity of lead drumming, the versatility of songsmiths, and the imaginative projections of poets—these and other aspects of African creativity need to continue to be analyzed within a cross-cultural framework. Although the theory deployed in such ventures, like all theoretical ventures, offers no ultimate guarantees as such, it gains in its principled resistance to the "ghettoizing" and patronizing temptations associated with ethno-theory. At this historical-political conjuncture, what we need in Africa are strong forms of conceptualization in the form of theory, not the titillating exoticisms associated with ethno-theory.

[42] Simha Arom, *African Polyphony and Polyrhythm*; David Locke, *Dum Gahu: An Introduction to African Rhythm* (Tempe, AZ: White Cliffs Media, 1998); Polo Vallejo, *Mbudi mbudi na mhanga: universo musical infantil de los Wagogo de Tanzania [The musical universe of the Wagogo children from Tanzania]* (Madrid: Edicion del autor, 2004); Willie Anku, *Structural Set Analysis of African Music 1: Adowa* (Legon, Ghana: Soundstage Production, 2002); Godfried Toussaint, *The Geometry of Musical Rhythm: What Makes a "Good" Rhythm Good?* (Bosa Roca: CRC Press, 2013); and Martin Scherzinger, "Negotiating the Music-Theory/African Music Nexus: A Political Critique of Ethnomusicological Anti-Formalism and a Strategic Analysis of the Harmonic Patterning of the Shona Mbira Song *Nyamaropa*," *Perspectives of New Music* 39 (2001): 5–118.

7

African Rhythm Studies

A Historical Sketch and a Critique

Every so often, a scholar who feels up to it takes stock of achievements in a given research area for the benefit of students and other scholars. The aim usually is to provide an overview of findings, recognize methodological trends, highlight the most influential work, and facilitate an assessment of what remains to be done. Outside of dictionary and encyclopedia entries, such panoramic viewing has happened only infrequently in Africanist ethnomusicology. The reasons are varied. Aside from the sheer scale of such an undertaking, scholarly production (on the continent especially, but outside it too) is diffuse and not always centralized institutionally. Then also, scholars come with different orientations, meta-languages, and professional skills, and their publications are addressed to different interpretive communities. Indeed, the presumption that all researchers share the same goals (or even similar goals) is embraced with widely divergent degrees of enthusiasm.

There are exceptions, however, and it is from these exceptions that I draw inspiration for the exercise undertaken in this chapter. In 1997, Gerhard Kubik assembled a conspectus of studies of multipart singing in Sub-Saharan Africa, their histories and systematics.[1] This survey has proved invaluable to students seeking broad acquaintance with the kinds of polyphonic thinking manifest in various African genres. In the same year, Kwabena Nketia provided an overview of scholarship on African music with special emphasis on the contributions of African scholars.[2] This unique survey, undertaken by an experienced senior scholar with an admirably broad perspective, offered a nuanced Africa-centered history while responding critically to competing ideologies of representation. Undoubtedly, the one subject that

[1] Gerhard Kubik, "Multipart Singing in Sub-Saharan Africa: Remote and Recent Histories Unravelled," in *Symposium on Ethnomusicology*, edited by A. Tracey, pp. 85–97 (Grahamstown, S.A.: International Library of African Music, 1997).

[2] J. H. Kwabena Nketia, "The Scholarly Study of African Music: A Historical Review," in *Africa: The Garland Encyclopedia of World Music*, edited by Ruth Stone, pp. 13–73 (New York: Garland, 1997).

On African Music. Kofi Agawu, Oxford University Press. © Oxford University Press 2023.
DOI: 10.1093/oso/9780197664063.003.0007

has tempted scholars to assess what has been done, and yet has remained intractable to cumulative, paradigm-falsifying inquiry, is rhythm. In 1980, ethnomusicologist Robert Kauffman undertook a state-of-the-art assessment of rhythm studies for the Society for Ethnomusicology's flagship journal, *Ethnomusicology*.[3] Touching on key concepts while raising basic questions about their applicability, Kauffman analyzed rhythmic construction in repertoire items from Eastern and Southern Africa, areas that not only fell within his own geo-cultural expertise but had hitherto not functioned centrally in representations of "African rhythm" as an essentialized, continent-wide phenomenon. A couple of years later, anthropologist Alan P. Merriam took on studies of time-reckoning, incorporating summaries of inquiries into African time by anthropologists while seeking an authentically African view of time as circular rather than linear or developmental.[4] And in a book first published in 1985 and translated into English six years later, ethnomusicologist-theorist Simha Arom offered a magisterial review of studies of nonspecialist as well as specialist accounts of African rhythm as a prelude to his own comprehensive theory of African polyphony and polyrhythm.[5]

Why rhythm? It bears repeating that the word *rhythm* does not occur in many of the indigenous languages of Africa. According to Kubik, rhythm "is not an emic category in Africa. No term has been isolated in any African language whose semantic field would be congruent with the Western notion 'rhythm.'"[6] The semantic field of a putative "African rhythm" encompasses qualities that fall within the domains of timbre, duration, accent, intonation, pattern, and grouping. Nevertheless, many Euro-American writers (who, after all, are numerically dominant in this field of research) have maintained that of all the dimensions of African music (melody, polyphony, harmony, timbre), rhythm or "the whole time aspect of music"[7] is the most distinctive and complex; it is also the most challenging for Western listeners.

[3] Robert Kauffman, "African Rhythm: A Reassessment," *Ethnomusicology* 24 (1980): 393–415.

[4] Alan P. Merriam, "Concepts of Time Reckoning," in *African Music in Perspective*, pp. 443–461 (New York: Garland, 1982).

[5] Simha Arom, *African Polyphony and Polyrhythm: Musical Structure and Methodology*; translated from French by Martin Thom, Barbara Tuckett, and Raymond Boyd, pp. 45–91 (Cambridge, UK: Cambridge University Press, 1991). See also Christopher Waterman, "The Uneven Development of Africanist Ethnomusicology: Three Issues and a Critique," in *Comparative Musicology and Anthropology of Music*, edited by Bruno Nettl and Philip V. Bohlman, pp. 169–186 (Chicago: University of Chicago Press, 1991).

[6] Kubik, *Theory of African Music*, vol. 2 (Chicago: University of Chicago Press, 2010), 5.

[7] Kerman, *Listen*, 3rd ed. (New York: Worth Publishers, 1980), 5.

Let's recall a few variations on the theme of Africa's rhythmic exceptionalism. Hornbostel, writing in 1928, found the parts in a piece of African drumming "syncopated past our comprehension."[8] Jones wrote in 1949 that "the outstanding characteristic of African music [is] . . . a highly developed rhythm." Andre Schaeffner suggested in 1956 that "rhythm in African music is more persuasive and more subtle than in any other music." Leopold Senghor identified imagery and rhythm as "the two fundamental characteristics of the African-Negro Style" and claimed, with an uncanny choice of words that anticipate the conduct of several post-independence African political regimes, that "nowhere else has rhythm reigned as despotically."[9] For Nketia, writing in 1974, "an understandable emphasis on rhythm" stems from the fact that "African music is predisposed towards percussion and percussive textures"; indeed, "rhythmic interest often compensates for the absence of melody or the lack of melodic sophistication."[10] In 1979 Chernoff claimed that "rhythmic complexity is the heart of African music,"[11] while Jon Pareles in 1998 identified the African continent as a place "where rhythm rules."[12] Gyimah Labi wrote in 2003 that "rhythmic sophistry constitute[s] the hallmark of African music,"[13] and according to Daniel Avorgbedor, "Musical rhythm is foremost among those African traits that have captured and qualified the sensations and narratives both of amateurs and scholars throughout the ages; it continues to dominate the current literature on African music."[14] David Temperley summed it up neatly in 2000: "That rhythm is of paramount importance in African music, and a major source of its richness and complexity, is a widespread popular notion, but one which has also received a good deal of scholarly affirmation."[15]

These comments could be multiplied, of course; they typify the consistently high, admiring, even ecstatic valuation of the rhythmic element in African music. In addition to qualitative, phenomenological, or experiential questions seeking access to the primal and spiritual dimensions of the

[8] Hornbostel, "African Negro Music," *Africa* 1 (1928): 52.

[9] Leopold Senghor, "Africa-Negro Aesthetics," *Diogenes* 16 (1956): 37, 30.

[10] Nketia, *The Music of Africa*, 125.

[11] Chernoff, *African Rhythm and African Sensibility*, 93.

[12] Jon Pareles, "The Rhythm Century: The Unstoppable Beat," *New York Times*, May 3, 1998, 1.

[13] Gyimah Labi, *Theoretical Issues in African Music: Exploring Resources Creatively* (Bayreuth: Bayreuth African Studies, 2003), 10.

[14] Avorgbedor, "East and West Africa," in *Oxford Bibliographies in Music*, accessed July 5, 2021, https://www.oxfordbibliographies.com/view/document/obo-9780199757824/obo-9780199757824-0175.xml.

[15] Temperley, "Meter and Grouping in African Music: A View from Music Theory," *Ethnomusicology* 44 (2000): 65.

rhythmic experience, there are narrowly technical ones dealing with meter and grouping, the location of "one" in the beat scheme, the number of meters operating simultaneously within a given composition or performance, and the principles by which the layers within a multi-layered work are coordinated. The fact that these issues return again and again throughout the history of writing on African rhythm may prompt some readers to ask why.

One obvious answer is that something in the phenomenon itself continues to intrigue us, to elicit attention. Is it Hornbostel's syncopation or motion, Brandel's hemiola, Jones's polyrhythm and polymeter, Locke's off-beat rhythms, multimeter, and simultaneous dimensionality, Nzewi's melorhythm and ETC (Ensemble Thematic Cycle), Kubik's "inverted perception," Anku's 12- and 16-set units, Betterman's "musical rhythms in heart period dynamics," or Friedson's ambiguity? As we will see, these and other traits have formed points of focus for many inquiries. A less obvious answer stems from the unequal power relations between Africa and the West. Here we might speculate that the underlying impulse behind some of these inquiries, knowingly or unknowingly, is less concerned with the pursuit of an ultimate empirical or analytically supported truth, than with a kind of ritual enactment of power in knowledge construction. Given the (colonial and postcolonial) historical, political, and institutional frameworks within which these inquiries are pursued, fixation on rhythm may be interpreted as an index of an unconscious desire to keep Africa permanently "un-understood" (or "under-understood" or misunderstood). As long as this strategic attribution of opacity obtains, the power differential is maintained, and Africa can remain a fertile and ready source for the enactment of various analytical fantasies, including racist text-making. The non-cumulative profile of the literature on African rhythm as a whole and the occlusion of movement and dance as powerful forces that have the potential to clarify rhythmic expression may lend support to this viewpoint.

Motivations are hard to prove, however, so although no one doubts the asymmetries of power that have shaped the library of African rhythm, there is no easy or collegially acceptable way to establish such causalities definitively. What is beyond dispute, as Avorgbedor has noted, is that research into this favorite subject has grown apace since the reviews of Kauffman and Arom in the 1980s. Therefore, another stock-taking exercise may be in order. My approach is a little different, however. I will be commenting informally on African rhythm scholarship for the benefit of the general student, not necessarily specialists. Within the framework of a simple periodization, I provide vignettes of selected scholarly contributions. Then, in an extended conclusion, I reflect broadly on the character of this scholarship and what it tells us about authorial priorities and strategies in this area of African musicology.

Two caveats about what follows: First, nothing I say here is intended to undermine the enduring belief that the domain of rhythm, however one configures it, is elaborated in interesting, creative, and ingenious ways by African composers and performers. Rhythm, however, is not the only dimension of African music that is subject to such nuanced treatment. Polyphonic procedures, language-based melodic patterning, and socially induced formal strategies all show high levels of imagination in a variety of genres and performances. Why these other dimensions are not similarly lauded remains an open question. For those who might want to right the priorities, the present focus on rhythm should properly be regarded as a first step toward a larger exploration of African creativity, one that will eventually extend to other musical dimensions. Second, I will be treating large bodies of scholarship in a brisk, cursory, and selective fashion. While the hoped-for payoff is a bird's-eye view of trends in discourse, the danger of a skewed or incomplete representation of the sometimes wide-ranging, nuanced, and evolving thinking of individual scholars is real. Alas, all synoptic views are always already in danger of being at once necessary and necessarily inadequate, so I can only hope that the benefits in this case outweigh the losses.

Figure 7.1 sets out basic information about Anglo-American scholarship on African rhythm in the twentieth and twenty-first centuries. Column 1 shows the decade in which a given work was produced, column 2 identifies scholars while column 3 lists one or more of their influential works.

1920s

William F. Ward (1900–1994). Historian, educator and amateur musician, Ward lived in the Gold Coast from 1924 to 1940, taught English, history, and music at Achimota School, and conducted fieldwork (including extensive oral interviews) in various parts of the country, especially among the Akan. He attended many live musical performances and made preliminary notations of some of the patterns he heard. A few of these are included in the important article published in 1927, "Music in the Gold Coast." In it Ward identified polyrhythm as a pertinent feature of African rhythm, understood that ensembles were organized hierarchically, and drew a distinction

Decade	Scholar	Principal Works
1920s	William F. Ward	"Music in the Gold Coast," 1927
	Erich von Hornbostel	"African Negro Music," 1928
1950s	Rev. A. M. Jones	"African Rhythm," 1954
		Studies in African Music, 2 vols. 1959
	John Blacking	"Some Notes on a Theory of African Rhythm Advanced by Hombostel," 1955
	Rose Brandel	"The African Hemiola Style," 1959
1960s	Rose Brandel	*The Music of Central Africa*, 1961
	Gerhard Kubik	"The Phenomenon of Inherent Rhythms in East and Central African Instrumental music," 1962
	J. H. Kwabena Nketia	African Music in Ghana, 1962
		Drumming in the Akan Communities of Ghana, 1963
	Gilbert Rouget	"African Traditional Non-Prose Forms," 1966
	John Blacking	*Venda Children's Songs*, 1967
1970s	James Koetting	"Analysis and Notation of West African Drum Ensemble Music," 1970
	Hewitt Pantaleoni	"Three Principles of Timing," 1972
	Mieczslaw Kolinski	"A Cross-Cultural Approach to Metro-Rhythmic Patterns," 1973
	J. H. Kwabena Nketia	*The Music of Africa*, 1974
	John Miller Chernoff	*African Rhythm and African Sensibility*, 1979
1980s	Alan P. Merriam	*African Music in Perspective*, 1982
	David Locke	"Principles of Offbeat Timing," 1982
		Drum Gahu, 1987
	Alfons M. Dauer	"Afrikanische Musik und völkerkundlicher Tonfilm," 1983
	Jeff Pressing	"Cognitive Isomorphisms between Pitch and Rhythm," 1983
	Simha Arom	*African Polyphony and Polyrhythm*, 1985 (Eng. Trans., 1991)
	Gerhard Kubik	"The Emics of African Musical Rhythm," 1985
	Ruth M. Stone	*Dried Millet Breaking*, 1988
	Marcos Branda-Lacerda	*Kultische Trommelmusik der Yoruba*, 1988
1990s	Meki Nzewi	*African Music: Theoretical Content*, 1991
	Akin Euba	*Yoruba Drumming*, 1991
	Willie Anku	*Structural Set Analysis of African Music I: Adowa*, 1992
	Gerhard Kubik	*Theory of African Music, volume 1*, 1994
		Africa and the Blues, 1999 (Chapter 3)
	Kofi Agawu	*African Rhythm: A Northern Ewe Perspective*, 1995
	Gilbert Rouget	*Un roi africain et sa musique de cour*, 1996

Figure 7.1 African rhythm scholarship in the twentieth and twenty-first centuries: A sketch

Decade	Scholar	Principal Works
2000s	David Termperley	"Meter and Grouping in African Music," 2000
	Willie Anku	*Structural Set Analysis 2: Bawa*, 2002
	Kofi Agawu	*Representing African Music*, 2003 (Chapters 3 and 4)
	Godfried Toussaint	"Classification and Phylogenetic Analysis of African Ternary Rhythm Timelines," 2003
	Polo Vallejo	*Mbudi Mbudi Na Mhanga: The Musical Universe of Wagogo Children*, 2004
	James Burns	*"The Beard Cannot Tell Stories to the Eyelash": Creative Transformation in an Ewe Funeral Dance-Drumming Tradition*, 2005
		Female Voices from an Ewe Dance-Drumming Community: Our Music Has Become a Divine Spirit, 2009
2010s	James Burns	"Rhythmic Archetypes in Instrumental Music from Africa and the Diaspora," 2010
	Rainer Polak	"Rhythmic Feel as Meter: Non-Isochronous Beat Subdivision in Jembe Music from Mali," 2010
		"The Lower Limit for Meter in Dance Drumming from West Africa," 2017
	Gerhard Kubik	*Theory of African Music, volume 2*, 2010
	David Locke	"*Yeweṿu* in the Metric Matrix," 2010
		The Metric Matrix: Simultaneous Multidimensionality in African Music," 2011
		"An Approach to Musical Rhythm in Agbadza," 2019
	Marcos Branda Lacerda	*Música Instrumental no Benim: Repertório Fon e Música Bàtá*, 2014
	Godfried Toussaint	*The Geometry of Musical Rhythm: What Makes a "Good" Rhythm Good?*, 2013
	Martin Scherzinger	"Mathematics of African Dance Rhythms," 2017
		"Temporalities," 2018

Figure 7.1 Continued

between foreground and background patterns. Ward's article, together with Hornbostel's 1928 essay, has proved immensely influential, and may, with hindsight, be said to have inaugurated the field of twentieth century African rhythm studies.

Erich von Hornbostel (1877–1935). An Austrian comparative musicologist of the Berlin School, Hornbostel never set foot on African soil; nevertheless, he managed to write insightfully about African music by studying materials brought over to Germany from the field, including sound recordings, musical instruments, and eyewitness accounts. In his often-cited 1928 article, he discusses melodic shape, mode, musical form, and rhythm. He also includes brief transcriptions in staff notation. Perhaps his most influential contribution was his claim that physical motion is a crucial component of African performance; indeed, motion is co-constitutive of musical elements. "We proceed from hearing, they from motion," he famously wrote, and in the process claimed a fundamental difference between African and European conceptions. The idea of motional patterns was subsequently taken up by other scholars, among them John Blacking, Ruth Stone, and Gerhard Kubik.

1950s

Rev. A. M. Jones (1889–1980). To Jones, an Englishman who spent twenty-two years in Zambia (then called Northern Rhodesia) as a missionary, we owe the first transcriptions *in extenso* of the polyrhythmic textures of African drum music. From his earliest studies of African music, including one entitled "African Rhythm," Jones incorporated notated samples of African drum music. But it was his two-volume *Studies in African Music* published in 1959 that provided the most comprehensive portrait of the music. Transcribing page upon page of master drum patterns, Jones facilitated a variety of analytical inquiries. One such inquiry was a motivic analysis of the ostensibly improvised patterns played by the mother drummer. This approach would later be deepened by David Locke, who also produced numerous transcriptions *in extenso* in his doctoral dissertation and in several books and journal articles; it would also be reformulated in terms of set manipulation by Willie Anku. Jones's material came from Zambia (where he had done fieldwork) and from the Gold Coast (where he had not, although it was his good fortune to have met and worked with Desmond Tay, a remarkably skilled and knowledgeable Ewe musician resident in London during the 1950s). Jones understood African ensemble music not only as polyrhythmic (a widely acknowledged structuring principle), but also, and misleadingly, as polymetric. Fabrice Marandola nicknamed him "the apostle of polymeter."

The debate about polymeter continues to this day. "In contrast to most Western music," wrote Chernoff in 1979, "African music cannot be notated without assigning different meters to the different instruments of an ensemble." Composer Steve Reich similarly modeled his transcriptions of Ewe dances Agbadza and Gahu on Jones's method, inserting bar lines before perceived accents, thus implying that each ensemble member had his own meter. A number of scholars have contested this idea (Nzewi, Agawu, Kolinski, Arom, Anku, Avorgbedor, Burns), arguing that ensemble performance is often constrained by a shared beat, and that the accompanying dance steps or choreographic supplement often reveal the metric feel. Nevertheless, the desire among writers to pluralize (or, as Anku once said to me, to *scatter*) the ensemble music is strong. The affordances of analytical readings that deny the existence of a centralized beat are more numerous because they allow the analyst to play with possibilities, not necessarily plausibilities. One can suggest a level of independence in the actions of players and singers, or claim a perceptual undecidability by invoking concepts like "multistability" or "simultaneous multidimensionality." Indeed, the idea of polymeter has made something of a comeback in recent years in the writings of Friedson, Locke, Chemillier, and Scherzinger. John Collins has gone further in interpreting multiplicities in various domains as conveying an essentialized African trait manifest in polyrhythm, polymeter, polytheism, polygamy, and polyglottism. Future research will require ethnographic support for, and empirical demonstrations of, how culture bearers and especially performers acknowledge and execute polymetric structures.

Throughout Jones's work, one finds an engagement with basic issues in rhythmic analysis, including concepts of stress, accent, duration, and meter. By embracing staff notation, he sought to render the material immediately comprehensible to a large number of metropolitan musicians. Few subsequent writers on African rhythm have been able to proceed without Jones's precedent. Although there are whiffs of missionary and colonial discourses in Jones's writing, his recognition of what is pertinent has stood the test of time. Jones's work does not necessarily follow ethnomusicological protocol; it is better thought of as a contribution to the wider field of African musical studies and music theory. Arom's 1985 assessment that *Studies in African Music* "remains to this day [1985] the major contribution to the technical study that is, the musicological study of African rhythm and polyrhythm" may not require much tweaking three decades later.[16]

Rose Brandel (1915–1993). Brandel was an influential American ethnomusicologist, composer, and teacher who studied, among others, various Central African repertoires, drawing from then available Smithsonian Folkways recordings. Her analyses were based on numerous transcriptions of songs and drum music made entirely by ear. Although she encountered African musicians in New York City, she was, like Hornbostel, an armchair ethnomusicologist. Again, like Hornbostel, she was knowledgeable about Western music and often sought comparisons between African music and

[16] Arom, *African Polyphony and Polyrhythm*, 80.

Europe's early music. Central to Brandel's theory of rhythm is the preponderance of so-called hemiolas (3 in the time of 2). In some of her transcriptions of Central African music, meter is represented as an additive rather than a divisive phenomenon. She created scores that resemble Stravinsky's scores, complete with series of irregularly alternating meters. For a comparison, see, for example, the following succession of meters starting at Rh 186-2 of *The Rite of Spring*: $\frac{3}{4}$, $\frac{2}{4}$, $\frac{5}{16}$, $\frac{4}{16}$, $\frac{2}{16}$, $\frac{2}{8}$ ($\frac{4}{16}$), $\frac{5}{16}$, $\frac{2}{8}$ ($\frac{4}{16}$), all unfolding in the space of eight bars.

1960s

Gerhard Kubik (b.1934). Kubik is an Austrian ethnologist, Africanist, ethnomusicologist, and trained psychoanalyst, and one of the best-known scholars of African music. He has done more time in the field than almost all of the outsiders on this list. His numerous recordings, made in some fifteen countries, are housed in the largest private archive of African oral data located at the Phonogrammarchiv in Vienna. Although Kubik's expertise extends well beyond the subject of rhythm, he has, since his earliest writings from the 1960s, advanced a number of influential notions about African rhythm. One is the distinction between what is played and what is heard: "The image as it is heard and the image as it is played are often different from each other [in African instrumental music]," he wrote. He was thinking specifically of styles of xylophone and lamellophone playing in Uganda, Mozambique, Zimbabwe, Angola, and elsewhere, in which successions of large intervals produce registrally separate melodies and cyclical but metrically unaccented patterns, often delivered at fast tempos. Kubik has also identified an African "oral notation" consisting of mnemonic devices or vocables with specific timbral properties.

Two volumes titled *Theory of African Music*, the first published in 1994 and the second in 2010, include definitive accounts of selected aspects of rhythm. One aspect stems from Hornbostel-inspired ideas about music and motion, the claim being that this particular conjunction is a feature "of pan-African validity." Another is a set of ideas pertaining to "the cognitive study of African musical 'rhythm.' " Kubik postulates a three-tiered framework for understanding the nature of rhythmic articulation: elementary pulsation (also referred to as "density referent" by Koetting and others), the reference beat (which may be closest to hand claps), and the cycle, a level of subjective timing "created by integrating the elementary pulsation, the beat and the basic theme of a musical piece" (typified by so-called time-line patterns). Kubik has long been fascinated by African time-line patterns, and he has studied their distribution throughout West and Central Africa, their striking absence from the United States but not the Caribbean, and their interesting mathematical properties. Another theory of which Kubik seems especially proud is the existence of an individual (as distinct from a shared) beat for certain ensemble performances, as for example the amadinda xylophone with multiple players. It was apparently A. M. Jones who first hit upon the idea, but Kubik rediscovered it and demonstrated its ramifications in other repertories. Aspects of rhythm including time, pedagogy, language, emic perception, and what Kubik calls inverted perception (contrasting Western and African perceptions of certain patterns) are elaborated along the way.

J. H. Kwabena Nketia (1921–2019). If Kubik is the best-known outsider researching African music, Nketia, who passed away only recently (2019), is his counterpart among insiders. Trained in linguistics, Nketia was active as a teacher, researcher, author, composer, and scholar. While—again like Kubik—he would probably not describe himself as a specialist in the narrower field of rhythm studies, his many writings, ranging from ethnographically focused studies of Akan culture (funeral dirges, drumming, folk songs) to broader studies of aesthetics and meaning in African music, and modern developments in choral and art music, frequently include significant attention to rhythm. Nketia was one of the first scholars to give serious attention to the rhythms of spoken language, a necessary topic for anyone studying the methods by which drummers think and talk within the constraints of the timbral, tonal, and articulative resources of their instruments (so-called *Atumpan* drums feature prominently in Nketia's work). An understanding of the rhythms of language can also illuminate ways in which songsmiths mold text into tune, or how lead singers improvise songs. In other publications, Nketia posited a distinction between free rhythm and strict rhythm, the former being declamatory and metrically unconstrained, the latter being subject to an explicit and often externalized metrical constraint. It was he who invented the now widely accepted term *time line* to describe bell patterns commonly used in ensemble music. Like Jones and Brandel, Nketia invested in additive rhythm as the hallmark of African music.

Gilbert Rouget (1916–2017). Rouget was a French linguist, anthropologist, and ethnomusicologist who took up the challenge of recording African music in what was then known as French West Africa. His 1996 book, *Un roi*

Africain et sa musique de cour: Chants et danses du palais à Porto-Novo sous le règne de Gbèfa (1948–1976), a highly detailed study of music at the court of King Gbèfa of Benin, displays Rouget's commitment to song style and function through meticulous transcriptions. Rouget shows that this mostly vocal court music, sung syllabically, is often metrically constrained by time lines played on bells and very occasionally on drums. There may be room for debate about the size of the metrical unit that Rouget identifies, but there is no disputing the cyclic nature of King Gbèfa's wives' performances. In other writings, Rouget showed a keen sense of the sound and sense of language, including the rhythms of language.

John Blacking (1928–1990). Blacking, an Englishman, was one of the leading scholars of his generation. An anthropologist and ethnomusicologist, Blacking's main fieldwork was carried out among the Venda of South Africa, whose children's songs formed the subject of his 1965 doctoral dissertation from the University of Witwatersrand. (The dissertation was subsequently published as a monograph in 1967 and reissued in paperback in 1995). Blacking ranged widely across various areas of ethnomusicological theory and analysis, often drawing on his Venda experience to counter many conventional ideas about human musicality, notably in his widely read book, *How Musical is Man?* Although he would probably not have considered himself a specialist on rhythm, Blacking was, among other things, intrigued by Hornbostel's notion that Africans proceed from motion while Europeans proceed from hearing, and he sought to test its validity on other terrain. By basing his study of Venda children's songs on copious transcriptions, Blacking opened the door to considerations of time and rhythm. While he was reticent about using time signatures, he took note of recurring hand claps, note groupings, and the dynamics of syllabic articulation. As part of a larger ideological stance, Blacking was adamant that researchers seek the views of the researched on such matters as the ontological differences between music and non-music. For the Venda, that particular distinction turned on the presence or absence of a regular beat, the former being speech, the latter music. These efforts to foreground an emic viewpoint contributed significantly to the cultivation of an ethno-theoretical discourse in Africanist ethnomusicology.

A tendency to reify difference, marked in Hornbostel's work, may be seen in some of Blacking's work, often in discussions bearing on music's temporal dimension. For example, Blacking once related an anecdote about a choral competition in Zimbabwe in the course of which the African conductors flipped notions of upbeat and downbeat entirely. They interpreted every first note of each phrase of the competition piece, "On Richmond hill there lives a lass," as a downbeat. Thus, instead of following the correct declamation (Version 1), the African conductors placed the accents at the beginning of each phrase (Version 2), thus misreading the anacrustic character of the tune:

Version 1
On **Richmond** hill there **lives** a lass
More **bright** than May Day **morn**
Whose **charms** all other **maids** surpass
A **rose** without a **thorn**

Version 2
On Richmond hill **there** lives a lass
More bright than May **Day** morn
Whose charms all **other** maids surpass
A rose without **a** thorn

The principle behind the confusion would later be explained by Lerdahl and Jackendoff as a conflation of grouping structure and metrical structure, grouping structure referring to the patterns initiated by onsets and beginnings of motivic and phrase groups, while metrical structure refers to a fixed grid of notionally strong and weak beats in alternation and marking regular periods of time. Blacking's claim was that the African conductors treated upbeats as downbeats, ascribed a nominal accent to the onset of each phrase, and thus marked the words *on*, *there*, *more*, *day*, *whose*, *other*, and *a* for attention. This kind of thinking, according to which European and African conceptions (particularly of rhythm and meter) are said to be diametrically opposite, occurs frequently in Africanist ethnomusicology. It is, of course, a fragile claim.

1970s

James Koetting (1939–1984). American ethnomusicologist Koetting died young, but he had already established himself as a clear-thinking ethnomusicologist who had studied with various master musicians at UCLA and followed that with fieldwork in Ghana. His 1970 article is widely cited because it is the first full exposition of the so-called Time Unit Box System (TUBS) of musical notation originally designed by Phillip Harwood at UCLA in the early 1960s. Its use is meant to minimize some of the a priori baggage that Western staff notation brings. TUBS, which carries an implicit critique of "Western" staff notation, has survived in the work of later rhythm theorists, including Stone, Arom, Kubik, Toussaint, and others. It is fair to say, however, that TUBS has not become the dominant mode of representing African rhythm. Koetting's article is noteworthy also in incorporating insights from learning to drum African music and paying attention to the words of his teachers, especially where those words contradicted the teacher's actions. The acquisition of this kind of ethno-theoretical knowledge is a theme in the writings of Blacking and Merriam. Finally, and as an aside, Koetting is responsible for one of the all-time favorite recordings of World Music used in courses in North America: a recording of postal workers at the University of Ghana canceling stamps in a catchy highlife rhythm.

Hewitt Pantaleoni (1929–1988). An American ethnomusicologist and educator, Pantaleoni studied Anlo drumming and developed views about its structural properties. He was one of the first scholars of African rhythm to seek to represent dance steps using a form of Labanotation, and to correlate these with rhythmic articulation. He wrote with an analytical focus rather than the broad brush of theory. While his work has not produced a school of thought, a number of his ideas about meter and rhythm and word accents have remained part of the discourse on African rhythm.

Mieczslaw Kolinski (1901–1981). A composer and scholar, indeed a composer who used non-Western materials (he is reported to have made over 2,000 transcriptions of music from Samoa, New Guinea, Suriname, West Africa, Haiti, and British Columbia), Kolinski sought an explicitly cross-cultural understanding of African rhythm. His comparativist forebears had brought various world musics together under one roof, so to speak, but there is a difference between the constellation-like comparative musicology of Hornbostel and his colleagues, and the more intense and compositionally mediated cross-cultural study that Kolinski and others practiced. His concise 1973 article introduces a useful distinction between commetric and contrametric accents, a distinction that would later be explored at length by Simha Arom in music from Central Africa. Arom shows that contrametric accents predominate over commetric accents in African music. Kolinski offered a passing critique of the notion of polymeter that would be elaborated in later writings by Arom, Anku, Nzewi, and myself.

John Miller Chernoff (b.1947). Chernoff studied theology and drumming, but he is really a writer at heart, and has written a highly successful account of his encounters with barmaids in Togo and Ghana. His 1979 book, *African Rhythm and African Sensibility* remains one of the most engaging studies of African music. After living in and exploring various parts of West Africa, mainly Ghana, Chernoff felt able to identify an African "sensibility" as it is manifest in rhythmic expression. His book is strong on the ethical as well as aesthetical values inscribed in various performances and repertoires. Although he includes a couple of tiny transcriptions in the book, his main concern is not with notation-based analysis (as we find, for example, in the publications of Jones and Locke) but with an understanding of rhythm informed by a performer's or learner's experience. Chernoff did not always resist the temptation to proceed from a premise of difference rather than sameness in constructing his ethnography ("The Western and African orientations to rhythm are almost opposite," he wrote), but it is entirely possible that embracing sameness would have knocked the bottom out of his project altogether, given that the very act of writing—evident in both his ethnomusicological and anthropological writings—is taken more seriously by him than by most scholars of African music.

1980s

Alan P. Merriam (1923–1980). Merriam, an anthropologically oriented ethnomusicologist who combined an interest in ethnographic studies (he did fieldwork among the Songye of the DRC and the Flathead Indians in the USA) with theoretical reflection on the field of ethnomusicology. An enduring aspect of his thought is the tripartite model for ethnomusicological research that has helped a generation of students frame their research. The model consists of the sounds themselves, behavior, and the conceptualizations of musicians and audiences. It acknowledges but does not necessarily privilege the kind of musical orientation that shaped the contributions to African rhythm that we are summarizing here. Again, Merriam would probably not consider himself a specialist of African rhythm, but his articles on the subject are significant. One such article is a summary and critique of African concepts of time reckoning. In it, Merriam contrasted the West's ostensibly linear time with Africa's ostensibly circular time. This dichotomy has been problematized recently by Martin Scherzinger. Merriam was reluctant to make certain assumptions about African rhythmic practice—for example, that it is based on a succession of equal pulses. Among concepts he endorsed was the contentious one of polymeter.

Alfons M. Dauer (1921–2010). Dauer's main writing is on jazz, but he also did fieldwork in Africa (Zimbabwe, Senegal, and Ghana). He researched the connections between African-American and African music. His interest was in time and rhythm, especially as revealed through moving images and various motoric actions. These elements are given a fuller airing in the work of Kubik.

Jeff Pressing (1946–2002). Pressing, an Australian-American psychologist and composer, studied African drumming at UC Berkeley and also in Australia. Drawing on tools from mathematical group theory, but combining these with exemplary sensitivity to cultural matters, Pressing wrote several original papers investigating the internal properties of African rhythmic patterns and their diasporic or Black Atlantic derivatives. His seminal 1983 article on "cognitive isomorphisms between pitch and rhythm" retrieves the spirit of comparison from comparative musicologists like Hornbostel from the early part of the twentieth century and moves the argument into the cognitive realm. For example, Pressing finds parallels between the structure of African time lines and Euro-American modes and scales. Thus the standard bell pattern [2-2-1-2-2-2-1] is held to be equivalent to (cognitively isomorphic with) the diatonic major scale, which has an identical intervallic profile. Although doubts have been expressed about the legitimacy of such isomorphisms, Pressing's insight and numerical representations have proven influential in recent work by theoretically minded scholars like Jay Rahn, Rick Cohn, and Godfried Toussaint.

David Locke (b.1949). With Locke, an American ethnomusicologist and performer who has done fieldwork among the Dagomba and Ewe, and who has on occasion brought the "field" to America by facilitating residencies for his African teachers, we can speak without hesitation of a specialist in African rhythm. In an impressive and widely read body of writings, Locke has emerged as the principal heir to A. M. Jones. Working on the basis of extensive transcriptions, Locke has provided the clearest articulation of the basic principles of West African ensemble drumming. Such principles as offbeat timing, meter, polyrhythm, and the accumulation of motifs in lead drum improvisation are well discussed in his work. Working with Ghanaian drummer Gideon Alorwoyie, he has made a special study of Agbadza. Recently, Locke's admiration for the multidimensionality of African rhythm has led him to explore analogies with cubist visual art and to revive previously discredited notions like polymeter or multimeter.

Simha Arom (b.1930). From a musicological or music-theoretical standpoint, the most rigorous and systematic characterization of the inner structure of African rhythm is found in the work of Simha Arom, an ethnomusicologist of Israeli and Belgian origins based in Paris. Arom's main fieldwork was in the Central African Republic, where he spent four years in the 1960s. His interests were divided equally between documentation, making high-quality recordings, and drawing aggressively on appropriate technology to illuminate performers' (and composers') conceptions of music-making. Like Jones, Anku and Locke, Arom is quite clearly a specialist in rhythm, although his contributions extend to other topics, such as polyphony and organology, and not only in Africa. (Georgian polyphony is a recent interest). His magnum opus, *African Polyphony and Polyrhythm* (1985, translated into English in 1991) is one of the key texts in the analysis of African rhythm (and for that matter, African music). Arom is without rival in the methodological explicitness of his approach, which has roots in the taxonomic-empirical methods that formed the earliest phases of structuralism and musical semiology. Arom has drawn on the performance of horn ensembles of the Banda-Linda to illuminate the foundations of polyrhythmic performance in Central Africa. In addition to caring about terminology, representation, methodology, Arom retains an interest in both the abstract possibilities and the concrete realizations of rhythmic patterns. He holds a deep conviction about what he has called "intelligence in traditional music." If theoretical abstractions took something of a back seat in ethnographically based work on African music in the 1960s and 1970s, they returned with a vengeance in Arom's work of the 1980s and beyond.[17]

Ruth M. Stone (b.1945). The daughter of missionaries to Liberia, Ruth Stone is an American ethnomusicologist whose mentors include the aforementioned scholars Brandel and Merriam. Her main fieldwork is among the Kpelle in Liberia, and she often draws on intimate knowledge of Kpelle language and cultural traditions to craft her ethnographies. Stone's first book, *Let the Inside Be Sweet*, was a study of what might be called the rhythmic life of African performance, and it is perhaps not surprising that this particular interest led her to issues of time, temporality, and performed language.

[17] Nattiez makes this point strongly in "Simha Arom and the Return of Analysis to Ethnomusicology," *Music Analysis* 12 (1993): 241–265.

Working with an admirably broad conception of rhythm, she is willing to venture beyond the narrow mechanics of strict rhythm to more elusive dimensions, such as ways in which Kpelle sculpt time in verbal as well as musical performance. A second book, *Dried Millet Breaking*, may be read as a meditation on various modes of temporal organization stemming from performed speech. And in the more recent *Music in West Africa* (2004), focused again on her Kpelle materials, discussion of rhythm encompasses not only the qualitative forms associated with language and narration derived from her earlier work, but explores the comparative alignment of various time-line patterns using TUBS notation.

Marcos Branda-Lacerda. A scholar from Brazil, Lacerda studied in Germany (Cologne and the Freie Universität Berlin) and did field work among the Fon in Benin. His work is laced with transcriptions of polyrhythmic music and analyses of lead-drum performance. He has a lot to say about meter, motifs, and grouping, and about the alignment of parts in a polyrhythmic texture, with due attention to on- and offbeatness. There is, in addition, exemplary awareness of spectral regions of instruments and empirical accounting for duration and articulations. Branda-Lacerda recognizes affinities between Fon and Ewe styles and so frequently incorporates dialogue with scholarship on Ewe music.

1990s

It is probably no more than mere coincidence that the 1990s in my periodization are dominated by Africa-born scholars. Although African contributions to rhythmic studies had begun as early as the 1950s and were subsequently developed in the writings of Sowande, Nketia, Cudjoe, Bebey, Ballanta, and Kyambiddwa, they had not attained much prominence in cosmopolitan spaces; nor had they become the basis for an internal (i.e., intra-African) critical discourse. But thirty years or so after independence, the cumulative significance of these contributions could no longer be hidden.

Meki Nzewi (b.1938). After early studies and professional activity in Nigeria, Nzewi took his PhD under the legendary John Blacking at Queens University in Belfast. He has been active as a performer, scholar, choreographer, and novelist. A unique voice among Africanists, Nzewi advocates an unabashed Africa-centered approach to all matters affecting our music. He is deeply skeptical of the views and theories of outsiders and Western-trained

Africans, and has devoted many pages to correcting various misperceptions, many of them having to do with the foundations of rhythmic organization. For example, in his 1991 book, Nzewi presented highly suggestive glosses on the basics of rhythmic organization. Rhythm, he maintains, is actually *melorhythm* (a term he invented for African musicology) because most expressions of rhythm on drums, insofar as they have more than one pitch, subtend a melodic element as well. So-called *cross rhythm*—or as he prefers to characterize it, "inter-rhythm"—expresses complementation rather than conflict. (Jones had claimed that "clash and conflict" were central to African rhythmic expression, and Chernoff has repeated that view several times). Cross rhythm is further analogous to spatial movement in which two separate moving bodies avert near collision as they travel through space. Nzewi argues that polyrhythm and polymeter are not valid concepts: polyrhythm misses the "melorhythmic essence" of ensemble performance, while polymeter misses the fundamental pulse that unites all ensemble participants. And regarding time lines, Nzewi prefers to call them "phrasing referents," and regards them as static, super-structural components that do not deserve half the attention given to them in the literature. The combative tone in some of Nzewi's writing is motivated in part by a struggle against English-language colonization of discourses about African music. Nzewi's work is at the frontline of postcolonial resistance and has gained in status as a rich, original, and thought-provoking body of work.

Akin Euba (1931–2020). Euba was a composer, performer, and ethnomusicologist who, after earlier training in Nigeria, the UK, and the USA as pianist and composer, took the PhD under Nketia at the University of Ghana, Legon. Euba's dual commitment to composition and scholarship has resulted in a wide and varied body of work. While he does not offer a theory of rhythm as such, he is alert to the mechanics and subtleties of rhythmic organization in the repertories he writes about. Notable among them is Yoruba dùndún drumming, the subject of his doctoral dissertation and subsequent book. Euba's work, too, is laced with transcriptions designed to support analytical claims. He demonstrates the interplay of strict and free rhythm and the affordances of $\frac{12}{8}$ meter in representations of dùndún drumming. Above all, perhaps, Euba's contribution to our understanding of African rhythm is inscribed in numerous original compositions produced since the 1960s.

Willie Anku (1949–2010). Anku, like others of his generation, studied composition, performance, and music education before settling into work as a theoretically inclined ethnomusicologist. After early training in Ghana, he studied in the United States, and returned to teach in Ghana before taking his PhD in ethnomusicology at the University of Pittsburgh under Nketia. Working in relative isolation at the University of Ghana, he drew on computer technology to extend our understanding of African rhythm. Anku's way was to make digital transcriptions of various ensemble pieces to support analysis. He was not interested in transcribing specific performances; rather, he insisted on reconstructing works like Adowa, Kpanlogo, Bawa, and Kete, in order to capture what was in the performer's head before he or she arrived at the performing arena. He was particularly interested in the lead drummer's art, which he explained by means of various set-theoretical operations, including the use of subsets and supersets in the disposition of rhythmic sets, variation, bridge patterns, and procedures of masking. Like Rycroft, Locke, Nzewi, and Toussaint, who have also gone down this path, Anku made considerable use of circles and cycles in depicting the procedures of African drumming. Although they are scattered among various publishing venues, Anku's writings have proved influential; indeed, he was the first continent-based scholar to put forward a theory of African rhythm (his "Structural Set Analysis of African Music") that attracted significant discussion among US music theorists.

Kofi Agawu (b.1956). My training was in composition, analysis, and later musicology, and my first book on African music sought a holistic view of African rhythm by exploring everything from the emerging rhythms of social discourse through the rhythms of speaking, singing, performing, and drumming/dancing. My second book on African music, *Representing African Music,* included two chapters on rhythm. The first, based on a previously published article entitled "The Invention of 'African rhythm,'" offered a postcolonial critique of the idea of "African rhythm," drawing on the work of African philosophers Mudimbe, Hountondji, Appiah, and Wiredu. The other chapter was a technical supplement to the one on invention. Following Nzewi, Arom, and Kolinski, I argued that notions like polymeter, additive rhythm, and cross rhythm were myths that had no reality in the conception and practice of African music. A subsequent article was devoted to a single rhythmic pattern, the so-called standard pattern [2-2-1-2-2-2-1]. I explored its phenomenological and structural properties, asking which of the many attributions it has attracted (rotational possibilities, additive conception, metrical undecidability) make sense from an African point of view. Most recently, in an introductory text to the African imagination in music, I have identified the following as key constituents of African rhythm: the interplay between free (or spoken or declamatory) rhythm and strict rhythm (measured, metronomically constrained); polyrhythm; the lead drummer's art along with a certain linguistic residue that enables the drummer's actions; and a generative approach, which reconstructs complex rhythms from simpler ones.

2000s

David Temperley (b.1963). Temperley is an American composer, cognitive scientist, and music theorist whose repertory interests extend beyond the usual classical confines to rock and non-Western music. In an important article published in 2000, Temperley, following Lerdahl and Jackendoff (Lerdahl was his mentor at Columbia), drew a fundamental distinction between meter and grouping. In the process, he shed much light on a fundamental feature of African rhythmic articulation, namely, the misalignment of motivic groups and the metrical grid. Incursions into African music studies by (Western) theorists like Temperley have grown in significance in recent years (see for example, papers by Cohn and Tenzer) and represent a positive trend toward cross-cultural understanding.

Godfried Toussaint (1944–2019). Toussaint, a mathematician who specialized in computational geometry, was also a practicing drummer. He published a number of studies in which the reality of African rhythm was distributed into various geometrical forms: circles, polygons, and TUBS. Toussaint was thus able to reveal interesting properties of various rhythmic patterns, including the rhythmic oddity property (a feature previously identified by Arom), maximal evenness (a feature noted by Pressing and others), offbeat rhythms (previously studied by David Locke), complexity, and the phylogenesis of rhythm as an evolutionary process, among numerous fascinating topics and processes. Detailed studies of time-line patterns enabled Toussaint to engage broader issues—why some time-line patterns endured while others disappeared, or what makes a rhythm "good." His 2013 book, *The Geometry of Musical Rhythm*, brings together this important body of studies. Although Toussaint, like Pressing and others, focuses on systematic rhythmic patterns as number and shape, his work has implications for aesthetic, stylistic, and historical understanding.

James Burns (b.1973). Burns is an American ethnomusicologist who studied with Lucy Durán at the School of Oriental and African Studies in

London (A. M. Jones's old school). He wrote a dissertation on Ewe drumming based on several years of fieldwork in West Africa, including an extended stint in the village of Dzodze, Ghana. In representing the rhythmic structure of African music, Burns uses a modified pulse notation to acknowledge groupings of 12 subdivided into 3s and 4s (and also into 2s and 6s), highlighting onsets only within the stream of eighth notes. This is an elegant way of displaying a grid of possibility while specifying patterns of articulation. In this way, readers can visually compare what is possible with what is activated in the course of a specific dance-music performance. Although some have countered the number 12 as the operative reference point, Burns's transcriptions—based, it should be said, on a highly secure understanding of the Dzodze community with which he worked in Ghana, extensive performing experience, and a wide acquaintance with World Music repertories—boast a new elegance, enhance appreciation, and deepen insight into the elements of African rhythm. Notable, too, is the fact that Burns's interests in recent work extend beyond African music to the Black Atlantic. A recent article addressing an audience of music theorists presents six rhythmic archetypes (or rhythmic tropes or phrase-building blocks) that link Black musical worlds on either side of the Atlantic. The archetypes model interlocking patterns that will be familiar to anyone who has direct experience performing African music. This important study identifies and carefully represents the named archetypes in notation and includes sound samples to aid the reader's comprehension.

Polo Vallejo (b.1959). Vallejo, a composer and ethnomusicologist from Spain, was trained by Simha Arom in Paris and later collaborated with his mentor in studies of Georgian polyphony. His main African work is on the Wagogo of Tanzania, although he has studied repertoires in several other places on the continent. Vallejo has recorded numerous Wagogo repertoires, among them children's music, and made numerous transcriptions in order to describe their rhythmic, melodic, and polyphonic systems. In 2012, he and his colleagues Javier Arias Bal, Pablo Vega, and Manuel Velasco released the film *Africa: The Beat*, a captivating portrait of the rhythmic life of a Tanzanian village, spectacularly presented as a multi-layered phenomenon constrained at the deepest level by a recurring beat.

Martin Scherzinger (b.1968). A wide-ranging scholar of South African origins with a background in composition and performance, Scherzinger's writings on African rhythm seek to convey their qualities through careful, number-based analysis of rhythm's properties, engagement with varieties of critical and philosophical theories ("Theory with a capital T," we might say), and a willingness to confront the political and ideological work that formalist analysis can do. A 2017 lecture to the Library of Congress, "Mathematics of African Dance Rhythms" (https://www.youtube.com/watch?v=2TgFp76Rnig), brings these theories into sharp focus in two African repertories, Zimbabwean mbira and matepe music. A recent essay, "Temporalities," incorporates observations about "double conceptions of rhythm and meter" in African music into a broader set of reflections on theories of time (musical as well as philosophical) encompassing the past two and a half centuries. Scherzinger ranges widely both historically and conceptually; at the same time, and perhaps reflecting his training as a music theorist, he often provides close readings to support his arguments. Working with xylophone and lamellophone music from Eastern and Southern Africa notable for its speed, multiple performers, and "digital" articulation, Scherzinger unveils a portrait of African rhythm different from the language-motivated, periodic structures of West Africa, with their choreographic supplement guaranteeing a stable background. It now appears that concepts that had previously seemed inadequate and thus abandoned (individual beats and polymeter, for example) may have been abandoned prematurely.

Rainer Polak (b.1966). Polak, a German teacher, performer on the jembe, and scholar, has made a special study of drumming in Mande repertories, notably those in Bamako, Mali. He has contributed a series of empirical studies that have brought to the fore aspects of micro-articulation that were previously underappreciated. Recent collaborations (with Justin London and Nori Jacoby) have provided further latitude for grounding claims about non-isochrony as an intentional feature of Malian drumming, and conceptions of swing as revealed in micro-timings. By bringing different Malian repertories into view, Polak has helped to diversify the roots of our theorizing. The range of African rhythmic practices is larger than we once thought.

Critique

These, then, are some of the main contributions to the technical study of African rhythm. There is surely a long list of absentees; mine includes writings by Richard Waterman, Christopher Waterman, Jay Rahn, C. K. Ladzekpo, Trevor Wiggins, Anthony King, Andre Schaeffner, Zabana Kongo, Marc Chemillier, Natalie Fernando, Justin London, Vijay Iyer, Eugene Novotney, and Chris Stover, among others. (See the book's bibliography for some of their works). The ideas described here, however, represent the principal trends. The danger of undercomplicating some formulations always attends this sort of exercise, but perhaps there'll be some value for nonspecialists or for those who seek a broad orientation. Let us now ask a few questions to help characterize the shape of the archive.

First, *Which Africa?* It is probably no accident that the works mentioned here deal mainly with West and Central Africa. While this may be no more than an accident of choice in this particular delineation of the field (not to mention the limits of my own knowledge), the list invites another consideration, namely, the theory that elaborate rhythm often stands in antithetical relationship to elaborate polyphony. To put it more colloquially: if God has given you rhythm, s/he will not give you elaborate polyphony as well; s/he likes to spread the wealth! The gift of rhythm, according to this theory, went to folks in West and Central Africa, while their relatives in Eastern and Southern African got harmony and polyphony. And an attempt could be made on a superficial level to support that view by contrasting the complex rhythms of say Ewe and Yoruba drumming with the complex polyphony exemplified in Wagogo and Luvale singing. But this line of argument will not get us very far. For one thing, complex rhythmic systems are known to exist in any number of Eastern and Southern African cultures as well (including Baganda drumming, Bemba and Lala drumming, xylophone playing among the Chopi, and Shona mbira music, to mention a few well-studied traditions). Similarly, rich polyphony is not out of the reach of West and Central African performers, as we know from vocal styles associated with the Anlo-Ewe, Baule, Aka, and BaAka, among others. What the broad attribution records, then, is not an essentialized difference between East/Southern and West/Central Africa, but simply the priorities of individual researchers (and groups of researchers) working within particular traditions of knowledge production in academia.

Special mention should be made of one group that has garnered a disproportionately large amount of attention: the Ewe in Ghana (and to a lesser extent Togo). For various reasons—not all of them accidental—there has emerged a concentration of rhythm studies based on Ewe music by scholars with different backgrounds. Some are born-in-the-tradition culture bearers, some did fieldwork in Eweland, and some have worked with Ewe musicians outside Ghana—in the UK, the United States, Canada, and Australia. They include Jones, Cudjoe, Pantaleoni, Locke, Pressing, Burns,

Fiagbedzi, Agawu, Amoaku, Younge, Dor, Avorgbedor, C. K. Ladzekpo, and Julian Gerstin, among others. Indeed, based on representations in the literature, one could be forgiven for thinking that African rhythm equals Ewe rhythm. Yet, this impression calls for considerable qualification. First, it is not all of Ewe music that has been subject to intense scrutiny; rather, it is drum ensemble music of the Southern Ewe localized in dances like Agbadza, Atsiagbekor, and Gahu. Second, familiarity with other idioms of Ghanaian music will show that the polyrhythmic textures admired in Southern Ewe music are by no means unique to them (similar performance styles are found among the Asante, Fante, Dagomba, and other groups in Ghana). There is, then, a certain precarity to the portrait of African rhythmic exceptionalism that emerges from current research. Were it possible to imagine a systematic study of rhythmic styles across the entire continent, we would have a more reliable portrait.[18]

Second, *Which music—traditional or popular?* The music that has occupied many theorists of African rhythm has been *traditional* African music, that is, orally and aurally cultivated repertoires of ostensibly pre-European origins, not urban popular music or the notated traditions of élite art music that emerged after colonialism and missionization. We may infer from this that the African music that most vividly displays the breadth and subtlety of our rhythmic imagination is that which owes little or nothing to Europe, not that which is built intentionally on hybrid foundations, fusing European and African elements. Hybridity in this understanding has led to a transformation—a few brave souls might even use the word impoverishment—of the original African resource. Putting the matter this way should not seem polemical; after all, parameters are prioritized differently in different musical styles. It is in the valuation of those prioritizations that polemics arise. From an intra-African point of view, the hard truth is that nobody goes to jùjú, soukouss, highlife, hiplife, benga, azonto, kwaito, fuji, mbalax, or afrobeats in search of African *rhythm* in its most sophisticated forms. As expressive fields, these genres of popular music offer other forms of titillation: comfort of the familiar in the form of closed harmonic patterns imported into Africa from Europe (listen, for example, to Davido's *Aye*); topical themes to both reflect, respond to, or construct a contemporary reality (Burna Boy's *20-10-2020*); easily recognized melodies and easily

[18] For a good example of such a distributive study, see Kubik, "Intra-African Streams of Influence," in Stone, *Africa: The Garland Encyclopedia of World Music*, 293–326.

imitated melodic refrains of tonal and modal origin; the energy of dance and dance grooves and the resultant socializing impulse; and the satisfaction of being part of a modern world, especially one which allows imitation of or localizing of hip cultures from Europe and America.[19]

Third, *Vocal or instrumental music?* There is an overwhelming preference among theorists for instrumental music over vocal music. And yet, we know that in the beginning was song, not the drum. Song in principle elevates the word beyond its spoken state. Song activates language, and language leaves a deep imprint on a great many instrumental forms (including drumming), all of which signify in one way or another. Why, then, haven't more scholars sought the foundations of African rhythmic expression where it matters most, namely, in texted music, or in the proto-music enshrined in the spoken word? One obvious reason is that many theorists (notably outsiders) are simply not equipped to employ a language-based approach because they do not know African languages. Then also, the sporadic attempts to take the rhythms of language seriously (by Ekundayo Phillips, Jones, Rouget, Nketia, Stone, Peter Cooke, Carter-Enyi, and others) have not been emulated as much as they might be. If anything, it is our colleagues in linguistics that we turn to for illumination on this point (see, for example, recent writings by Kathryn Franich and Laura McPherson). Another reason may be purely practical, namely, the wish to dispense with the additional layers of complexity stemming from word accents, lingual rhythm, intonational patterns, and vocal timbre in order to focus on features like meter, accent, duration, pattern, and grouping, features that seem more obviously tied to music. This bias is not a feature of theorizations of African rhythm alone; with a few exceptions, recent theorizing of European rhythm by American music theorists has not necessarily placed language at the center of their efforts either (exceptions include Yonathan Malin, Harald Krebs, Stephen Rodgers, John Halle, and Fred Lerdahl, among others). Given the deep ties that bind language and music together in the African context, however, African musicology cannot afford to occlude the linguistic dimension from its vision of rhythm.

Fourth, *Where is the dance?* Although a great many of the traditional repertories studied by scholars are dance repertories, the dimensions of physical movement and embodiment that dance entails have—again with

[19] See Eric Charry, ed., *Hip Hop Africa: New African Music in a Globalizing World* (Bloomington: Indiana University Press, 2012), and Catherine Appert, *In Hip Hop Time: Music, Memory, and Social Change in Urban Senegal* (New York: Oxford University Press, 2018).

exceptions—not always been factored into theorizations of rhythm. This is a striking omission. "Watch the dance feet, the *pieds de danse*," should be inscribed in every rhythm theorist's notebook. When faced with a daunting population of onsets in African ensemble music, attention to the way that culture bearers domesticate the rhythms using their bodies is often (alas, not always, and certainly not in a mechanical way) a helpful indication of their understanding of rhythmic order. Foot movement, for example, defines or at least provides clues to definitions of metrical structure. While indigenous theorists often take this supplementary knowledge for granted, unenculturated scholars or those not familiar with such co-constitutive movements often miss out on the disambiguating role of movement. By ignoring the dance, they miss the synthetic response expressed by the body; the music's essential beat or gross pulse eludes them.

It is just possible that the light that dance shines on rhythmic structure, the orientation that the body provides, under-complicates African rhythm for some theorists. Preferring to bask in the plethora of (apparently) irregularly positioned accents, or displacements between meter and grouping, or the sheer multiplicity of onsets in ensemble music, some writers are drawn to ambiguity and undecidability. Friedson, for example, denies that there is a "one" in Southern Ewe drumming. Martin Scherzinger argues for a multiplicity of reference in the highlife *topos* even though the dance, known by specialists and amateurs alike, discloses a duple metrical framework. And David Locke, previously committed to metrical exactitude in his influential transcriptions from the 1980s and 1990s of Gahu, Agbadza, Damba, and other Ghanaian dances, now emphasizes "simultaneous multidimensionality" as a feature of African rhythm. Locke has found an ally in Friedson, whose portrait of Ewe life as unpredictable he cites in support of his contention that there is no one correct way to hear the music of Agbadza:

> Ewe culture seems to thrive on uncertainty, ambiguity, disputation, rivalry, unreconcilable antimony, paradox, enigma. In many aspects of life in Eweland, one can never be too sure of anything (see Friedson 2009). As my musical analysis has emphasized, the sonic surface of a song or drum phrase can be heard in different ways.[20]

[20] Locke, "An Approach to Musical Rhythm in Agbadza," in *Thought and Play in Musical Rhythm*, edited by Richard Wolf, Stephen Blum and Christopher Hasty, p. 145 (New York: Oxford University Press, 2019).

This extraordinary analogy between life (social, economic, religious) and the organization of a popular dance apparently empowers listeners to hear the music "in different ways." One wonders whether (Agbadza) performers are free to play "in different ways"? And, to the extent that composers form a separate entity, whether they assemble their music "in different ways" to elicit different hearings? Or is this perceptual flexibility only granted to listeners? Do culture bearers also hear "in different ways"? We await empirical research data that will help answer these questions definitively.

The embrace of ambiguity and multidimensionality may also reflect a belief in the mystical and mysterious, in the meaningfulness of those things that lie beyond number. And by downplaying rules and clear premises, analysts are effectively guaranteed permanent stakes in future acts of theorization. After all, if no one person has the correct answer, if we can hear "in different ways," then there is permanent room for multiple viewpoints. How does one balance the undoubted richness of African ensemble performance against the undoubted order that structurally underpins it and guarantees its continued performance? Some scholars have argued that the complexity of African rhythm is a rational complexity, that African genres are built on specifiable "background" structures that support myriad forms of play, planned accidents, and contingencies. To deny, mystify, or loosely pluralize those foundations undermines the incredible discipline, dedication, and sheer creativity that inform performance. Listeners are of course free to enact their fantasies about African rhythm, but if we have learned anything from a century of theorization, it is the power of African rhythm's generative principles.

Fifth, *Difference or sameness?* These terms should always be understood contextually, of course; indeed, rather than represent fixed positions in a firm oppositional framework, difference and sameness harbor degrees of salience. But no matter how finely we qualify the opposition, its coordinates in a given situation are normally specifiable. It matters, therefore, whether an individual theorist proceeds from an ideology of difference or one of sameness. Hornbostel began his famous 1928 article by declaring that African music and European music are based "on entirely different principles." Numerous others have either echoed his words or adopted a similar belief to guide their research. While the choice of an initial stance is merely ideological, it is important to be alert to the consequences of adopting either premise. In the field of rhythm studies for example, operating with a premise of difference can obscure certain shared organizational principles while a premise of sameness can illuminate those same principles and—paradoxically, perhaps—show where the difference lies. For example, in the designation "African $\frac{4}{4}$ " introduced casually by Locke in his study of Gahu, he acknowledges that African musicians deploy cycles of four beats but treat its normative accentual patterns in a way that distinguishes their usage from a putative "European $\frac{4}{4}$." Difference and sameness are thus signaled simultaneously, and within the broad prospect of cross-cultural understanding, the specific prospect of an enhanced understanding of $\frac{4}{4}$ meter in *both* European and African music becomes real.

In an early article, Bruno Nettl noticed "the relatively similar musical styles of Africa and Europe (viewed on a broad scale) as compared to the musical contrast between the African Negroes and the physically similar Melanesians."[21] That African and European music can be considered "similar" in any context may come as a surprise to some readers, but for scholars like Nettl who embraced comparative thinking on a global scale, such affinities were plausible. Locke's "African $\frac{4}{4}$" registers such affinities without erasing differences, whereas theorists who reject the applicability of European time signatures like $\frac{4}{4}$ or $\frac{12}{8}$ to African music altogether run the risk of de-emphasizing the shared cyclical processes and exaggerating differences in the normative succession of strong and weak beats in either repertory.

For some people, the sound of African music is so self-evidently different from European music that it would seem almost perverse to suggest otherwise. The point here concerns not the immediate sound, not the material vehicles that create the soundscape, not the actual surface configurations; the point is rather about underlying *frameworks* for organizing material into motives, metrical units, periods, and so on. It is at this sub-surface or background level that one sometimes observes deep parallels between musical styles. The argument for a contextualized sameness cannot be won at an abstract level, however. Presuming sameness is really a call to a proceeding, an invitation to adopt a certain attitude or certain premises that may then lead to useful discoveries. In the end, it is really an argument for *both* sameness and difference. But how we get to these final states may differ radically depending on whether we take a principled stance to resist sameness, as Erlmann recommends.[22]

[21] Bruno Nettl, "Historical Aspects of Ethnomusicology," *American Anthropologist* 60 (1958): 44.

[22] See Veit Erlmann, "Resisting Sameness—À propos Kofi Agawu's 'Representing African Music,'" *Music Theory Spectrum* 26 (2004): 291–304.

Sixth, *Which audience?* Many writings on African rhythm are aimed at Euro-American audiences, not African ones, and this accounts in part for the language and methodologies employed, and the framing of research results. It might also explain the reticence to proceed from certain shared assumptions and presumptions and the not infrequent reinvention of certain wheels. Sometimes, acts of theorization seem stuck at elementary levels, burdened by yet another (ritual) rehearsal of the basics. Time was when it made sense to provide such knowledge for readers with no prior familiarity with a subject—maps, digital addresses, population statistics, descriptions of marriage customs and kinship systems, photographs of instruments featured in an ensemble, and so on. But after more than a century of rehearsing these contexts, beginning at the beginning does not always seem necessary. (Think how tedious it would be if you had to describe the viola every time you wrote about an orchestral piece by Haydn, Bruckner, or Mahler!) What happened to local, knowledgeable audiences, audiences comprising of students, teachers, or just curious individuals familiar enough with the basic mechanisms of African rhythmic production to be able to appreciate a new theory or deliver informed critique? Again, the point here is not to deny new knowledge its contexts; it is rather to lament the tendency to overlook or undervalue accumulated knowledge.

Seventh, *Compared to what?* Among its goals, the ethnomusicological intervention in the construction of knowledge about African music in the 1960s and after sought to replace an earlier comparative framework with a more in-depth ethnographic approach. The comparative impulse never really disappeared, however; it remained implicit in the ethnographic construction.

And with that came both gains and losses. One obvious gain was in the depth of inquiry and in the accumulation of data. A not-so-obvious loss came with the muting of associationism. Where previously a scholar like Hornbostel could speak freely of resonances among works of diverse origin, thus placing African music in a comparative framework, the new regime dis-privileged the making of such connections. The idea was to eliminate anachronism; if we must compare, then let's be sure to compare like with like. Not much was made of the losses entailed in discouraging erudite scholars from hearing across repertoires—hearing contrapuntally, as we discussed in Chapter 5. Nor was much made of the temptations to narcissism that the ethnographic approach sometimes delivers. This new, solipsistic approach was caught in a contradiction, however, because all acts of verbal description retain an implicit comparative element. Our language is freighted, permanently marked by other usages. To refer to a "rattle" or "story-song" or "lamellophone" is to call on larger worlds. Comparison is built into the very act of representation. So the question is whether one wants to, as it were, be upfront about an individual author's horizon of comparison (complete with its systematic and historical factors), or whether one prefers to let that horizon remain implicit in what one says.

In some recent studies of African rhythm, the comparative element has returned in a way that will be welcomed by advocates of cross-cultural analysis. I'm thinking of the work of Jeff Pressing (who identified "cognitive isomorphisms" in world musics), Godfried Toussaint (who undertook a phylogenetic analysis of African rhythms and, in a related project, distributed the shapes of these rhythms into geometrical shapes thus inviting comparison with, for example, the geometrical treatment of harmony in the extended common practice by Dmitri Tymoczco), and James Burns (who has recently linked six rhythmic archetypes originating in Africa with various Black Atlantic replicas or derivatives).[23] In lamenting the muting of the comparativist impulse from the 1960s on, I do not mean to downplay the very reasonable urge to counter inappropriate or unfavorable comparisons, especially those beholden to evolutionary frameworks that portray Africa as lagging behind her historical oppressors. Nor do I mean to overlook the important contributions of an individual scholar like Gerhard Kubik, who has long been interested in intra-African stylistic comparison informed by the latest developments in psychology and cognition. I mean only to tout the virtues of laying bare our frames of comparison. Signs of an emerging new comparative musicology (in writings by Michael Tenzer, for example, and in the work of the larger Analytical Approaches to World Music movement [discussed in Chapter 5]) give us reason to be optimistic.

[23] Jeff Pressing, "Cognitive lsomorphisms between Pitch and Rhythm in World Musics: West Africa, the Balkans and Western Tonality," *Studies in Music* 17 (1983): 38–61; Godfried Toussaint, *The Geometry of Musical Rhythm: What Makes a "Good" Rhythm Good?* (Bosa Roca: CRC Press, 2013).. James Burns, "Rhythmic Archetypes in Instrumental Music from Africa and the Diaspora," *Music Theory Online* 16, no. 4 (2010), accessed May 16, 2022, http://mto.societymusictheory.org/issues/mto.10.16.4/mto.10.16.4.burns.html. See also Julian Gerstin, "Comparisons of African and Diasporic Rhythm: The Ewe, Cuba, and Martinique," *Analytical Approaches to World Music*, no. 5 (2017), accessed July 9, 2021, http://www.aawmjournal.com/articles/2017b/Gerstin_AAWM_Vol_5_2.pdf; Vijay S. Iyer, *Microstructures of Feel, Macrostructures of Sound: Embodied Cognition in West African and African-American Musics* (PhD diss., University of California, Berkeley, 1998); and David Penalosa, *The Clave Matrix: Afro-Cuban Rhythm: Its Principles and African Origins* (Redway, CA: Bembe Books, 2012).

Eighth and finally, *To cite or not to cite?* A final feature of the literature on theories of African rhythm is its apparently non-cumulative nature. If you assumed that writers in the 1950s digested the writings of their predecessors from the 1920s before advancing their own theories, or that people writing in the 1980s had done their homework by reading previous publications (including publications bearing directly on their own research), or that twenty-first-century rhythm research builds systematically on its twentieth-century antecedents, you would be mistaken. For various reasons, the literature on African rhythm has been slow to acquire a genuine cumulative profile. As such, instead of continuous growth in understanding based on the falsification of previous concepts, ideas and results, wheels are regularly being reinvented. This failure to digest and cite—unthinkable in scientific research—is not restricted to work on African rhythm. Ethnomusicologist Timothy Rice once undertook a systematic study of writings on *music and identity* published in the journal *Ethnomusicology* in the period 1982–2006 and discovered, among other things, that authors routinely ignored previous work on the subject. He thought this a "fundamental weakness in ethnomusicology." He did not, however, entertain the possibility that strategic amnesia might actually be an enabling condition for the production of certain kinds of knowledge. If indeed such amnesia is strategic for writers on African rhythm, then it would be helpful to acknowledge it openly.[24]

Conclusion

It has been my task to describe some of the principal contributions to the subject of African rhythm and to comment on the overall character of the resulting literature. That rhythm remains an intriguing and vital component of African music, and that we are nowhere near exhausting the challenges it offers is abundantly clear. As we expand the geo-cultural reach of rhythm studies, and as more and more scholars develop new and systematic ways of analyzing rhythm, acquainting ourselves with past triumphs and failures will ensure that we're not in danger of tripping over the same stone twice.

[24] On the politics of citation, see Agawu, "To Cite or Not to Cite? Confronting the Legacy of (European) Writing on African Music," *Fontes Artis Musicae* 54 (2007): 254–262.

Epilogue

The magnificent music of the African continent—our continent—so diverse in its idiomatic manifestations, so generous in the paths it opens up for all music-makers, amateur and professional alike, and so consistent in its underlying grooves based on some of the most imaginative ways of negotiating repetition known in human history—this music continues to engage African communities, their diasporic kin, and the global community, from casual consumers and music lovers to students, critics, scholars, seasoned dancers, and composers. African music's present is alive, its future guaranteed.

My goal in these seven simple essays has been to shed light on a handful of animating structures, enhance appreciation for African creativity, and engage with aspects of the scholarship. I began with the minimalist impulse (how we make much out of little) and the prevalent use of iconicity (how notions of resemblance shape many an expressive action), and continued with adaptations of tonality (how European tonality has been put in circulation alongside various indigenous tone systems). My examples included not only traditional music (music that belongs to the sphere of old and continuing Africa and encapsulates our inalienable contribution to the world of music) but also the modern tradition of African pianism, itself a subset of African art music (the written tradition of composition that has produced sonatas, operas, chamber music, art songs and choral music by individual composers in possession of both African and European Tekhné). Ways in which the discipline of music theory (study of the principles underlying the structure of music) might benefit from African musical aid were outlined, and I broached conceptual and ideological issues raised by ethno-theory (indigenous conceptualizations of music and music-making ostensibly innocent of outside influences). The closing chapter considered evolving changes in the discourse on African rhythm (that dimension of music that deals with timing, accent, and periodicity).

It would be normal to try and tie the various strands of the discussion together at this point. However, I fear that no grand, synthesizing statement can do justice to these fragmentary conversations. Not only are the critical, aesthetic, and analytical issues raised by the collective repertoires simply too rich and diverse for a pat, synoptic statement, but our interpretive communities are widely dispersed while the meta-languages deployed within each community are not always built upon the same or even comparable premises.

There are nevertheless a few recurring *topoi* across the book. One of them is the centrality of natural language to musical understanding. We see and hear this in the shaping of melody in response to linguistic tone, the use of ideophones to enliven speech, the rendering of sung song as wordless melody on instruments, and in the formulation of theoretical ideas and concepts. Recognizing these affinities is not, however, a prescription for erasing or even downplaying the significant differences between the two semiotic systems. On the contrary, thinking about language and music in tandem invariably underlines their ultimate non-identity. Thus, while the mirroring property associated with iconicity, for example, is manifest in the systems of language, music, and the visual arts, the informational redundancy of music—acquired from unavoidably extensive use of repetition—stands in contrast to the semantically explicit universes of natural-language composition.

Methodologically, I have followed a loosely postcolonial approach in these essays. Such an approach takes the historical contingencies of precolonial and colonial pasts as given, and proceeds to work within the constraints and affordances of those pasts, pasts that continue to influence and direct a lot of what we do today. The (imagined) precolonial is not comprehensible without the mediation of the colonial; nor is the colonial meaningful without a precolonial horizon. The term *postcolonial*, however, sometimes registers different priorities depending on the heritage and disciplinary orientation of individual scholars. Add to this the recent emergence of a non-identical *decoloniality* in writings by Latin American theorists advocating a de-linking from the hegemonic West, and you begin to appreciate the conceptual diffuseness of postcolonialism. I'd like to believe that nothing in these essays is rendered opaque on account of my not spending pages trying to unpack the various meanings of postcoloniality.[1]

[1] On decoloniality, see among others Walter Mignolo and Madina Tlostanova, "Theorizing from the Borders Shifting to Geo- and Body-Politics of Knowledge," *European Journal of Social Theory* 9, no. 2 (2006), 205–221; Anibal Quijano, "Coloniality of Power, Ethnocentrism, and Latin America." *NEPANTLA* 1, no. 3 (2000), 533–80; and Rámon Grosfoguel, "Decolonizing Post-Colonial Studies and Paradigms of Political-Economy: Transmodernity, Decolonial Thinking, and Global Coloniality," *Transmodernity: Journal of Peripheral Cultural Production of the Luso-Hispanic World*, 1, no. 1 (2011), 1–38. On the postcolonial, see Kwame Anthony Appiah, *In My Father's House: Africa in the Philosophy of Culture* (New York: Oxford University Press, 1992); Gayatri Spivak, *The Post-Colonial Critic: Interviews, Strategies, Dialogues* (New York: Routledge, 1990); Kwasi Wiredu, *Cultural Universals and Particulars: An African Perspective* (Bloomington: Indiana University Press, 1996); V. Y. Mudimbe, *The Invention of Africa: Gnosis, Philosophy, and the Order*

Whatever else the label postcolonial might signify, it has been appropriated here in the context of analysis within African musicology. Analysis is sometimes regarded as a contested practice, while African musicology is thought to be exclusionary, so it will be well to say a few things about them.

Analysis typically involves taking something apart in order to explain its inner workings. Analysis has been a mainstay of a variety of disciplines, from anthropology and philosophy through linguistics and literary studies to music studies, and its objects have included poems, myths, folk tales, novels, funeral dirges, sentences in language, songs, piano pieces, or even entire performances. When I began writing about African music in the 1980s, it was not common for writers to embark on extensive close readings of individual repertory items. There was nothing in the literature on African music like Jean-Jacques Nattiez's 100-page analysis of a solo flute piece by Varèse, in which every note, configuration, and phrase is examined, competing analyses critically discussed, and the entire analytical proceeding conducted with exemplary methodological self-awareness. Yet there were countless solo instrumental and vocal pieces in the African corpus that could have been fruitfully analyzed following Nattiez's example.[2]

More common in those days was the making of inventories of scales and intervals, summaries of gross features, and theorizations of rhythm based on recurring principles.[3] The apparently indulgent act of listening into the interior of, say, a single dirge or play song or piece of dance-drumming and subjecting it to detailed analysis seemed dissonant with the ostensibly communalistic production processes said to be characteristic of African creativity. The practice of close reading was further held to be suspect because it

of Knowledge (Bloomington: Indiana University Press, 1988); Achille Mbembe, *On the Postcolony* (Berkeley: University of California Press, 2001); and Gaurav Desai, *Subject to Colonialism: African Self-fashioning and the Colonial Library* (Durham, NC: Duke University Press, 2001).Within the sphere of African music studies, pertinent recent discussions include Lee Watkins, Elijah Madiba, and Boudina McConnachie, "Rethinking the Decolonial Moment Through Collaborative Practices at the International Library of African Music (ILAM), South Africa," *Ethnomusicology Forum*, 30 (2021), 20–39; and Noel Lobley, *Sound Fragments: From Field Recordings to African Electronic Stories* (Middletown, CT: Wesleyan University Press, 2022). Also of considerable interest is Olúfẹ́mi Táíwò, *Against Decolonisation: Taking African Agency Seriously* (London: Hurst & Company, 2022).

[2] Jean-Jacques Nattiez, "Varèse's *Density 21.5*: A Study in Semiological Analysis," translated by Anna Barry, *Music Analysis* 1, no. 3 (1982), 243–340.

[3] See for example, John Blacking, *Venda Children's Songs: A Study in Ethnomusicological Analysis* (Chicago: University of Chicago Press, 1995 [1967]); and J. H. Kwabena Nketia, *The Music of Africa* (New York: Norton, 1974). Simha Arom's *African Polyphony and Polyrhythm: Musical Structure and Methodology* (Cambridge, UK: Cambridge University Press, 1991 [1985]) is frequently cited for its inventories of rhythmic devices.

was too readily reminiscent of the individualistic approaches of Western musicology. When I included a five-page analysis of an Ewe lament in a book on African rhythm published in 1995, one reviewer complained that the analysis "veers perilously close to [a point of diminishing returns]."[4] What to do with the surplus of detail found in analytical writing has been an issue for readers (less so for writers), so the reviewer's remark was not entirely surprising. But this is not a problem for African musicology alone. Moreover, given the then-prevalent tendency to construct African music as always already different from European music, the last thing that authorities wished to recommend was the application of a "Western" analytical approach to African music.

Yet the distinction between Western and African approaches has always been fragile. For one thing, its construction too often gives short shrift to the African side of the equation. Instead of providing strong models of African introspection that students might emulate, critics (of certain disciplinary persuasions) were more likely to decry the merest sign of supposedly "Western" influence on a writer's work. These were acts of prohibition, not constructive acts. And they were ultimately produced within a censorious discourse less committed to entering deeply and speculatively into African worlds than to checking credentials at the door. It is gratifying today to see that the embrace of a postcolonial historical reality and the celebration of Afrofuturist prospects have begun to move us beyond the simple binaries of the past.

Regarding the trope of communalism, we know that although dirges, for example, are typically performed by groups of people, their ontological origins lie in specific creative acts undertaken by individuals for specific purposes and under specific circumstances. The functional presence of an individual is a practical necessity for creation. So, the theory that composition in traditional society is communal is only an artifact of discourse, itself shaped by an anti-individualist ideology. The desire to present Africa as communal in contrast to the many individualistic regimes that rule in the West is a permanent temptation for some writers on traditional African music. Yet, the shaping hand of one individual or another is evident in practically every creative act.

Analysis makes a reciprocal contribution by presenting readers with one individual's introspection about a given song or item of dance-drumming.

[4] Roger Vetter, "Review of Agawu, *African Rhythm: A Northern Ewe Perspective*," *Journal of the American Musicological Society* 51 (1998), 161.

Aesthetic considerations shape such analyses in ways that differentiate them from taxonomies exemplifying predetermined structural features. I hope that the analyses of such pieces/performances as Aly Keita's *Farafinko* (in the chapter on minimalism) or Nketia's *Volta Fantasy* (in the chapter on African pianism) will contribute in a small way to appreciation of these products of the African musical imagination and perhaps encourage previously hesitant students to undertake their own close readings. We stand to learn a great deal from the interpretive insights of individual culture-bearers.

Invoking the label "African musicology" in the Introduction to this book was not intended to be polemical. Some readers have wondered why I don't simply call what I'm doing ethnomusicology, especially since ethnomusicology covers all World Music and has been the main home for a good deal of the research into African music. Two responses may be given. First, we may wish to speak of musicology in the African context rather than African musicology. In that way, we can acknowledge the impact of all kinds of contexts (cultural, institutional, linguistic, even class) on the work of scholars active on the continent. Second, we might wish to recall that some knowledge is produced under the sign of area studies, whose premises are not identical to those of particular disciplines. In the case of African music, one may speak of an African musicology where one's orientation is to any and all products of the African musical imagination. This body of work sports a methodological plurality, is welcoming of less wrought, even journalistic writing, and is willing to express value-laden opinions. Knowledge produced under the sign of ethnomusicology, by contrast, will normally observe ethnomusicological protocol as detailed in any number of the discipline's theory texts. It assumes the notional equality of all works, eschews value judgments, insists on context, and frequently invokes the authority of fieldwork. No doubt, the line between an African-musicological approach and an ethnomusicological one is not hard and fast, but the two traditions of knowledge production remain ultimately distinct.

I would not normally dwell on this point, preferring to let the work speak for itself. But since at least one anonymous reader's reaction to the manuscript was to question my use of the rubric "African musicology" and to demand that I address the disciplinary politics implicit in my text, it will be well to clarify this briefly.

In its broadest sense, African musicology could mean one of two things: first, if musicology is the scholarly study of music, then African musicology can be defined simply as the scholarly study of African music; second, by using the qualifier "African" (as distinct from say Indian, Chinese, Middle Eastern, or European), African musicology might be understood as the scholarly study of music undertaken by African people. The first definition is object-centered, the second incorporates the scholar's identity. Historically, the term has gone through several iterations at the hands of scholars like Wachsmann, Nketia, Euba, Djedje, Nzewi, and Mapaya; there was also a short-lived journal by that name in the 1980s.[5] What unites these various usages is a shared desire to recognize creative intellection about African music using whatever tools one deems appropriate. While it is nowadays expedient and politically progressive to reject the essentialism enshrined in the second definition (by arguing, for example, that African musicology has been produced by non-Africans, or that African scholars also write about other music), it would be bizarre to hide or even underplay the fact that the urge to proclaim an African musicology was always beholden to the expression of a "nationalist" impulse. Accordingly, it has been felt most keenly by born-in-the-tradition African intellectuals. While this may be no more than a sociological fact, it seems to unsettle some non-African white scholars who, although fully aware of persistent historical inequities in the opportunities available for the production of knowledge, still manage to feel excluded or underappreciated whenever strategic essentialism of this sort is invoked.

An analogous situation obtained in the field of African philosophy, where the main players in the 1980s and after were individuals from countries like Nigeria, Senegal, Kenya, Benin, Ghana, Cameroon, the DRC, and elsewhere.[6] Their training and experiences shaped the topics that were being debated in those days, including the foundational question of whether an African philosophy was possible in the first place. And the question of what it meant for a born-in-the-tradition African philosopher to do philosophy

[5] On African musicology, see Klaus Wachsmann, "The State of African Musicology," in *African Studies of Makerere 1961–66: A Report* (Kampala: Makerere University College, 1967); Jacqueline Djedje and William G. Carter, "African Musicology: An Assessment of the Field," in *African Musicology: Current Trends*, Vol. 1, edited by Jacqueline Codgell Djedje and William G. Carter, pp. 39–44 (Los Angeles: African Studies Center, University of California, 1989); J. H. Kwabena Nketia, "Perspectives on African Musicology," in *Africa and the West: The Legacies of Empire*, edited by Isaac James Mowoe and Richard Bjornson, pp. 215–253 (Westport, CT: Greenwood Press, 1986); and Geoff Madimabe Mapaya, "African Musicology: Towards Defining and Setting Parameters of the Study of the Indigenous African Music," *Anthropologist* 18, no. 2 (2014), 619–627; *African Musicology Online*, accessed May 26, 2022, https://africanmusicology.online/publications/. See also Agawu, "Meki Nzewi and the Discourse of African Musicology: A 70th Birthday Appreciation," *Journal of the Musical Arts of Africa* 5, no. 1 (2008), 1–18.

[6] For a brisk survey, see Harry Ballen, *A Short History of African Philosophy* (Bloomington: Indiana University Press, 2009). See also various writings by Hountondji, Kagame, Mudimbe, Wiredu, Appiah, and Oruka, and others.

was part of the conversation. As far as I can tell, few "outsiders" complained that African philosophy was exclusionary. Whatever seemed to matter to individual African scholars doing what they called philosophy was considered legitimate. (Apparently the same privilege is not to be afforded to African musicologists!). Today's globalizing trends may blur the line between an African philosophy and a European or World philosophy, but it is not at all clear that regional characterizations have outlived their usefulness. Perhaps such characterizations should *not* be retired if only because they lend a hand to efforts to resist the dominating force of globalization.

As writers on African music who occasionally get caught up in debates like these, we may sometimes forget that when all is said and done, our discourses pale in comparison to the numerous acts of daily music-making sponsored by thriving performing traditions. We may lose sight of the extraordinary influence that African music has exerted on countless musical traditions around the world, or take for granted the amazing constellation of elements, procedures, and new patterns of parametric co-presence that animate these collective repertoires in the first place. Let me close, then, by saying—once again—that the future of African music is secured by the strength of its underlying routines and possibilities. Out of many such routines, I chose only a handful for elaboration in the foregoing essays. We noted the extraordinary ability of African musicians to make much out of little (minimalism) and to derive meaning from varieties of sameness (groove) even while deploying differentiating procedures to generate narratives. We recognized different ways of coming to terms with European tonality, from uncritical acceptance through incorporation into a system of indigenous modal organization to strategic relativization. We recognized ingenious ways of negotiating temporality in art music, including speech-inflected articulation and varieties of pulse orientation. We touched on the richness of our ideational worlds without succumbing to the temptation to reify them as self-sufficient theory. And we finished by revisiting various scholars' fantasies about African rhythm, a dimension that was there in the beginning and is often considered essential to the African musical imagination. Ultimately, words about music are most meaningful when they return the gaze (or its auricular equivalent) to the sounding forms themselves.

Bibliography

AAWM [Analytical Approaches to World Music]. 2011. http://journal.iftawm.org/.

Adams, Kyle. 2008. "Aspects of the Music/Text Relationship in Rap." *Music Theory Online* 14 (2).

Afa Songs. n.d. Compact Disc. Recorded by James Burns. Unpublished.

African Musicology Online. Accessed May 26, 2022. https://africanmusicology.online/publications/.

Agawu, Kofi. 1990. "Variation Procedures in Northern Ewe Song." *Ethnomusicology* 34 (2): 221–243.

Agawu, Kofi. 1995. *African Rhythm: A Northern Ewe Perspective*. Cambridge, UK: Cambridge University Press.

Agawu, Kofi. 2003. *Representing African Music: Postcolonial Notes, Queries, Positions*. New York: Routledge.

Agawu, Kofi. 2004. "How We Got Out of Analysis and How to Get Back in Again." *Music Analysis* 23 (2/3): 267–286.

Agawu, Kofi. 2006. "Structural Analysis or Cultural Analysis? Competing Perspectives on the 'Standard Pattern' of West African Rhythm." *Journal of the American Musicological Society* 59 (1): 1–46.

Agawu, Kofi. 2007. "To Cite or Not to Cite? Confronting the Legacy of (European) Writing on African Music." *Fontes Artis Musicae* 54 (3): 254–262.

Agawu, Kofi. 2008. "Meki Nzewi and the Discourse of African Musicology: A 70th Birthday Appreciation." *Journal of the Musical Arts of Africa* 5 (1): 1–18.

Agawu, Kofi. 2016. *The African Imagination in Music*. New York: Oxford University Press.

Agawu, Kofi. 2020. *L'Imagination africaine en musique*. Paris: Philharmonie.

Agawu, Kofi. 2020. "Rethinking Ligeti's (and Reich's) African Affiliations." In *A Tribute to György Ligeti in his Native Transylvania*, edited by Bianca Ţiplea Temeş and Kofi Agawu, pp. 103–129. Cluj-Napoca, Romania: MediaMusica.

Agawu, Kofi. 2021. "Lives in Musicology: My Life in Writings." *Acta Musicologica* 93: 1–18.

Ames, David W., and Anthony V. King. 1971. *A Glossary of Hausa Music and Its Social Contexts*. Evanston, IL: Northwestern University Press.

Ampene, Kwasi. 2005. *Female Song Tradition and the Akan of Ghana: The Creative Process in Nnwonkoro*. Aldershot, UK: Ashgate.

Ampene, Kwasi. 2020. *Asante Court Music and the Verbal Arts in Ghana: The Porcupine and the Gold Stool*. SOAS Studies in Music Series. London: Routledge.

Ampene, Kwasi, and Nana Kwadwo Nyantakyi III. 2016. *Engaging Modernity: Asante in the Twenty-First Century*. Ann Arbor, MI: University Lithoprinters.

Amu, Misonu. 1997. "Glossary of Ewe Musical Terms." Institute of African Studies, University of Ghana. *Research Review* 13: 27–45.

Anku, Willie. 2002. *Structural Set Analysis of African Music 1: Adowa*. Legon, Ghana: Soundstage Production.

Anku, Willie. 2002. *Structural Set Analysis 2: Bawa*. Legon, Ghana: Soundstage Production.

Appert, Catherine. 2018. *In Hip Hop Time: Music, Memory, and Social Change in Urban Senegal*. New York: Oxford University Press.

Appiah, Kwame Anthony. 1992. *In My Father's House: Africa in the Philosophy of Culture*. New York: Oxford University Press.

Appiah, Anthony. 1984. "Structures on Strictures: The Prospects for a Structuralist Poetics of African Fiction." In *Black Literature and Literary Theory*, edited by Henry-Louis Gates Jr., pp. 127–150. New York: Methuen.

Arom, Simha. 1991 [1985]. *African Polyphony and Polyrhythm: Musical Structure and Methodology*, translated from French by Martin Thom, Barbara Tuckett, and Raymond Boyd. Cambridge, UK: Cambridge University Press.

Arom, Simha. 1994. "Intelligence in Traditional Music." In *What is Intelligence?* (Darwin College Lectures 1992), edited by Jean Khalfa, pp. 137–160. Cambridge, UK: Cambridge University Press.

Askew, Kelly. 2002. *Performing the Nation: Swahili Music and Cultural Politics in Tanzania*. Chicago: University of Chicago Press.

Avorgbedor, Daniel Kodzo. 2012. "The Place of the Visual in Constructing and Extending Affect and Meaning in Ewe Performance Traditions with Attention to *Dufozi*: Some Theoretical and Methodological Implications." Paper Read at the International Symposium, African Music in the 21st Century—An Iconic Turn? Mainz.

Avorgbedor, Daniel. 2016. "East and West Africa." In *Oxford Bibliographies Online*. Accessed May 17, 2022. https://www-oxfordbibliographies-com.ezproxy.princeton.edu/view/document/obo-9780199757824/obo-9780199757824-0175.xml.

Ballen, Harry. 2009. *A Short History of African Philosophy*. Bloomington: Indiana University Press.

Bates, Eliot. 2012. "The Social Life of Musical Instruments." *Ethnomusicology* 56 (3): 363–395.

Bent, Ian, and Anthony Pople. 2001 [1980]. "Analysis." In *Grove Music Online*. Accessed July 9, 2021. https://www-oxfordmusiconline-com.ezproxy.princeton.edu/grovemusic/view/10.1093/gmo/9781561592630.001.0001/omo-9781561592630-e-0000041862.

Berger, Anna Maria Busse. 2013. "Spreading the Gospel of *Singbewegung*: An Ethnomusicologist Missionary in Tanganyika of the 1930s." *Journal of the American Musicological Society* 66 (2): 475–522.

Berger, Anna Maria Busse. 2020. *The Search for Medieval Music in Africa and Germany, 1891–1961: Scholars, Singers, Missionaries*. Chicago: University of Chicago Press.

Berliner, Paul. 1978. *The Soul of Mbira: Music and Traditions of the Shona People of Zimbabwe*. Berkeley: University of California Press.

Berliner, Paul. 2020. *The Art of Mbira: Musical Inheritance and Legacy*. Chicago: University of Chicago Press.

Berry, David Carson. 2004. *A Topical Guide to Schenkerian Literature: An Annotated Bibliography with Indices*. Hillsdale, NY: Pendragon Press.

Best of Ladysmith Black Mambazo. 1992. Compact Disc. [US]: Shanachie Entertainment.

Betterman, Henrik, et al. 1999. "Musical Rhythms in Heart Period Dynamics: A Cross Cultural and Interdisciplinary Approach to Cardiac Rhythms." *Proceedings of the American Physiological Society* 277, H1762–H1770.

Blacking, John. 1955. "Some Notes on a Theory of African Rhythm Advanced by Hornbostel." *African Music* 1 (2): 12–20.

Blacking, John. 1973. *How Musical Is Man*? Seattle: University of Seattle Press.

Blacking, John. 1995 [1967]. *Venda Children's Songs: A Study in Ethnomusicological Analysis*. Chicago: University of Chicago Press.

Blacking, John. 1995. *Music, Culture and Experience: Selected Papers of John Blacking.* Chicago: University of Chicago Press.

Boahen, A. Adu. 1987. *African Perspectives on Colonialism.* Baltimore, MD: Johns Hopkins University Press.

Brandel, Rose. 1959. "The African Hemiola Style." *Ethnomusicology* 3 (3): 106–117.

Brandel, Rose. 1961. *The Music of Central Africa: An Ethnomusicological Study.* The Hague: Martinus Nijhoff.

Brandilly, Monique. 1997. *Introduction aux musiques Africaines.* Arles: Cité de la musique/Actes Sud.

Burns, James. 2005. *The Beard Cannot Tell Stories to the Eyelash: Creative Transformation in an Ewe Funeral Dance-Drumming Tradition.* PhD diss., University of London, School of Oriental and African Studies.

Burns, James. 2009. *Female Voices from an Ewe Dance-Drumming Community: Our Music Has Become a Divine Spirit.* Farnham, UK: Ashgate.

Burns, James. 2010. "Rhythmic Archetypes in Instrumental Music from Africa and the Diaspora." *Music Theory Online* 16 (4). Accessed May 16, 2022. http://mto.societymusictheory.org/issues/mto.10.16.4/mto.10.16.4.burns.html.

Carter-Ényì, Aaron. 2016. *Contour Levels: An Abstraction of Pitch Space Based on African Tone Systems.* PhD diss., Ohio State University.

Carter-Ényì, Aaron. 2020. "Tones and Tunes: Melody and Part Writing Exercises based on Ìgbò and Yorùbá Lyrics." In *Engaging Students: Essays in Music Pedagogy* 8. http://dx.doi.org/10.18061/es.v7i0.

Carter-Ényì, Aaron, and Quintina Carter-Ényì. 2020. "Melodic Language and Linguistic Melodies: Text Setting in Igbo." *SMT-V* 6 (5). https://vimeo.com/448178213.

Centrafrique: pygmées Aka (Chants de chasse, d'amour et de moquerie. 1998. Compact Disc. Paris: Ocora.

Charry, Eric. 2000. *Mande Music: Traditional and Modern Music of the Maninka and Mandinka of Western Africa.* Chicago: University of Chicago Press.

Charry, Eric. 2012. *Hip Hop Africa: New African Music in a Globalizing World.* Bloomington: Indiana University Press.

Chemillier, Marc. 2004. "Musical représentations and mathematical representations." *L'Homme* 171–172: 267–284.

Chernoff, John Miller. 1979. *African Rhythm and African Sensibility: Aesthetics and Social Action in African Musical Idioms.* Chicago: University of Chicago Press.

Chikowero, Mhoze. 2015. *African Music, Power, and Being in Colonial Zimbabwe.* Bloomington: Indiana University Press.

Childs, Tucker G. 1994. "African Ideophones." In *Sound Symbolism*, edited by Leanne Hinton, Johanna Nichols, and John J. Ohala, pp. 178–204. Cambridge, UK: Cambridge University Press.

Christensen, Thomas, ed. 2006. *The Cambridge History of Western Music Theory.* Cambridge, UK: Cambridge University Press.

Christensen, Thomas. 2019. "Tonality." In *Oxford Bibliographies Online.* Accessed June 15, 2021. https://www-oxfordbibliographies-com.ezproxy.princeton.edu/view/document/obo-9780199757824/obo-9780199757824-0252.xml.

Christensen, Thomas. 2019. *Stories of Tonality in the Age of François-Joseph Fétis.* Chicago: University of Chicago Press.

Chung, Andrew J. 2022. "Music Theory Splintered Up, Not Broken Down." *Music Theory Spectrum* 44 (1): 173–186.

Comaroff, Jean, and John Comaroff. 1991. *Of Revelation and Revolution: Christianity, Colonialism and Consciousness in South Africa.* Chicago: University of Chicago Press.

Comaroff, Jean, and John Comaroff. 2012. *Theory from the South: Or, How Euro-America Is Evolving Toward Africa*. Boulder, CO: Paradigm Publishers.

Composers Under the Tree of God: Art-Music in Ghana. 1995. Film. Berlin: Bavarian TV.

Cooke, Peter. 1969. "Ganda Xylophone Music: Another Approach." *African Music* 4 (4): 62–80.

Coplan, David. 1978. "'Go To My Town, Cape Coast!': The Social History of Ghanaian Highlife." In *Eight Urban Musical Cultures*, edited by Bruno Nettl, pp. 96–114. Urbana: University of Illinois Press, 1978.

Curry, Ben. 2012. "Resituating the Icon: David Osmond-Smith's Contributions to Music Semiotics." *Twentieth Century Music* 9 (1–2): 177–200.

Damschroder, David, and David Russell Williams. 1990. *Music Theory from Zarlino to Schenker: A Bibliography and Guide*. Stuyvesant, NY: Pendragon Press.

Dauer, Alfons M. 1983. "Afrikanische Musik und völkerkundlicher Tonfilm." In *Musik in Afrika. 20 Beiträge zur Kenntnis traditioneller afrikanischer Musikkulturen*, edited by Artur Simon, pp. 189–201. Berlin: Staatliche Museen Preussischer Kulturbesitz.

Davidson, Basil. 1984. *Africa: A Voyage of Discovery*. Video recording. Chicago: Home Vision Select.

Denning, Michael. 2015. *Noise Uprising: The Audiopolitics of a World Musical Revolution*. London: Verso.

Desai, Gaurav. 2001. *Subject to Colonialism: African Self-Fashioning and the Colonial Library*. Durham, NC: Duke University Press.

De-Souza, Dorothy Enam Esi. 2020. *A Study of the Ghanaian Classics Recording Project by the Ghana National Symphony Orchestra*. M. Phil. thesis, University of Ghana, Legon.

Dingemanse, Mark. 2010. *The Meaning and Use of Ideophones in Siwu*. PhD diss., Max Plank Institute for Psycholinguistics.

Djedje, Jacqueline. 2008. *Fiddling in West Africa: Touching the Spirit in Fulbe, Hausa, and Dagbamba Cultures*. Bloomington: Indiana University Press.

Djedje, Jacqueline. 2008. *Fiddling in West Africa (1950s–1990s): The Songbook*. Los Angeles, CA: UCLA Ethnomusicology Publications.

Djedje, Jacqueline, and William G. Carter. 1989. "African Musicology: An Assessment of the Field." In *African Musicology: Current Trends*, vol. 1, edited by Jacqueline Codgell Djedje and William G. Carter, pp. 39–44. Los Angeles: African Studies Center, University of California.

Dolan, Emily. 2013. *The Orchestral Revolution: Haydn and the Technologies of Timbre*. Cambridge, UK: Cambridge University Press.

Dor, George. 2004. "Communal Creativity and Song Ownership in Anlo-Ewe Musical Practice: The Case of Havolu." *Ethnomusicology* 48 (1): 26–51.

Dor, George Dor. 2005. "Uses of Indigenous Music Genres in Ghanaian Choral Art Music: Perspectives from the Works of Amu, Blege, and Dor." *Ethnomusicology* 49 (3): 441–475.

Dor, George. 2015. "Exploring the Ontology and Application of the 'Nketia Dominant Seventh Chord.'" In *Discourses in African Musicology*, edited by Kwasi Ampene et al., pp. 350–371. Ann Arbor: Michigan Publishing.

Dor, George Worlasi Kwasi. 2015. "Exploring Indigenous Interpretive Frameworks in African Music Scholarship: Conceptual Metaphors and Indigenous Ewe Knowledge in the Life and Work of Hesinɔ Vinɔkɔ Akpalu." *Black Music Research Journal* 35 (2): 149–183. doi:10.5406/blacmusiresej.35.2.0149.

Dor, George. 2014. *West African Drumming and Dance in North American Universities: An Ethnomusicological Perspective*. Jackson: University of Mississippi Press.

Eco, Umberto.1973. "Introduction to a Semiotics of Iconic Signs." *Versus* 2: 1–15.

Edwards, Brent. 2016. "The Sound of Anticolonialism." In *Audible Empire: Music, Global Politics, Critique*, edited by Ronald Radano and Tejumola Olaniyan, pp. 269–291. Durham, NC: Duke University Press.

Ekwueme, Lazarus. 1973–1974. "African Music in Christian Liturgy: The Igbo Experiment." *African Music* 5: 12–33.

Erlmann, Veit. 1996. *Nightsong: Performance, Power and Practice in South Africa*. Chicago: University of Chicago Press.

Erlmann, Veit. 1999. *Music, Modernity, and the Global Imagination: South Africa and the West*. New York: Oxford University Press.

Erlmann, Veit. 2004. "Resisting Sameness: À propos Kofi Agawu's 'Representing African Music.'" *Music Theory Spectrum* 26 (2): 291–304.

Euba, Akin. 1989. *Essays in African Music*, vol. 2. Lagos: Elekoto Music Centre.

Euba, Akin. 1991. *Yoruba Drumming: The Dùndún Tradition*. Lagos and Bayreuth: Elokoto Music Centre and Bayreuth African Studies Series.

Euba, Akin. 1993. *Modern African Music: A Catalogue of Selected Archival Materials at Iwalewa-Haus, University of Bayreuth, Germany*. Bayreuth: Iwalewa-Haus.

Euba, Akin. 2014. *J. H. Kwabena Nketia: Bridging Musicology and Composition: A Study in Creative Musicology*. Richmond, CA: MRI Press.

Everett, Yayoi Uno, and Frederick Lau, eds. 2004. *Locating East Asia in Western Art Music*. Middletown, CT: Wesleyan University Press.

Ewe Drumming from Ghana: The Soup Which Is Sweet Draws the Chairs Closer. 2005. Compact Disc. London: Topic Records.

Ewell, Philip. 2020. "Music Theory and the White Racial Frame." *Music Theory Online* 26 (2). https://mtosmt.org/issues/mto.20.26.2/mto.20.26.2.ewell.html.

Eybl, Martin. 1995. *Ideologie und Methode: Zum ideengeschichtlichen Kontext von Schenkers Musiktheorie*. Tutzing: Schneider.

Eyre, Banning. 2015. *Lion Songs: Thomas Mapfumo and the Music that made Zimbabwe*. Durham, NC: Duke University Press.

Fanon, Frantz. 1968 [1952]. *Black Skin, White Masks*. Translated by Charles Lam Markmann. London: MacGibbon and Kee.

Feld, Steven. 1981. "'Flow Like a Waterfall': The Metaphors of Kaluli Musical Theory." *Yearbook for Traditional Music* 13: 22–47.

Feld, Steven. 1982. *Sound and Sentiment: Birds, Weeping, Poetics, and Song in Kaluli Expression*. Philadelphia: University of Pennsylvania Press.

Feld, Steven. 1987. "Dialogic Editing: Interpreting How Kaluli Read *Sound and Sentiment*." *Cultural Anthropology* 2 (2): 190–210.

Feld, Steven. 2012. *Jazz Cosmopolitanism in Accra: Five Musical Years in Ghana*. Durham, NC: Duke University Press.

Fernando, Nathalie. 2011. *Polyphonies du Nord-Cameroun*. Société d'Etudes Linguistiques et Anthropologiques de France. Paris: Peeters/SELAF.

Fiagbedzi, Nissio. 2015. "J. H. Kwabena Nketia's *Republic Suite*: An Analytical Portrait of Movement 1." In *Discourses in African Musicology*, edited by Kwasi Ampene et al., pp. 306–329. Ann Arbor: Michigan Publishing.

Fink, Robert, and Cecilia Sun. 2016. "Minimalism." In *Oxford Bibliographies Online*. Accessed July 8, 2021. https://www-oxfordbibliographies-com.ezproxy.princeton.edu/view/document/obo-9780199757824/obo-9780199757824-0188.xml.

Forte, Allen. 2003. "The Founding of the Society for Music Theory." *Music Theory Online* 9. https://www.mtosmt.org/issues/mto.03.9.1/mto.03.9.1.forte.php.

Franich, Kathryn, and Ange B. Lendja Ngnemzué. 2021. "Feeling the Beat in an African Tone Language: Rhythmic Mapping Between Language and Music." *Frontiers in Communication* 6. Accessed May 17 2022. https://doi.org/10.3389/fcomm.2021.653747.

Friedson, Steven. 1996. *Dancing Prophets: Musical Experience in Tumbuka Healing*. Chicago: University of Chicago Press.

Friedson, Steven. 2009. *Remains of Ritual: Northern Gods in a Southern Land*. Chicago: University of Chicago Press.

Frozen Brass: Africa and Latin America. 1993. Compact Disc. Leiden: Pan.

Fürniss, Suzanne. 2006. "Aka Polyphony." In *Analytical Studies in World Music*, edited by Michael Tenzer, pp. 163–204. New York: Oxford University Press.

Gabon: Music of the Bibayak Pygmies: Epic Cantors. 2001. Compact Disc. France: Ocora.

Gbagbo, Divine. 2021. *Recreation, Rites, and Rulership: Postcolonial Christianity in Ewe Music of Ghana*. PhD diss., Ohio University.

George, Olakunle. 2003. *Relocating Agency: Modernity and African Letters*. Albany: State University of New York Press.

Gerstin, Julian. 2017. "Comparisons of African and Diasporic Rhythm: The Ewe, Cuba, and Martinique." *Analytical Approaches to World Music* 5 (2). Accessed July 9, 2021. http://www.aawmjournal.com/articles/2017b/Gerstin_AAWM_Vol_5_2.pdf.

Geurts, Kathryn Linn. 2002. *Culture and Senses: Bodily Ways of Knowing in an African Community*. Berkeley: University of California Press.

Gopinath, Sumanth. 2020. "Steve Reich and the Politics of Race with Sumanth Gopinath." Accessed May 17, 2022. https://www.buzzsprout.com/1114601/5410909.

Grauer, Victor. 2009. "Concept, Style and Structure in the Music of African Pygmies and Bushmen: A Study in Cross-Cultural Analysis." *Ethnomusicology* 53 (3): 396–424.

Gray, John. 2018. *Music of Sub-Saharan Africa: An International Bibliography and Resource Guide*. Nyack, NY: African Diaspora Press.

Greer, Taylor. 1998. *A Question of Balance: Charles Seeger's Philosophy of Music*. Berkeley: University of California Press.

Grosfoguel, Rámon. 2011. "Decolonizing Post-Colonial Studies and Paradigms of Political-Economy: Transmodernity, Decolonial Thinking, and Global Coloniality." *Transmodernity: Journal of Peripheral Cultural Production of the Luso-Hispanic World* 1 (1): 1–38.

Gunderson, Frank. 2010. *Sukuma Labor Songs from Western Tanzania: "We Never Sleep, We Dream of Farming."* Leiden and Boston: Brill.

Gunderson, Frank. 2018. *The Legacy of Tanzanian Musicians Muhidin Gurumo and Hassan Bitchuka: Rhumba Kiserebuka!* Lanham, MD: Lexington Books.

Halle, John, and Fred Lerdahl. 1993. "A Generative Text-Setting Model." *Current Musicology* 55: 3–26.

Hornbostel, Erich M. von. 1928. "African Negro Music." *Africa* 1 (1): 30–62.

Horton, Julian. 2020. "On the Musicological Necessity of Musical Analysis." *Musical Quarterly* 103: 62–104. Accessed July 2021. https://doi-org.ezproxy.princeton.edu/10.1093/musqtl/gdaa005.

Hountondji, Paulin. 1996 [1983]. *African Philosophy: Myth and Reality*. 2nd edition. Translated by Henry Evans with Jonathan Rée. Bloomington: Indiana University Press.

Hyer, Brian. 2006. "Tonality." In *The Cambridge History of Western Music Theory*, edited by Thomas Christensen, pp. 726–752. Cambridge, UK: Cambridge University Press.

Impey, Angela. 2018. *Song Walking: Women, Music and Environmental Justice in an African Borderland*. Chicago: University of Chicago Press.

Irele, Abiola. 1993. "Is African Music Possible?" *Transition* 61: 56–71.

Irele, Abiola. 2001. *The African Imagination: Literature in Africa and the Black Diaspora.* Oxford, UK: Oxford University Press.

Irele, F. Abiola. 2001. "Editorial: The Landscape of African Music." *Research in African Literatures* 32 (2): 1–2.

Ishola, Haruna and His Apala Group. 2010. *Oluwa Nikan Loba.* LP. Lagos: Star Label.

Iyer, Vijay S. 1998. *Microstructures of Feel, Macrostructures of Sound: Embodied Cognition in West African and African-American Musics.* PhD diss., University of California, Berkeley.

Jackson, Timothy L. 2019. "A Preliminary Response to Ewell." *Journal of Schenkerian Studies* 12: 157–166.

Jaji, Tsitsi. 2014. *Africa in Stereo: Modernism, Music, and Pan-African Solidarity.* Oxford, UK: Oxford University Press.

Jakobson, Roman. 1971. "Language in Relation to Other Communication Systems." In *Selected Writings*, vol. 2, pp. 697–708. The Hague: Mouton.

Jones, A[rthur]. M[orris]. 1954. "African Rhythm." *Africa* 24 (1): 26–47.

Jones, A[rthur]. M[orris]. 1959. *Studies in African Music.* 2 vols. London: Oxford University Press.

Jones, A[rthur]. M[orris]. 1976. *African Hymnody in Christian Worship: A Contribution to the History of Its Development.* Mambo Occasional Papers. Gwelo, Rhodesia: Mambo.

Kafumbe, Damascus. 2018. *Tuning the Kingdom: Kawugulu Musical Performance, Politics, and Storytelling in Baĝanda.* Rochester, NY: University of Rochester Press.

Kagame, Alexis. 1976. *La philosophie Bantu Comparée.* Paris: Présence Africaine.

Kauffman, Robert. 1980. "African Rhythm: A Reassessment." *Ethnomusicology* 24 (3): 393–415.

Keil, Charles. 1979. *Tiv Song: The Sociology of Art in a Classless Society.* Chicago: University of Chicago Press.

Keïta, Aly. 2010. *Farafinko.* Compact Disc. Vodelée, Belgium: Studio Contre-Jour.

Kerman, Joseph. 1980. "How We Got into Analysis." *Critical Inquiry* 7 (2): 311–331.

Kerman, Joseph. 1980. *Listen.* 3rd edition. New York: Worth Publishers.

Kerman, Joseph. 1986. *Contemplating Music: Challenges to Musicology.* Cambridge, MA: Harvard University Press.

Khumalo, Andile. 2018. "Reading for 'African Spectralism' in Latozi Mphahleni's 'Modokali.'" *SAMUS: South African Music Studies* 38 (1): 137–158.

Kidula, Jean Ngoya. 2013. *Music in Kenyan Christianity: Logooli Religious Song.* Bloomington: Indiana University Press.

Kimberlin, Cynthia, and Akin Euba. 2005. *Towards an African Pianism: Keyboard Music of Africa and the Diaspora.* Richmond, CA: MRI Press.

King, Anthony. 1960. "Employments of the Standard Pattern in Yoruba Music." *African Music* 2 (3): 51–54.

King, Roberta, Jean Ngoya Kidula, James R. Krabill, and Thomas A. Oduro. 2008. *Music in the Life of the African Church.* Waco, TX: Baylor University Press.

Kisliuk, Michelle. 1998. *Seize the Dance! BaAka Musical Life and the Ethnography of Performance.* New York: Oxford University Press.

Klein, Tobias. 2008. *Moderne Traditionen: Studien zur postkolonialen Musikgeschichte Ghanas.* Berlin: Peter Lang.

Klein, Tobias Robert. 2018. "Preview for Spirits and Ancestors: Representations of Ghanaian School Life in Audiovisual and Electronic Media." *Africa Today* 64 (4): 53–73.

Koetting, James. 1970. "Analysis and Notation of West African Drum Ensemble Music." *Selected Reports in Ethnomusicology* 1 (3): 115–146.

Koetting, James. 1985. "Sub-Saharan Africa." *Ethnomusicology* 29 (2): 314–317.

Kolinski, Mieczyslaw. 1973. "A Cross-Cultural Approach to Metro-Rhythmic Patterns." *Ethnomusicology* 17 (3): 494–506.

Kongo, Zabana P. 1997. *African Drum Music [Slow Agbekor, Adowa, Kpanlogo, Agbadza]*. Accra, Ghana: Afram Publications.

Konye, Paul. 2007. *African Art Music: Political, Social, and Cultural Factors Behind Its Development and Practice in Nigeria*. New York: Edwin Mellen Press.

Krebs, Harald. 2009. "The Expressive Role of Rhythm and Meter in Schumann's Late Lieder." *Gamut* 2 (1): 267–298.

Kronos Quartet. 1992. *Pieces of Africa*. Compact Disc. New York: Elektra Nonesuch.

Kubik, Gerhard. 1962. "The Phenomenon of Inherent Rhythms in East and Central African Instrumental Music." *African Music* 3 (1): 33–42.

Kubik, Gerhard. 1985. "The Emics of African Rhythm." In *Cross Rhythms* 2, edited by Daniel Avorgbedor and Kwesi Yankah, pp. 26–66. Bloomington, IN: Trickster Press.

Kubik, Gerhard. 1985. "African Tone Systems: A Reassessment." *Yearbook for Traditional Music* 17: 31–63.

Kubik, Gerhard. 1987. "African Space/Time Concepts and the 'Tusona' Ideographs in Luchazi Culture: With a Discussion of Possible Cross-Parallels in Music." *African Music* 6 (4): 53–89.

Kubik, Gerhard. 1994. *Theory of African Music*, vol. *1*. Wilhelmshaven: Florian Noetzel Verlag.

Kubik, Gerhard. 1997. "Multipart Singing in sub-Saharan Africa: Remote and Recent Histories Unravelled." In *Symposium on Ethnomusicology*, edited by A. Tracey, pp. 85–97. Grahamstown, SA: International Library of African Music.

Kubik, Gerhard. 1997. "Intra-African Streams of Influence." In *Africa: The Garland Encyclopedia of World Music*, edited by Ruth Stone, pp. 293–326. New York: Garland.

Kubik, Gerhard. 1999. *Africa and the Blues*. Jackson: University Press of Mississippi.

Kubik, Gerhard. 2010. *Theory of African Music*, vol. *2*. Chicago: University of Chicago Press.

Kyker, Jennifer. 2016. *Oliver Mtukudzi: Living Tuku Music in Zimbabwe*. Bloomington: Indiana University Press.

Labi, Gyimah. 2003. *Theoretical Issues in African Music: Exploring Resources Creatively*. Bayreuth: Bayreuth African Studies.

Lacerda, Marcos Branda. 1988. *Kultische Trommelmusik der Yoruba in der Volksrepublik Benin: Bata-Sango und Bata-Egungun in den Städten Pobè und Sakété*. 2 vols. Hamburg: Verlag der Musikalienhandlung Karl Dieter Wagner.

Lacerda, Marcos Branda. 2007. "Instrumental Texture and Heterophony in a Fon Repertoire for Drums." *Revista Transcultural de Música* [*Transcultural Music Review*] 11. Accessed July 24, 2021. http://www.sibetrans.com/trans/a127/instrumental-texture-and-heterophony-in-a-fon-repertoire-for-drum.

Lacerda, Marcos Branda. 2014. *Música Instrumental no Benim: Repertório Fon e Música Bàtá*. São Paulo: Editoria la Universidade de São Paulo.

Lachmann, Kathryn. 2014. *Borrowed Forms: The Music and Ethics of Transnational Fiction*. Liverpool, UK: Liverpool University Press.

Ladzekpo, C. K. 1996. *Cultural Understanding of Polyrhythm*. Accessed November 2022. http://home.comcast.net/~dzinyaladzekpo/PrinciplesFr.html.

Ladzekpo, C. K., and Richard Hodges. 1995. *Foundation Course in African Dance Drumming*. Accessed May 17, 2022. http://www.richardhodges.com/ladzekpo/.

Larson, Steve. 2012. *Musical Forces: Motion, Metaphor, and Meaning in Music*. Bloomington: Indiana University Press.

Legendary Wulomei. 2000. Compact Disc. Accra: Sam Records.

Lewin, David. 1969. "Behind the Beyond: A Response to Edward T. Cone." *Perspectives of New Music* 7: 59–69.

Ligeti, György. 1991. "Foreword." In Simha Arom, *African Polyphony and Polyrhythm: Musical Structure and Methodology*, pp. xvii–xviii. Cambridge, UK: Cambridge University Press.

Locke, David. 1982. "Principles of Offbeat Timing and Cross Rhythm in Southern Ewe Dancing." *Ethnomusicology* 26: 217–246.

Locke, David. 1992. *Drum Kpegisu: A War Drum of the Ewe*. Tempe, AZ: White Cliffs Media Company.

Locke, David. 1998. *Dum Gahu: An Introduction to African Rhythm*. Tempe, AZ: White Cliffs Media.

Locke, David. 2011. "The Metric Matrix: Simultaneous Multidimensionality in African Music." *Analytical Approaches to World Music* 1. Accessed May 17, 2022. http://www.aawmjournal.com/articles/2011a/Locke_AAWM_Vol_1_1.htm.

Locke, David. 2010. "Yeweyu in the Metric Matrix." *Music Theory Online* 16 (4). https://www.mtosmt.org/issues/mto.10.16.4/mto.10.16.4.locke.html.

Locke, David. 2019. "An Approach to Musical Rhythm in Agbadza." In *Thought and Play in Musical Rhythm*, edited by Richard Wolf, Stephen Blum, and Christopher Hasty, pp. 100–145. New York: Oxford University Press.

London, Justin. 2012. *Hearing in Time: Psychological Aspects of Musical Meter*. 2nd edition. New York: Oxford University Press.

Lucia, Christine. 2008. "Back to the Future? Idioms of 'Displaced Time' in South African Composition." In *Composing Apartheid: Music for and against Apartheid*, edited by Grant Olwage, pp. 11–34. Johannesburg: Wits University Press.

Lucia, Christine. 2017. "'Yet None with Truer Fervour Sing': Coronation Song and the (De)colonization of African Choral Composition." *African Music: Journal of the International Library of African Music* 10 (3): 23–44.

Malin, Yonatan. 2010. *Songs in Motion. Rhythm and Meter in the German Lied*. Oxford Studies in Music Theory. Oxford, UK: Oxford University Press.

Mapaya, Geoff Madimabe. 2014. "African Musicology: Towards Defining and Setting Parameters of the Study of the Indigenous African Music." *Anthropologist* 18 (2): 619–627.

Mbembe, Achille. 1997. "The 'Thing' and its Double in Cameroonian Cartoons." In *Readings in African Popular Culture*, edited by Karin Barber, pp. 151–163. Bloomington: Indiana University Press.

Mbembe, Achille. 2001. *On the Postcolony*. Berkeley: University of California Press.

McClary, Susan. 1987. "The Blasphemy of Talking Politics during Bach Year." In *Music and Society: The Politics of Composition, Performance and Reception*, edited by Richard Leppert and Susan McClary, pp. 13–62. Cambridge, UK: Cambridge University Press.

McCreless, Patrick. 1997. "Rethinking Contemporary Music Theory." In *Keeping Score: Music, Disciplinarity, Culture*, edited by David Schwarz and Anahid Kassabian, pp. 1–49. Charlottesville: University of Virginia Press.

McPherson, Laura. 2019. "The Talking Balafon of the Sambla: Grammatical Principles and Documentary Implications." *Anthropological Linguistics* 60 (3): 255–294.

McPherson, Laura, and Lucas James. 2021. "Artistic Adaptation of Seenku Tone: Musical Surrogates vs. Vocal Music." In *Celebrating 50 Years of ACAL: Selected Papers from the 50th Annual Conference on African Linguistics*, edited by Akinbiyi Akinlabi, et al., pp. 203–223. Contemporary African Linguistics 7. Berlin: Language Science Press. DOI: 10.5281/zenodo.5578772.

Meintjes, Louise. 2006. Review of *Representing African Music* by Kofi Agawu. *Journal of the American Musicological Society* 59 (3): 769–777.

Meir, Irit, and Oksana Tkachman. 2014. "Iconicity." In *Oxford Bibliographies Online*. Accessed May 17, 2022. https://www-oxfordbibliographies-com.ezproxy.princeton.edu/view/document/obo-9780199772810/obo-9780199772810-0182.xml.

Memmi, Albert. 1965. *The Colonizer and the Colonized*. Translated by Howard Greenfield. Boston: Beacon.

Merriam, Alan P. 1964. *The Anthropology of Music*. Evanston, IL: Northwestern University Press.

Merriam, Alan P. 1982. "Concepts of Time Reckoning." In Merriam, *African Music in Perspective*, pp. 443–461. New York: Garland.

Mignolo, Walter, and Madina V. Tlostanova. 2006. "Theorizing from the Borders Shifting to Geo- and Body-Politics of Knowledge." *European Journal of Social Theory* 9 (2): 205–221.

Monts, Lester P. 1990. *An Annotated Glossary of Vai Musical Language and Its Social Contexts*. Paris: Peters-SELAF.

More Than 50 Most Loved Hymns. 2004. Compact Disc. Hollywood, CA: Liberty Records.

Morey, Stephen, and Jürgen Schöpf. 2012. "Tone in Speech and Singing: A Field Experiment to Research Their Relation in Endangered Languages of North East India." *Language Documentation and Description* 10 (0): 37–60. DOI: https://doi.org/10.25894/ldd188.

Morgan, Robert P. 2000. "Circular Form in the *Tristan* Prelude." *Journal of the American Musicological Society* 53 (1): 69–103.

Moyo, Dambisa. 2009. "Why Foreign Aid Is Hurting Africa." *Wall Street Journal*, March 21. https://www.wsj.com/articles/SB123758895999200083.

Mudimbe, V. Y. 1988. *The Invention of Africa: Gnosis, Philosophy, and the Order of Knowledge*. Bloomington: Indiana University Press.

Mukherji, Somangshu. 2014. *Generative Musical Grammar: A Minimalist Approach*. PhD diss., Princeton University.

Mukherji, Somangshu. 2022. "Language Models and World Music Analysis." In *Trends in World Music Analysis*, edited by Lawrence Beaumont Shuster, Somangshu Mukherji and Noé Dinnerstein, pp. 283–331. London: Routledge.

Muller, Carol. 1999. *Rituals of Fertility and the Sacrifice of Desire: Nazarite Women's Performance in South Africa*. Chicago: University of Chicago Press.

Music of Africa Series: 30 Musical Instruments 4 Flutes and Horns. n.d. Compact Disc. Grahamstown: International Library of African Music.

Music of our Century. 1988. Compact Disc. Mainz: Wergo.

Musiques du monde. 1989. Compact Disc. France: Playa Sound.

Nannyonga-Tamusuza, Sylvia. 2005. *Baakisimba: Gender in the Music and Dance of Baganda People of Uganda*. New York: Routledge.

Nattiez, Jean-Jacques. 1982. "Varèse's *Density 21.5*: A Study in Semiological Analysis," translated by Anna Barry. *Music Analysis* 1 (3): 243–340.

Nattiez, Jean-Jacques. 1990. *Music and Discourse: Toward a Semiology of Music*. Translated by Carolyn Abbate. Princeton, NJ: Princeton University Press.

Nattiez, Jean-Jacques. 1993. "Simha Arom and the Return of Analysis to Ethnomusicology." *Music Analysis* 12 (2): 241–265.

Ndaliko, Chérie Rivers. 2016. *Necessary Noise: Music, Film, and Charitable Imperialism in the East of Congo*. New York: Oxford University Press.

Nettl, Bruno. 1958. "Historical Aspects of Ethnomusicology." *American Anthropologist* 60: 518–532.

Nettl, Bruno. 2001. "Colonialism." *Grove Music Online*. Accessed June 15, 2021. https://doi.org/10.1093/gmo/9781561592630.article.46822.

Nketia, J. H. Kwabena. 1949. *Akanfo nwom bi [Akan songs]*. London: Oxford University Press.

Nketia, J. H. Kwabena. 1963. *Folk Songs of Ghana*. Legon: University of Ghana.

Nketia, J. H. Kwabena. 1962. *African Music in Ghana*. Evanston, IL: Northwestern University Press.

Nketia, J. H. Kwabena. 1963. *Drumming in Akan Communities of Ghana*. Edinburgh: Thomas Nelson and Sons.

Nketia, J. H. Kwabena. 1974. *The Music of Africa*. New York: Norton.

Nketia, J. H. Kwabena. 1986. "Perspectives on African Musicology." In *Africa and the West: The Legacies of Empire*, edited by Isaac James Mowoe and Richard Bjornson, pp. 215–253. Westport, CT: Greenwood Press.

Nketia, J. H. Kwabena. 1997. "The Scholarly Study of African Music: A Historical Review." In *Africa: The Garland Encyclopedia of World Music*, edited by Ruth Stone, pp. 13–73. New York: Garland.

Nketia, J. H. Kwabena. 2004. *The Creative Potential of African Art Music in Ghana: A Personal Testimony*. Companion Booklet to ICAMD CDs of music by Nketia. Accra: Afram Publications.

Nketia, J. H. Kwabena. 2016. *Reinstating Traditional Music in Contemporary Context*. Akropong-Akuapem, Ghana: Regnum Africa Publications.

No Boundaries: Ladysmith with the English Chamber Orchestra. 2004. Compact Disc. Cleveland, OH: Heads Up International, 2004.

Nöth, Winfried. 1995. *Handbook of Semiotics*. Bloomington: Indiana University Press.

Novotney, Eugene D. 1998. *The Three against Two Relationship as the Foundation of Timelines in West African Musics*. Urbana, IL: University of Illinois.

Nyaho, William Chapman, ed. 2009. *Piano Music of Africa and the African Diaspora*. New York: Oxford University Press.

Nyanyui Hame Hadzigbalẽ Gã, 5th edition. 2002. Maharashtra, India: Evangelical Presbyterian Church, Ghana and Eglise Evangélique Presbytérienne du Togo.

Nzewi, Meki. 1974. "Melo-Rhythmic Essence and Hot Rhythm in Nigerian Folk Music." *Black Perspective in Music* 2 (1): 23–28.

Nzewi, Meki. 1991. *Musical Practice and Creativity: An African Traditional Perspective*. Bayreuth, Germany: IWALEWA-Haus, University of Bayreuth.

Nzewi, Meki. 1997. *African Music: Theoretical Content and Creative Continuum: The Culture-Exponent's Definitions*. Olderhausen, Germany: Institut für populärer Musik.

Nzewi, Meki. 2010. *Musical Sense and Musical Meaning: An Indigenous African Perception*. Amsterdam: Rozenberg Publishers.

Olaniyan, Tejumola. 2004. *Arrest the Music!: Fela and His Rebel Art and Politics* Bloomington: Indiana University Press.

Olaniyan, Tejumola. 2002. "Cartooning Nigerian Anticolonial Nationalism." In *Images and Empires: Visuality in Colonial and Postcolonial Africa*, edited by P. S. Landau and D. D. Kaspin, pp. 124–140. Berkeley: University of California Press.

Omojola, Bode. 1994. "Contemporary Art Music in Nigeria: An Introductory Note on the Works of Ayo Bankole." *Africa* 64 (4): 533–543.

Omojola, Bode. 1995. *Nigerian Art Music, with an Introductory Study of Ghanaian Art Music*. Ibadan: Institut Français de Recherche en Afrique, University of Ibadan.

Omojola, Bode. 2009. *The Music of Fela Sowande: Encounters, African Identity and Creative Ethnomusicology*. Richmond, CA: MRI Press.

Omojola, Bode. 2012. *Yorùbá Music in the Twentieth Century: Identity, Agency, and Performance*. Rochester: University of Rochester Press.

Oruka, Odera. 1990. *Sage Philosophy: Indigenous Thinkers and Modern Debate*. Leiden: E. J. Brill.

Oxford Bibliographies Online (http://www.oxfordbibliographies.com.)

Ozah, Marie Agatha. 2008. *Égwú Àmàlà: Women in Traditional Performing Arts in Ogbaruland*. PhD diss., University of Pittsburgh.

Ozah, Marie Agatha. 2013. "Building Bridges Between Traditional and Western Art Music: A Study of Joshua Uzoigwe's *Egwu Amala*." *Analytical Approaches to Western Music Journal* 3. Available at http://www.aawmjournal.com/articles/2014a. Accessed June 2021.

Palisca, Claude. 2001 [1980]. "Theory." In *Grove Music Online*. Accessed May 17, 2022.

Pan-African Orchestra. 1995. *Opus 1*. Compact Disc. New York: Real World.

Pantaleoni, Hewitt. 1970. "Takada Drumming." *African Music* 4 (4): 6–31.

Pantaleoni, Hewitt. 1972. "Three Principles of Timing in Anlo Dance Drumming." *African Music* 5 (2): 50–63.

Pareles, Jon. 1998. "The Rhythm Century: The Unstoppable Beat." *New York Times*. May 3: 1. Accessed January 10, 2023. http://www.nytimes.com/1998/05/03/arts/pop-jazz-the-rhythm-century-the-unstoppable-beat.html?scp=1&sq=PARELES, Jon. The Rhythm Century&st=cse.

Passler, Jann. 2013. "Sacred Music in the African Missions: Gregorian Chant, Cantiques, and Indigenous Expression." *Atti del Congresso Internazionale di Musica Sacra*, 1287–1309. Rome: Libreria Editrice Vaticana.

Patel, Anirudh. 2007. *Music, Language, and the Brain*. Oxford, UK: Oxford University Press.

Peirce, Charles Sanders. 1931–1935. "*What Is a Sign?*" In *Collected Papers of Charles Sanders Peirce*, vol. 2, edited by C. Hartshone and P. Weiss, pp. 281, 285, and 297–302. Cambridge, MA: Harvard University Press.

Penalosa, David. 2012. *The Clave Matrix: Afro-Cuban Rhythm: Its Principles and African Origins*. Redway, CA: Bembe Books, 2009.

Perlman, Marc. 2004. *Unplayed Melodies: Javanese Gamelan and the Genesis of Music Theory* (Berkeley-London: University of California Press).

Perman, Tony. 2020. *Signs of the Spirit: Music and the Experience of Meaning in Ndau Ceremonial Life*. Champaign, IL: University of Illinois Press.

Phillips, Thomas Ekundayo. 1953. *Yoruba Music; African; Fusion of Speech and Music*. Johannesburg: African Music Society.

Plesch, Melanie. 2017. "Decentring Topic Theory: Musical Topics and Rhetorics of Identity in Latin American Art Music." *Portuguese Journal of Musicology/Revista Portuguesa de Musicologia* 4: 27–32.

Plesch, Melanie. 2019. "The West and the Rest: Some Reflections on Ex-Centric Art Musics." Unpublished keynote address to the workshop, "Musicology or Ethnomusicology? Discussing Disciplinary Boundaries in Non-Western Art Music." Cambridge University, Faculty of Music, 22 March 2019.

Polak, Rainer. 2010. "Rhythmic Feel as Meter: Non-Isochronous Beat Subdivision in Jembe Music from Mali." *Music Theory Online* 16. Accessed May 17, 2022. https://www.mtosmt.org/issues/mto.10.16.4/mto.10.16.4.polak.html.

Polak, Rainer. 2017. "The Lower limit for Meter in Dance Drumming from West Africa." *Empirical Musicology Review* 12 (3–4): 205–226.

Poole, Geoffrey. 1999. "Black-White-Rainbow: A Personal View on What African Music Means to the Contemporary Western Composer." In *Composing the Music of Africa: Composition, Interpretation and Realisation*, edited by Malcolm Floyd, pp. 295–334. Aldershot, UK: Ashgate.

Potter, Keith. 2013. "Minimalism." *Grove Music Online*. Accessed May 17, 2022. https://doi-org.ezproxy.princeton.edu/10.1093/gmo/9781561592630.article.A2257002.

Pressing, Jeff. 1983. "Cognitive Isomorphisms between Pitch and Rhythm in World Musics: West Africa, the Balkans and Western Tonality." *Studies in Music* 17: 38–61.

Quijano, Anibal. 2000. "Coloniality of Power, Ethnocentrism, and Latin America." *NEPANTLA* 1 (3): 533–580.

Quinn, Ian. 2006. "Minimal Challenges: Process Music and the Uses of Formalist Analysis." *Contemporary Music Review* 25 (3): 283–294.

Radano, Ronald, and Tejumola Olaniyan, eds. 2016. *Audible Empire: Music, Global Politics, Critique*. Durham, NC: Duke University Press.

Rae, Caroline. 2009. "Review of *Piano Music of Africa and the African Diaspora*, vols. 1–3, ed. William Chapman Nyaho." *Ethnomusicology* 53 (1): 146–151.

Rahn, Jay. 1983. *A Theory for All Music: Problems and Solutions in the Analysis of Non-Western Forms*. Toronto: University of Toronto Press.

Ratner, Leonard. 1980. *Classic Music: Expression, Form and Style*. New York: Schirmer.

Reed, Daniel. 2003. *Dan Ge performance: Masks and Music in Contemporary Côte d'Ivoire*. Bloomington: Indiana University Press.

Rehding, Alex, and Steven Rings, eds. 2015 online; 2020 in print. *The Oxford Handbook of Critical Concepts in Music Theory*. New York: Oxford University Press. https://doi.org/10.1093/oxfordhb/9780190454746.001.0001.

Reich, Steve, ed. 2002. *Writings on Music, 1965–2000*. Edited with an introduction by Paul Hillier. Oxford; New York: Oxford University Press.

Revuluri, Sindhumathi. 2016. "Orientalism and Musical Knowledge: Lessons from Edward Said." *Journal of the Royal Musical Association* 141: 205–209.

Rhyn, Chris van. 2013. *Towards a Mapping of the Marginal: Readings of Art Songs by Nigerian, Ghanaian, Egyptian and South African Composers*. PhD diss., Stellenbosch University.

Rodney, Walter. *How Europe Underdeveloped Africa*. London: Bogle-L'Ouverture, 1972.

Rogers, Stephen. 2011. "Thinking (and Singing) in Threes: Triple Hypermeter and the Songs of Fanny Hensel." *Music Theory Online* 17 (1). Accessed May 17, 2022. https://www.mtosmt.org/issues/mto.11.17.1/mto.11.17.1.rodgers.html.

Rouget, Gilbert. 1966. "African Traditional Non-Prose Forms: Reciting, Declaiming, singing and Strophic Structure." In *Proceedings of a Conference on African Languages and Literatures, Northwestern University*, edited by Jack Berry et al., pp. 45–58. Evanston, IL: Northwestern University Press.

Rouget, Gilbert. 1996. *Un roi Africain et sa musique de cour: Chants et danses du palais à Porto-Novo sous le règne de Gbèfa (1948–76)*. Paris: CNRS Éditions.

Russell, David Williams, and C. Matthew Balensuela. 2008. *Music Theory from Boethius to Zarlino: A Bibliography and Guide*. Stuyvesant, NY: Pendragon Press.

Sadoh, Godwin. 2004. "Intercultural Creativity in Joshua Uzoigwe's Music." *Africa* 74 (4): 633–661.

Sadoh, Godwin. 2010. "African Musicology: A Bibliographical Guide to Nigerian Art Music (1927–2009)." *Notes* 66 (3): 485–502.

Said, Edward. 1978. *Orientalism*. New York: Vintage Books.

Said, Edward. 1994. *Culture and Imperialism*. New York: Vintage Books.

Sakata, Lorraine. 1983. *Music in the Mind: The Concepts of Music and Musician in Afghanistan*. Kent, OH: State University.

Savage, Patrick E., and Steven Brown. 2013. "Toward a New Comparative Musicology." *AAWM Journal* 2 (2). Accessed May 17, 2022. http://iftawm.org/journal/oldsite/articles/2013b/Savage_Brown_AAWM_Vol_2_2.html.

Schaeffner, André. 1936. *Origine des instruments de musique. Introduction ethnologie à l'histoire de la musique instrumentale*. Paris: Payot.

Schachter, Michael. 2015. "Structural Levels in South Indian Music." *Music Theory Online* 21 (4). Accessed May 17 2022. https://mtosmt.org/issues/mto.15.21.4/mto.15.21.4.schachter.php.

Schenker, Heinrich. 1987 [1910]. *Counterpoint: A Translation of Kontrapunt*, vol. 1. Translated by John Rothgeb and Jürgen Thym. Edited by John Rothgeb. New York: Schirmer Books.

Schenker, Heinrich. 2004 [1921–23]. *Der Tonwille: Pamphlets in Witness of the Immutable Laws of Music: Offered to a New Generation of Youth*, volume 1, issues 1–5 (1921–1923). Edited by William Drabkin, translated by Ian Bent et al. Oxford, UK: Oxford University Press.

Schenker, Heinrich. 2012. *Schenker Documents Online*. In collaboration with the Department of Digital Humanities, King's College London. Accessed July 9, 2021. https://schenkerdocumentsonline.org/index.html.

Scherzinger, Martin Rudolf. 2001. "Negotiating the Music-Theory/African Music Nexus: A Political Critique of Ethnomusicological Anti-Formalism and a Strategic Analysis of the Harmonic Patterning of the Shona Mbira Song *Nyamaropa*." *Perspectives of New Music* 39 (1): 5–118.

Scherzinger, Martin Rudolf. 2001. "Review of *Music, Modernity, and the Global Imagination* by Veit Erlmann." *Journal of the Royal Musical Association*, 126 (1): 117–114.

Scherzinger, Martin Rudolf. 2004. "Art Music in a Cross-Cultural Context: The Case of Africa." In *The Cambridge History of Twentieth-Century Music*, edited by Nicolas Cook and Anthony Pople, pp. 584–613. Cambridge, UK: Cambridge University Press.

Scherzinger, Martin Rudolf. 2005. "*Masanga* for Two Pianos (1998)." In *Towards an African Pianism: Keyboard Music of Africa and the Diaspora*, edited by Cynthia Tse Kimberlin and Akin Euba, pp. 289–310. Point Richmond, CA: MRI Press.

Scherzinger, Martin Rudolf. 2006. "György Ligeti and the Aka Pygmies Project." *Contemporary Music Review* 25 (5–6): 227–262.

Scherzinger, Martin Rudolf. 2017. "Mathematics of African Dance Rhythms." Accessed May 17, 2022. Washington, D.C. Library of Congress Lecture. https://www.loc.gov/today/cyberlc/feature_wdesc.php?rec=7988.

Scherzinger, Martin Rudolf. 2018. "Temporalities." In *The Oxford Handbook of Cultural Concepts in Music Theory*, edited by Alex Rehding and Steven Rings. New York: Oxford University Press. Online publication.

Scherzinger, Martin Rudolf. 2019. "Afro-Electric Counterpoint." In *Rethinking Reich*, edited by Sumanth Gopinath and Pwyll ap Siôn, pp. 259–302. New York: Oxford University Press.

Schmalfeldt, Janet. 2019. "Phrase." In *The Oxford Handbook of Critical Concepts in Music Theory*, edited by Alexander Rehding and Steven Rings. New York: Oxford University Press. Online publication.

Secretan, Thierry. 1995. *Going into Darkness: Fantastic Coffins from Africa*. London: Thames and Hudson.

Seminary Tunes. 1907. Akropong, Ghana: Basel Mission.

Senghor, Leopold. 1956. "Africa-Negro Aesthetics." *Diogenes* 16: 23–38.

Senku: Piano Music by Composers of African Descent. 2003. Compact Disc. S.I.: Musicians Showcase Recordings.

Serwadda, Moses, and Hewitt Pantaleoni. 1968. "A Possible Notation for African Dance Drumming." *African Music* 4 (2): 47–52.

Smith, David Osmond. 1975. "Iconic Relations within Formal Transformations." In *Actes du 1er congress international de sémiotique musicale* (Proceedings of the 1st International Congress on Semiotics of Music), Belgrade 1973, edited by Gino Stefani, pp. 45–55 (Pesaro: Centro di Iniziativa Culturale, 1975).

Smith, Sandra. 1982. "The Constituents of Music Ethnotheory: An Example from the Kuna of Panama." In *Ethnotheory*, edited by Maria Herndon, pp. 1–16. Dorby: Norwood Editions.

Spivak, Gayatri. 1990. *The Post-Colonial Critic: Interviews, Strategies, Dialogues*. New York: Routledge.

Steingo, Gavin. 2016. *Kwaito's Promise: Music and the Aesthetics of Freedom in South Africa*. Chicago: University of Chicago Press.

Stevens, Robin, and Eric Akrofi. 2004. "Tonic Sol-fa in South Africa—A Case of Endogenous Musical Practice." In *Australian Association for Research in Music Education: Proceedings of the XXVIth Annual Conference, 25–28 September 2004*. Southern Cross University, Tweed-Gold Coast Campus, New South Wales, Australia, September 25–28 (Clayton, Victoria: Australian Association for Research in Music Education), 301–314.

Stock, Jonathan.1993. "The Application of Schenkerian Analysis to Ethnomusicology: Problems and Possibilities." *Music Analysis* 12 (2): 215–240.

Stockhausen, Karlheinz. 1957. ". . . How Time Passes," translated by Cornelius Cardew. *Die Reihe* 3: 10–43.

Stokes, Martin. 2008. "John Blacking and Ethnomusicology." In *The Queen's Thinkers: Essays on the Intellectual Heritage of a University*, edited by David N. Livingstone and Alvin Jackson, pp. 168–169. Belfast: Blackstaff.

Stone, Ruth M. 1982. *Let the Inside Be Sweet: The Interpretation of Music Event Among the Kpelle of Liberia*. Bloomington: Indiana University Press.

Stone, Ruth M. 1988. *Dried Millet Breaking: Time, Words, and Song in the Woi Epic of the Kpelle*. Bloomington: Indiana University Press.

Stover, Chris. 2012. "Review of David Penalosa, *The Clave Matrix*." *Latin American Music Review* 33: 131–140.

Stover, Chris. 2017. "Eight Axioms for a Theory of Timeline Space." Invited Talk, University of Oslo. Accessed November 2022. https://www.chrisstovermusic.com/eight-axioms

Taiwo, Olufemi. 2010. *How Colonialism Preempted Modernity in Africa*. Bloomington: Indiana University Press.

Táíwò, Olúfémi. 2022. *Against Decolonisation: Taking African Agency Seriously*. London: Hurst & Company.

Talabi, Grace. 2020. *A Study of the Music and Social Meaning of Selected Choral Works from Dayo Oyedun's Cantata*. PhD diss., Stellenbosch University.

Tang, Patricia. 2007. *Masters of the Sabar: Wolof Griot Percussionists of Senegal*. Philadelphia: Temple University Press.

Taruskin, Richard. 2005. *The Oxford History of Western Music*. New York: Oxford University Press.

Taruskin, Richard. 2016 [1996]. *Stravinsky and the Russian Traditions*, vol. 2. Berkeley and London: University of California Press.

Tedlock, Barbara. 1980. "Songs of the Zuni Kachina Society: Composition, Rehearsal and Performance." In *Southwestern Indian Ritual Drama*, edited by Charlotte Frisbie, pp. 7–35. Albuquerque: University of New Mexico Press.

Tempels, Placide. 1959. *Bantu Philosophy*. Paris: Présence africaine.

Temperley, David. 1998. "Review of *African Rhythm: A Northern Ewe Perspective* by K. Agawu." *Current Musicology* 62: 69–83.

Temperley, David. 2000. "Meter and Grouping in African Music: A View from Music Theory." *Ethnomusicology* 44 (1): 65–96.

Tenzer, Michael. 2003. "José Maceda and the Paradoxes of Modern Composition in Southeast Asia." *Ethnomusicology* 47 (1): 93–120.

Tenzer, Michael. 2017. "In Honor of What We Can't Groove to Yet." In Robin Moore, edited by *College Music Curricula for a New Century*, pp. 169–190. Oxford, UK: Oxford University Press.

Tenzer, Michael. 2017. "Transforming African Musical Cycles." *Music Theory Spectrum* 39 (2): 139–157.

Tenzer, Michael. 2019. "That's All It Does: Steve Reich and Balinese Gamelan." In *Rethinking Reich*, edited by Sumanth Gopinath and Pwyll ap Siôn, pp. 303–322. New York: Oxford University Press.

Thiel, Paul van. 1977. *Multi-Tribal Music of Ankole: An Ethnomusicological Study Including a Glossary of Musical Terms*. Tervuren: Musée royal de l'Afrique central.

Thompson, Robert Farris. 1984. *Flash of the Spirit: African and Afro-American Art and Philosophy*. New York: Vintage Books.

Tiersot, Julien. 1905. *Notes d'ethnographie musicale*. 2 vols. Paris: Fischbacher.

Toussaint, Godfried. 2003. "Classification and Phylogenetic Analysis of African Ternary Rhythm Timelines." Meeting Alhambra, ISAMA-BRIDGES Conference Proceedings, 25–36.

Toussaint, Godfried. 2013. *The Geometry of Musical Rhythm: What Makes a "Good" Rhythm Good?"* Bosa Roca: CRC Press.

Tunes for the Use of the Seminary: Twi Version. 1907. Akropong: [Basel Mission].

Turino, Thomas. 1999. "Signs of Imagination, Identity and Experience: A Peircian Semiotic Theory for Music." *Ethnomusicology* 43 (2): 221–255.

Tymoczko, Dmitri. 2011. *A Geometry of Music: Harmony and Counterpoint in the Extended Common Practice*. New York: Oxford University Press.

Uzoigwe, Joshua. 1992. *Akin Euba: An Introduction to the Life and Music of a Nigerian Composer*. Bayreuth: E. Breitinger, University of Bayreuth.

Vallejo, Polo. 2004. *Mbudi mbudi na mhanga: universo musical infantil de los Wagogo de Tanzania* (The musical universe of the Wagogo children from Tanzania). Madrid: Edicion del autor.

Vallejo, Polo. 2007. *Patrimonio musical Wagogo: Contexto y sistematica*. Madrid: Fundación Sur.

Van den Toorn, Pieter C. 2017. "The Rite of Spring Briefly Revisited: Thoughts on Stravinsky's Stratifications, the Psychology of Meter, and African Polyrhythm." *Music Theory Spectrum* 39 (2): 158–181.

Vetter, Roger. 1998. "Review of Agawu, *African Rhythm: A Northern Ewe Perspective*," *Journal of the American Musicological Society* 51 (1): 158–163.

Villepastour, Amanda. 2010. *Ancient Text Messages of the Yoruba Bàtá Drum: Cracking the Code*. Farnham, UK: Ashgate.

Wachsmann, Klaus. 1967. "The State of African Musicology." In *African Studies of Makerere 1961–66, A Report*, pp. 82–93. Kampala: Makerere University College.

Wachsmann, Klaus P. 1982. "The Changeability of Musical Experience." *Ethnomusicology* 26 (2): 197–215.

Ward, William E. F. 1927. "Music in the Gold Coast." *Gold Coast Review* 3: 199–223.

Waterman, Christopher. 1990. *Jùjú: A Social History and Ethnography of an African Popular Music*. Chicago: University of Chicago Press.

Waterman, Christopher. 1991. "The Uneven Development of Africanist Ethnomusicology: Three Issues and a Critique." In *Comparative Musicology and Anthropology of Music*, edited by Bruno Nettl and Philip V. Bohlman, pp. 169–186. Chicago: University of Chicago Press.

Waterman, Richard A. 1948. "Hot Rhythm in Negro Music." *Bulletin of the American Musicological Society* 1 (1): 24–37. doi: https://doi.org/10.2307.

Watkins, Lee, Elijah Madiba, and Boudina McConnachie. 2021. "Rethinking the decolonial moment through collaborative practices at the International Library of African Music (ILAM), South Africa." *Ethnomusicology Forum* 30: 20–39.

Watson, J. R. 2002. *An Annotated Anthology of Hymns*. Oxford, UK: Oxford University Press.

Waugh, Linda. 1992. "Let's Take the Con Out of Iconicity: Constraints on Iconicity in the Lexicon." *American Journal of Semiotics* 9 (1): 7–48.

Webb, Gavin Elliot. 2011. *The Wulomei Ga Folk Group: A Contribution Towards Urban Ethnomusicology*. PhD diss., University of Ghana, Legon.

Westermann, Dietrich Frederich. 1928. *Ewefiala or Ewe-English Dictionary*. Berlin: Reimer.

Widdess, Richard, and Ritwik Sanyal. 2004. *Dhrupad: Tradition and Performance in Indian Music*. Aldershot, UK: Ashgate.

Wiggins, Trevor. 1999. "Drumming in Ghana." In *Composing the Music of Africa: Composition, Interpretation and Realisation*, edited by Malcolm Floyd, pp. 45–65. Aldershot: Ashgate, 1999.

Wiggins, Trevor. 1999. "The Xylophone Tradition of North-West Ghana." In *Composing the Music of Africa: Composition, Interpretation and Realisation*, edited by Malcolm Floyd, pp. 67–89. Aldershot, UK: Ashgate.

Williams, David Russell, and C. Matthew Balensuela. 2008. *Music Theory from Boethius to Zarlino: A Bibliography and Guide*. Stuyvesant, NY: Pendragon Press.

Wilson, Olly. 1974. "The Significance of the Relationship Between Afro-American Music and West African Music." *Black Perspective in Music* 2 (1): 3–22.

Wintle, Christopher. 1980. "Review of Heinrich Schenker, *Free Composition*." *Times Literary Supplement* 79 (4042): 1046.

Wiredu, Kwasi. 1980. *Philosophy and an African Culture*. Cambridge, UK: Cambridge University Press.

Wiredu, Kwasi. 1996. *Cultural Universals and Particulars: An African Perspective.* Bloomington: Indiana University Press.

Wiredu, Kwasi, ed. 2004. *A Companion to African Philosophy*. Oxford, UK: Wiley-Blackwell.

Yoruba Drums from Benin, West Africa. 1996. Compact Disc. Washington, DC: Smithsonian/Folkways.

Zbikowski, Lawrence. 2005. *Conceptualizing Music: Cognitive Structure, Theory, and Analysis.* New York: Oxford University Press.

Zemp, Hugo. 1979. "Aspects of 'Are'are Musical Theory." *Ethnomusicology* 23 (1): 6–48.

Zemp, Hugo. 1978. "'Are'are Classification of Musical Types and Instruments." *Ethnomusicology* 22 (1): 37–67.

Index

For the benefit of digital users, indexed terms that span two pages (e.g., 52–53) may, on occasion, appear on only one of those pages.